A Garland Series

Nineteenth-Century Book Arts
and Printing History

Twenty-Six Texts reprinted in
Twenty-Three Volumes, mostly relating to
Papermaking, Book Illustration, Type Design,
Typefounding, and the Practice of Printing
during the Industrial Revolution.

Edited by

John Bidwell

Typographia:
or
The Printer's Instructor

by

Thomas F. Adams

with a new introduction by

John Bidwell

GARLAND PUBLISHING, INC.

New York   1981   *London*

**For a complete list of the titles in this series,
see the final pages of this volume.**

Introduction copyright © 1981 by John Bidwell

Bibliographical note: this facsimile has been made
from a copy in the Library of Congress (Z244.A2A2.1844).

Library of Congress Cataloging in Publication Data

Adams, Thomas F
Typographia : or The printer's instructor.

(Nineteenth-century book arts and printing history)
Reprint of the 1844 ed. published in Philadelphia.
1. Printing, Practical.   2. Printing—History.
I. Title.   II. Series.
Z244.A2A2   1981   686.2'24   78-74409
ISBN 0-8240-3893-2

The volumes in this series are printed on acid-free,
250-year-life paper.

Printed in the United States of America

Introduction

Authors of early English and American printers' manuals casually appropriated text from their predecessors. This practice, common enough not to require explanation or acknowledgement (much less apology), was documented by Lawrence C. Wroth in 1935.[1] Citing borrowed passages and devising a literary family tree, Wroth measured the original work of typographical writers from Moxon (1683) to De Vinne (1900–1904), with much praise for them but with less for those in between. Thomas F. Adams, whose *Typographia* (Philadelphia, 1844) is reprinted here, was found to be the worst and boldest of offenders.

Adams, Wroth observed, had the "effrontery" to point out the plagiarism of others. "Compelled to admit some degree of impatience" with the *Typographia*, Wroth impatiently examined only a few of the at least thirteen editions, his indictment misdating three textual changes.[2] Even more unfair, a recent article traces a passage from Smith's manual of 1755 through the 1837 *Typographia*, "a classic instance of the rampant plagiarism in nineteenth-century printer's manuals," when in fact this passage was specifically omitted by Adams.[3] Much of the *Typographia* was indeed derived from other works, but it has been judged in undue haste and on insufficient evidence.

Most likely, Wroth would not have been so hard on the

Typographia if he had understood that it began as an abridged reprint (1828) of John Johnson's *Typographia* (London, 1824) and that it was then gradually revised and supplemented from one edition to the next. It was as "compiler" that Adams substituted his own name for Johnson's on the 1837 title page, and he did not claim authorship until the completely reset 1844 edition, abridged in some places and enlarged in others. The 1844 edition was stereotyped and regularly reprinted for twenty years, the plates changed frequently but only for minor, mostly commercial reasons. As Wroth himself noticed, the chapter on printing presses was the most conscientiously updated section during the later years.

The first version of the *Typographia* is accurately titled *An Abridgment of Johnson's Typographia, or the Printers' Instructor*, Boston: C. L. Adams, 1828. Even the ornamental typography imitates Johnson's, and there is little new here except for remarks on skin rollers and an appended chapter on printing presses. Thomas, probably the son or younger brother of the publisher, Charles L. Adams, must have at least edited this volume, since he calls it "our former edition" in the 1837 *Typographia*.[4]

The real first edition, Philadelphia, "printed and published by the compiler" in 1837, was mostly based on Johnson but with many substituted passages from Thomas C. Hansard's *Typographia* (London, 1825). Adams also used Isaiah Thomas's *History of Printing in America* (Worcester, 1810) and Senefelder's *Complete Course of Lithography* (London, 1819), perhaps indirectly. He contributed an original section, "Of Filling in and Pressing Sheets" (pp. 346–347); new technical terms, "Hell" and "Ratting"; his own proposed improvement of the lay of the case (pp. 132–136); and some new imposition schemes. The purpose of "imposing from the centre," the solid outside pages of the form acting as bearers for blank or thinly-set inner pages, was not explained until the 1844 edition (p. 118). Adams made changes in terminology (for instance, "division" to "hyphen," "crotchet" to "bracket," "scale-board" to "lead" or "leads," and "m rule" to "m dash") and also in two of the typographical marks (nos. 10 & 18). A three-page "Scale of Prices Adopted by the Philadelphia Typographical Association, June 1, 1836," was appended to this edition.

Several sections were rewritten to keep pace with improvements in the hand press and in inking. "Setting Up a Press" (pp. 279–280) no longer applied to the two-pull wooden press but to the metal press, and inking was now accomplished more with composition rollers than with the traditional pelt-covered balls. Instructions for preparing composition included his own recipe as well as Hansard's and, with reservations, Sherman's.[5]

The 1844 edition, reproduced here, was again revised and also abridged, eliminating many passages derived from Johnson and Hansard. None of these omissions are really significant. However, those studying the printer's attitude towards accidentals may want to note that Adams decided to pass over a paragraph from Johnson (II, 55–56; 1837 ed., p. 74) advising authors to point their copy precisely since some compositors were not well trained enough to punctuate for them.

Johnson's list of type sizes, somewhat expanded and Americanized for the 1837 edition, was again revised in 1844. A typographical mark for broken letters was added, and the use of metal furniture and quoins noted; E. M. Maeder's Iron

Screw Quoin (p. 225), a "recent invention . . . not yet . . . offered to the trade" in 1844, remained so in every edition through 1864, Adams's later publishers either too thrifty or too careless to change the plate. Several new sections were inserted: "Sizes of Paper as Made by Machinery" (p. 279); "Making Up" (p. 222); "Printing Engravings on Wood" (pp. 251–252); and "Ornamental Printing" (pp. 252–254). These last two were featured in his 1844 preface, and Adams's interest in this sort of printing is indicated by many smaller insertions, for instance: "The variety and richness of the designs [for printers' flowers] recently introduced by some of our founders, seems to have occasioned a desire on the part of several printers to introduce the old mode of ornamenting" (p. 76).

Some remarks on the abuse of electrotyping matrices were inserted in this edition (p. 45). Adams suggests that this useful typefounder's shortcut (both a technological one, a means of casting type without having to cut punches, and an ethical one, a device for pirating type designs) had already started a price war. Successful experiments in duplicating matrices by this method were reported as early as 1840, and a patent for an "Improvement in Preparing Matrices for Type by the Electrotyping Process" was granted to Thomas W. Starr in 1845.[6] Although Adams contributes some confusion to the chronology of this invention, casually mentioning its ill effects a year before it was patented, his account does indicate that the trade immediately recognized its potential and its threat.

Another interesting change in the 1844 edition concerns the overseer's role in making the *revise*. As early as Stower (1808)[7] an overseer, present in some shops with four or five presses,[8] will make a last-minute check of the proofs before a form goes to press; these passages descend almost intact to the 1844 edition (pp. 213 & 195) by way of Johnson (II, 484 & 236). By substituting "clean proof" (1844 ed., p. 192) for "revise" (1837 ed., p. 239) and by making the revise a specific duty of the overseer (1844 ed., p. 195), now a regular member of the shop, and of the pressman (1837 ed., p. 292; 1844 ed., p. 239), Adams codifies an additional step in the proofreading routine. After the form has been placed on the press, a proof is pulled for the overseer. He is responsible for any accidents that might have happened while the form was locked up or on its way to the press or during make ready: crooked lines, letters missing or battered, or "*bite* from the frisket." If all is well, "Revise" is written in the margin, and the proof is returned to the pressman.

All succeeding editions seem to have been printed from the 1844 plates, probably made by Adams himself, who advertised "Stereotyping in all its branches executed in the best manner, and at the lowest prices" at the end of this edition. The copyright was transferred to the publishers of the next, 1845, edition, James Kay, Jun. and Brother, and it was listed as such up through the last, 1864, edition.

These plates served long and hard, and changes in them were motivated almost solely by the commercial interests of their later owners. References to Adams's Printers' Warehouse were eliminated, and blurbs for the products of L. Johnson & Co., the Philadelphia typefounding firm, were inserted. John Johnson's fulminations against the "chicanery of the priests" and other such reformation rhetoric (I, 77; 1844 ed., p. 41) were censored in the 1858 edition. One disinterested change in the plates, an added footnote on p. 117, was made sometime before the 1854 edition: "It was formerly the custom to omit the letters, J, V, and W, in the list of signatures. But the greater convenience attending the use of twenty-five letters has recently induced several of our largest establishments to omit the letter J only."

The most rewritten and revised chapter of the *Typographia* was "Improved Presses." This was where printing technology was most obviously changing and where printers were most likely to insist on up-to-date information. Many were ruined by investing in needlessly expensive, obsolete, or inappropriate equipment. Adams's 1828 abridged reprint of Johnson could not have competed against Van Winkle's second edition of 1827 without its appended state-of-the-art account of currently available presses. Since printing machinery was sold by Adams, and by some of the *Typographia*'s later publishers, advertisements in this chapter, some more subtle than others, were inserted and removed from one edition to the next. The most important revisions were made in the editions of 1837, 1844, and 1856. In 1844 "Improved Presses" included, with somewhat different emphasis, every item mentioned in 1837 except for the Ruthven Press. A section on "Machine Printing" was added. Presumably, this chapter was rewritten and updated in 1856 for the R. Hoe & Co. edition of that year. The following list of presses has been prepared to show where they appear in the *Typographia* (1837–1864) and in Adams's appendix to the *Abridgment* of 1828:

Adams, Isaac & Co., "the best power-press for book-work" (1856–1864; the Adams firm, however, was bought up by R. Hoe & Co. in April, 1859[9])

Adams, Seth & Co., "the best platen power press now in use" (1844–1854). This press, essentially the same as the above, was invented by Isaac Adams in 1830 and was manufactured by him in partnership with his brother Seth.

Adams, machine job press (1856–1864)

Albion (1828)

American (1837–1854)

Columbian (1828–1864)

Couillard (1828)

Gordon, machine job press (1856–1864)

Hoe & Co., "prominent manufacturers of Double and Single Cylinder Presses" (1844–1845)

Hoe, machine job press (1856–1864)

Hoe's Eight-Cylinder Type-Revolving Machine, also with four impression cylinders (1856–1864)

Hoe's Single Small Cylinder Press (1856–1864)

Lawyer, machine job press (1856–1864)

Philadelphia (1837–1854)

Ramage (1837–1854)

Ruggles, machine job press (1856–1864)

Ruthven (1837)

Smith (1828–1864)

Stanhope (1828)

Taylor, A. B. & Co., double cylinder printing press "justly entitled to our preference [to that of Hoe & Co.] . . . and for sale by T. F. Adams, Philadelphia" (1844–1845)

Washington (1828–1864)

Wells (1828–1854)

Williams, C. G., "New Printing Machine" (1828)

So far, I have located thirteen editions of the *Typographia*. My list includes eight editions published by L. Johnson & Co., of which six are mentioned in the firm's manuscript ledgers at Columbia University. The date for each entry in these ledgers, L. Johnson & Co.'s edition number, size of the edition, printer, and, whenever possible, the price of paper and presswork combined are reported below after the citation *ledger*. Editions of five hundred copies were printed in twenty-four tokens at forty cents a token. I am much indebted to Peter M. VanWingen (Rare Book and Special Collections Division, Library of Congress) for providing this valuable and, in the bibliography of early printers' manuals, certainly uncommon information.

1837. Philadelphia, Printed and Published by the Compiler.

1844. Second Edition, with Numerous Emendations and Additions. Philadelphia, Published at No. 118 Chesnut St. [business address of Charles L. Adams] and No. 8 Franklin Place [business address of Thomas F. Adams] and for Sale at the Principal Type Foundries.

1845. Third Edition . . . Philadelphia, James Kay, Jun. & Brother; Pittsburgh, C. H. Kay.

1851. Fourth Edition . . . Philadelphia, Peck & Bliss.

1851. Fourth Edition . . . Philadelphia, L. Johnson & Co.

1853. Fourth Edition . . . Philadelphia, L. Johnson & Co. *ledger* 24 Jan. 1853: second edition [that is, L. Johnson & Co.'s second edition] 500 copies printed by Kite & Walton. $49.92.[10]

1854. Fourth Edition . . . Philadelphia, L. Johnson & Co. *ledger* 25 May 1854: [their] third edition, 500 copies printed by Kite & Walton.

1856. New York, R. Hoe & Co.[11]

1856. Philadelphia, L. Johnson & Co. *ledger* 20 June 1856: [their] fourth edition, 750 copies printed by Kite & Walton.

1857. Philadelphia, L. Johnson & Co. *ledger* 14 March 1857: [their] fifth edition, 500 copies printed by Kite & Walton. $55.10.

1858. Philadelphia, L. Johnson & Co. *ledger* 15 Sept. 1858: [their] sixth edition, 500 copies printed by H. B. Ashmead and bound, at 11¢ a copy, by Ducomb. $55.10.

1861. Philadelphia, L. Johnson & Co. *ledger* 14 Sept. 1860: [their] seventh edition, 500 copies. This entry records, as in other editions of five hundred copies, the purchase of seven reams of 24″ × 38″ paper, but details about

       printing and binding were never filled in. [$55.10?]
1864.   Philadelphia, L. Johnson & Co.

Along with type and printing supplies, the *Typographia* must have been kept systematically in stock by L. Johnson & Co. (parent of MacKellar, Smiths & Jordan and ultimately of the American Type Founders Company). The firm also offered to put together "complete outfits . . . comprising every requisite, from a steam-power press to a bodkin" (1864 ed., p. 285). Surely there were occasions when a salesman would formally present (with best wishes) a copy in sober blind-stamped cloth to some eager printing novice, successfully induced to purchase the makings of an entire country newspaper office: everything necessary to profit from a new territory's literary cravings, and then some.

The company's *Typographic Advertiser*, edited by Thomas MacKellar, advertised the *Typographia* as "always on hand" from October 1858 through January 1864 and gave it a full-length blurb as early as its fourth issue (Jan. 1856):

> In the compass of less than 300 pages, this book contains every thing essential to the well-ordering of a printing office, as well as a sketch of the origin, rise, and progress of the typographic art. The apprentice who wishes to become master of his profession should study it; and the oldest printer will find advantage in its numerous schemes for imposing sheets, which it is difficult, if not impossible, to retain in the memory. Authors, too, will be not a little benefited by its proof-reading directions; and a general acquaintance with it will enable publishers to transact business with printers in a business-like way. We sell it at $1 per copy. For $1.15 we send it, post-paid, to any place.

A late, if not the last, advertisement for the *Typographia*, in the 1864 combined April and July issues, was rather neatly phrased, perhaps by MacKellar himself: "PRINTERS' GUIDE.—Adams's Typography [*sic*], a useful manual for the instruction of apprentices, as well as remembrancer for old professors of the printing art. Price, $1.25. . . ."

When the *Typographia* finally became irredeemably obsolete, MacKellar's own classic manual was introduced deferentially (April, 1866):

> We have just issued a Manual of Typography, called *The American Printer*, which we offer as a substitute for Adams's Typographia, the book formerly published by us. The latter, having been prepared many years ago, had gradually become less valuable as a guide for printers, and the plates had begun to show signs of wear: we determined, therefore, to get up a volume that should more adequately meet the requirements of the day.

In the *American Dictionary of Printing and Bookmaking* (1894) Adams is remembered only as the author of the *Typographia*, "a writer on printing, [who] carried on the art in Philadelphia for a number of years." Some biographical clues can be extracted from his writing, which, along with information available in city directories, can at least outline his business activities. His observations on composition rollers in 1837 (p. 313), based on nearly thirteen years of printing experience, revised to nearly twenty years in 1844 (p. 260), suggest that he entered the trade sometime around 1824. Since he was approximately seventy years old when he died in 1881,[12] he must have been apprenticed at the age of thirteen, presumably to Charles L. Adams. His extreme youth might explain why his name appears nowhere in the *Abridgment*, published when he was seventeen, and why his technique for printing two colors in one impression, invented at the age of sixteen, was neither protected nor promoted as aggressively as his "Polychromatic Printing" of 1844.[13]

Charles L. Adams was listed as printer at various addresses in Boston directories from 1825 through 1832. He next appeared in Philadelphia directories 1835–1857, first as "printer" and then as "printer, cards." When, in 1844, Thomas F. Adams set up his "Printers' Furnishing Warehouse" at No. 8 Franklin Place, Charles took over his old 118 Chestnut Street business address and his card manufacturing business along with it. In 1845 Charles printed a *Philadelphia Street Directory* and, on the back wrapper, advertised his services as "Card Printer" at 118 Chestnut Street. This address precedes Thomas's new one in the imprint of the 1844 *Typographia*.

Except for the *Abridgment* no book or pamphlet is recorded from the shop of Charles L. Adams in the *Checklist of American Imprints* from 1825 through 1828. Since Thomas, most likely his apprentice or assistant at this time, claimed to have been "almost exclusively engaged" in ornamental printing for nearly twenty years by 1844[14] and to have advanced this art in 1827 by inventing a means of printing two colors in one impression,[15] job work and card printing must have been the main ingredients of Charles's business both in Boston and Philadelphia.

No doubt Thomas followed Charles to Philadelphia from Boston in 1835 or thereabouts. He went into business on his own in 1837, listed in directories for that year through 1843 as "printer," "fancy printer," or "printer, cardmaker, &c." In the 1844 edition (p. 253) he remarked that there were two small card printing machines in his shop.

Judging from the directories, Thomas's venture into "printers' findings," as advertised at the end of this volume, lasted from 1844 through 1846. In 1847 he had a "printers' ink manufactory," and then after two years listed simply as "printer" he became a "printing ink manuf." in 1850 and then "lampblack manuf.," "merchant," an associate of the printing ink manufacturer L. Martin & Co., and "pres." through 1880. His thirty years or so in the ink business seem to have been prosperous. By 1859 L. Martin & Co.'s products were promoted with some regard to Adams's literary fame:

> There are now five establishments in this city engaged in making Printing Inks . . . The youngest of these enterprising firms, Messrs. L. MARTIN & Co., have very politely proposed to furnish a fair sample of Philadelphia Ink for use in these pages . . . Mr. Adams, the author of the well-known "Adams' Typographia," is associated in this firm, and has succeeded in producing a very superior article, of which the one-dollar quality has been used side by side with English four-dollar Ink, and the difference is imperceptible to an unpracticed eye.[16]

As to his personal life, I can find nothing except that he was secretary to the Philadelphia Artists & Amateurs Association in 1843.[17]

The *Typographia* remains as the best testament of Adams's printing career. All of its first-person biographical statements seem to apply to him except a complaint derived from Johnson (II, 222) about the inconveniences occasioned by dilatory proofreading, "having not only repeatedly witnessed it, but also greatly suffered from it ourselves" (p. 184). Certainly, enough of his personal experience went into the successive revisions of the *Typographia* to justify keeping it in print for so long. It was easily the most popular American manual of its day, perhaps because it was the most comprehensive one available. Considering that MacKellar took both format and text from it, Adams can be said to have influenced more than a half century of American graphic arts.

JOHN BIDWELL

William Andrews Clark Memorial Library

I would like to acknowledge the assistance of Terry Belanger, Bruce L. Johnson, Jennifer Lee, Alice Schreyer, Daniel Traister, and Peter M. Van Wingen. Carey S. Bliss very kindly let me use his notes on the *Typographia*, and Alexander S. Lawson lent me his copy of the 1837 edition. I am also indebted to the American Antiquarian Society's Daniels Fellowship program, which gave me an opportunity to investigate printers' manuals in the Society's library.

1. Lawrence C. Wroth, "Corpus Typographicum: A Review of English and American Printers' Manuals," *The Dolphin* 2 (1935): 157–170.

2. The paragraph quoted by Wroth (pp. 167–168), an "addition . . . to his preface of 1864," can be found twenty years earlier in the edition reprinted here. Wroth noted that "Adams' book takes its place among the documents that mark the development of printing facilities in the nineteenth century" because it included "new features in the field of mechanical appliances in its successive editions of 1837, 1845, and 1864" (p. 168). These "new features," printing presses, first appeared in the editions of 1837, 1844, and 1856.

3. John Bush Jones, "Victorian 'Readers' and Modern Editors: Attitudes and Accidentals Revisited," *PBSA* 71 (1977): 50–51.

4. Thomas F. Adams, *Typographia* (Philadelphia, 1837), p. 335.

5. A. N. Sherman, *The Printer's Manual* (New York, 1834), pp. 52–55.

6. Rollo G. Silver, "Trans-Atlantic Crossing: The Beginning of Electrotyping in America," *JPHS* 10 (1974/5): 100–102. According to A. F. Johnson's revised and enlarged edition of Talbot Baines Reed, *A History of the Old English Letter Foundries* (London, 1952), p. 368, electrotyping of matrices was practised, and regretted, in America by 1851.

7. Caleb Stower, *The Printer's Grammar* (London, 1808), pp. 381–382 & 397.

8. *Ibid.*, p. 376.

9. James Moran, *Printing Presses* (Berkeley & Los Angeles, 1973), p. 115.

10. Another Peck & Bliss "fourth edition" may have been published in

this year. See Sinclair H. Hitchings's catalogue of printers' manuals appended to Herbert Davis, "The Art of Printing: Joseph Moxon and His Successors," *PaGA* 5 (1957):29.

11. The edition statement on the title page, by now meaningless, was omitted in this and in all succeeding editions. Perhaps some copies from L. Johnson & Co.'s unusually large 1856 edition were meant to be distributed by R. Hoe & Co. and were accordingly furnished with a special title page and appropriate advertisements.

12. See his obituaries in *The Printers' Circular* 15 (Jan., 1881): 268 and in the [Philadelphia] *Public Ledger*, 17 Jan. 1881, p. 2.

13. *Typographia* (Philadelphia, 1844), p. 254. "A patent for Polychromatic printing, by which it is claimed any number of colors may be printed at one impression by a series of separate and complete inking fountains" was granted to Thomas F. Adams on Sept. 17, 1844. See J. Luther Ringwalt, ed., *American Encyclopaedia of Printing* (Philadelphia, 1871), p. 222.

14. *Typographia* (Philadelphia, 1844), pp. 252–253.

15. *Ibid.*, p. 254.

16. Edwin T. Freedley, *Philadelphia and its Manufactures* (Philadelphia, 1859), p. 175.

17. An "Extract from the Minutes" of the association, dated March 1, 1843, and signed by Adams, is held by the Historical Society of Pennsylvania.

TYPOGRAPHIA:

OR THE

PRINTER'S INSTRUCTOR;

A BRIEF SKETCH OF THE

ORIGIN, RISE, AND PROGRESS

OF THE

TYPOGRAPHIC ART,

WITH

**PRACTICAL DIRECTIONS FOR CONDUCTING EVERY
DEPARTMENT IN AN OFFICE,**

HINTS TO AUTHORS, PUBLISHERS, &c.

SECOND EDITION,
WITH NUMEROUS EMENDATIONS AND ADDITIONS.

BY THOMAS F. ADAMS,

TYPOGRAPHER.

PHILADELPHIA:

PUBLISHED AT No. 118 CHESNUT ST. AND No. 8 FRANKLIN PLACE,

AND FOR SALE

AT THE PRINCIPAL TYPE FOUNDRIES.

1844.

TO THE

PHILADELPHIA

TYPOGRAPHICAL SOCIETY,

THIS WORK

IS MOST RESPECTFULLY

DEDICATED

PREFACE.

In presenting another edition of our work for public favor, we cannot forego the opportunity of acknowledging our obligations to the profession, for the very liberal and flattering testimonials of their approbation heretofore extended us, as well as to those who have taken so warm an interest in the appearance of the present edition.

Very many of the works heretofore published on this subject, in a practical point of view, have been little else than reprints of old Grammars, chiefly of Smith's, published in London, 1755; although we have in many instances adopted the language of our predecessors, still we have in general not only compressed the information contained in it, but have in all cases made it subservient to our own views and experience.

It was our intention when we commenced the preparation of the copy for this volume, to reduce the work in size and consequently in price, by the exclusion of every thing not of practical utility, but upon more mature reflection we became impressed with the belief that a brief sketch of the origin, rise and progress of the Art, could not fail to be appreciated by every one who feels sufficiently interested in the Art, to *study* it; and, that by reducing the size of the type, and rendering our emendations and additions as concise as possible, the work could be afforded, as it now is, at about one half the cost of the former edition.

Among the numerous additions which have been made, and which now appear in print for the first time, we would direct attention particularly to the articles on Gold, Bronze,

Card and Xylographic printing, and last though not least in
importance, the printing of Wood Engravings, a branch
which when properly executed is eminently calculated to
elevate the art in public estimation, and to secure for the
best productions extensive patronage as works of Art.   Until
recently but little attention has been bestowed upon it in this
country, and as the attention of the profession has now been
turned to it, we have thought proper to make our observations
on the subject full and comprehensible.

   The Literati, and in fact every one in any way connected
with the publishing and printing business, will find suitable
directions for their guidance in preparing copy, making calculations, corrections, &c. &c.

   The practical directions for conducting every department
in an office, will, we trust, be found more complete than any
heretofore published, giving all the necessary information
for Composing, Imposing, Fine Presswork, Ornamental
Printing, and a minute account of the best modes of making
and managing composition rollers.

   In our endeavors to furnish the profession with an Assistant, we have borne in mind the wants of beginners, and
might, perhaps, in some instances be charged with unnecessary prolixity ; but is it not better to lay before the general
reader information which he already possesses, than to
withhold such minutiæ from the rising generation, who by
a proper appreciation of it, and attention to business may become ornaments to the profession they have embraced?

   Should our humble endeavors to promote a knowledge
of the Art meet the approbation of its enlightened professors, then shall we receive that reward for our labors which
is the utmost bounds of our wishes.

ORIGIN, RISE, AND PROGRESS,

TYPOGRAPHIC ART.

" Th' Inventor of this noble Art to find,
Has long engag'd the Antiquary's mind ;
To question dates, on books and records pore,
To draw the veil Obscurity's cast o'er ;
Vain are his efforts, 'tis beyond his might,
To fix in truth, on man, or place the right:
Doubts still exist to whom the palm is due,
Partisans for each their claims pursue :
But metal types the honor all confer,
On both the Guttembergs, Faust and Schœffer."

THIS noble invention, which is one of the greatest blessings heaven has bestowed, cannot fail exciting a considerable degree of interest in the rising generation, to be informed when, and by whom, it was first discovered, and brought into general use. Though printing be considered a modern invention, it is allowed to have been practised in the East from a very early period, in a similar manner to our first essays. It has been contended, that the remoteness and seclusion of the Chinese prevented our gaining any information from them: but Mr. W. Y. Ottley, and Mr. S. W. Singer, concur in opinion, that the art of engraving in wood was known in Europe in the thirteenth century: that it was brought from Asia by the Venitian merchants, whose intercourse with that territory was frequent, by way of Constantinople, from a very early period. As to the silence of Marco Polo upon this subject, in his account of the marvels he had witnessed in China, having resided at the court of the great Chan of Tartary for seventeen years, 1295: Mr. O. conceives that the author thought it of little interest, as the art had been long practised in Venice. Many writers have ascribed this invention to an earlier period than the Christian era; Father Couplet states the year 930: Father du Halde fixes it fifty years prior

to the former period, under the reign of Ming Tsong I. the second Emperor of the Tartarian dynasty: and Father le Compte
contends, that it has been practised in China from all ages: he
adds that the only difference between the European and Chinese methods, consist in the former being able, from the small
number of letters in their alphabet, to print voluminous works,
the letters of the first sheet, from a re-arrangement, serving for
all the succeeding ones: whereas, from the prodigious number
of characters in the Chinese alphabet, (some accounts state them
at eighty thousand) they contend that it is much easier and less
expensive to have their pages cut on wood; thus having as many
blocks as there are leaves in the book. Father du Halde gives
the following particulars relative to Chinese printing:

"The work intended to be printed is transcribed by a careful
writer upon a thin transparent paper: the engraver glues each
of these written sheets, with its face downwards upon a smooth
tablet of pear or apple-tree, or some other hard wood; and then,
with gravers and other instruments he cuts the wood away in
all those parts upon which he finds nothing traced; thus leaving
the transcribed characters ready for printing: in this manner he
prepares as many blocks as there are written pages. He then
prints the number of copies immediately wanted; for he can always print more, if they are required, without the labor of re-
composition necessary in typography: nor is any time lost in
correcting the proof sheets, for, as he is guided in his engraving
by the strokes of the written copy, or perhaps the original of the
author himself, it is impossible for him to make any mistakes,
if the copy is written with exactness. When once, however,
the blocks are engraved, the paper is cut, and the ink is ready,
one man with his brush can, without fatigue, print ten thousand
sheets in a day. The block to be printed must be placed level,
and firmly fixed. The man must have two brushes, one of them
of a stiffer kind, which he can hold in his hand, and use at either
end. He dips it into the ink, and rubs the block with it; taking
care not to wet it too much, or to leave it too dry: if it were wetted
too much, the characters would be slurred; if too little, they
would not print. When the block is once got into a proper
state, he can print three or four sheets following without dipping

his brush into the ink. The second brush is used to rub over the paper, with a small degree of pressure, that it may take the impression: this it does easily, for, not being sized with alum, it receives the ink the instant it comes in contact with it. It is only necessary that the brush should be passed over every part of the sheet with a greater or smaller degree of pressure, and repeated in proportion as the printer finds there is more or less ink upon the block. This brush is soft, and of an oblong form."

The discovery of Printing, having been made so lately as the fifteenth century, it is matter of surprise that no certain record has been handed down fixing the precise time when, the person by whom, and the place whence this Art received its birth. The abilities of the literary Antiquaries of different nations have been called forth, in order that the palm may be ceded to those, who not only merited so well of their own country, but also of every other portion of the civilized globe. These researches have not satisfactorily determined the point; the affair still remains involved in a certain degree of mystery; although it must be admitted, that great probability appears in the theories of some of those who have investigated this difficult subject.

Two reasons may be assigned for this obscurity; viz. the imperfect state of printing while it remained in the possession of its inventor. 2d. Pecuniary motives induced the first printers (from the large sums which were usually paid for manuscripts) to sell their works as such; so that printing was, for a period, as much the counterfeit as the substitute for writing, it being a *fac-simile* of the most approved Scribes. The few persons concerned kept the art a secret for some time, till their funds not being sufficient to answer the necessary expenses, these ingenious men were thus compelled to associate with persons of property, from the union of whose names a degree of doubt has arisen to whom the merit really belongs.

A competition for this distinguished honor now took place between Hærlem, Mentz, Strazburg, and Venice; partizans arose in favor of Laurensz Jansz Coster, of Hærlem; John Guttemberg and others of Mentz; Guttemberg and Mentilius, of Strazburg; and Nicolas Janson, of Venice; others ascribing the discovery to John Guttemberg, or Geinsfleich, junior.

The claims of Laurentius Coster, of Hærlem, depend principally on the authority of the celebrated historian of Holland,
Hadrianus Junius, or Adrian Young, who took up his residence
at Hærlem in 1560. He died 1575, having just finished his
work intituled "Batavia," which appeared in 1578, and from
which it is considered that all Coster's partizans have taken
their ground of argument. The following particulars, supposed
to have been written in 1568, he states were related by his tutor,
Nicholas Galius, an old gentlemen of very tenacious memory,
who stated, that when a boy, he had often heard one Cornelius,
a bookbinder, (then upwards of eighty years of age, who had,
when a youth, assisted at the printing office of Coster,) describe
with great earnestness the numerous trials and experiments
made by his master in the infancy of the invention : when he
came to that part of his narrative touching the robbery, he
would burst into tears, and curse, with the greatest vehemence,
those nights in which he had slept with so vile a miscreant;
and that, were he still alive, he could with great pleasure
execute the thief with his own hands. Junius states that he
received a similar account from Quirinus Talesius, the Burgo-
master, who declared that it was recited to him by the said
Cornelius :—

"About 120 years ago, Laurence Zanssen Coster, inhabited
a decent and fashionable house in the city of Hærlem, situated
on the market-place, opposite the royal palace. The name of
Coster was assumed, and inherited from his ancestors, who had
long enjoyed the honorable and lucrative office of Coster or
Sexton to the church. This man deserves to be restored to the
honor of being the first inventor of printing, of which he has
been unjustly deprived by others, who have enjoyed the praises
due to him alone. As he was walking in the wood contiguous
to the city, which was the general custom of the richer citizens
and men of leisure, in the afternoon and on holidays, he began
to cut letters on the bark of the beech ; with these letters he
enstamped marks upon paper in a contrary direction, in the
manner of a seal; until at length he formed a few lines for his
own amusement, and for the use of the children of his brother-
in-law. This succeeding so well, he attempted greater things;

and being a man of genius and reflection, he invented, with the aid of his brother or son-in-law, Thomas Pietrison, a thicker and more adhesive ink, as the common ink was too thin and made blotted marks. With this ink he was able to print blocks and figures, to which he added letters. I have seen specimens of his printing in this manner: in the beginning he printed on one side only. This was a Dutch book, entitled *Spiegal enser Behoudenisse.* That it was one of the first books printed after the invention of the art, appears from the leaves, which are pasted together, that the naked sides might not be offensive to the eyes; and none at first were printed in a more perfect manner. As this new species of traffic attracted numerous customers, thus did the profits arising from it increase his love for the art, and his diligence in the exercise of it.

" He engaged workmen, which was the source of the mis-chief. Among these workmen was one Jan ——, whether his surname be that of Faust, or any other, is of no great importance to me; as I will not disturb the dead, whose consciences must have smote them sufficiently while living. This Jan, who assisted at the printing-press under oath, after he had learned the art of casting the types, setting them, and other articles belonging to the art, and thought himself sufficiently instructed, having watched the opportunity, as he could not find a better, he packed up the types and the other articles on Christmas eve, while the family was engaged in celebrating the festival, and stole away with them. He first fled to Amsterdam, thence to Cologne, until he could establish himself at Mentz, as a secure place, where he might open shop, and reap the fruits of his knavery. It is a known fact, that within the twelve months, that is, in the year 1440, he published the *Alexandri Galli Doctrinale,* a grammar at that time in high repute, with *Petri Hispani Tractatibus Logicis,* with the same letters which Laurens had used. These were undoubtedly the first products of his press. These are the principal circumstances that I have collected from creditable persons far advanced in years, which they have transmitted like a flaming torch from hand to hand; I have also met with others who have confirmed the same," &c. &c.

Ulric Zell, father of the Cologne press, was a native of Germany, and is said to have gained his knowledge of the art at Mentz. In the Cologne Chronicle of 1499, he gives the following testimony:

"ITEM : This most revered art was first discovered at Mentz, in Germany ; and it is a great honor to the German nation, that such ingenious men were found in it. This happened in the year of our Lord MCCCCXL; and from that time, till the year MCCCCL, the art, and what belongs to it, was rendered more perfect. In the year of our Lord MCCCCL, which was a golden year, then men began to print, and the first book printed was a Bible in Latin, and it was printed in a larger character than that with which men now print mass-books. ITEM: although this art was discovered at Mentz at first, in the manner in which it is now commonly used, yet the first example of it was found in Holland, in the Donatuses which were before printed there. And thence is derived the beginning of this art, and it is more masterly and subtle than the ancient manner was, and by far more ingenious: but the first inventor of printing was a citizen of Mentz, and was born at Strasbourg, and was called John Gudenburch. ITEM: from Mentz, the before-mentioned art first came to Cologne, thence to Strasbourg, and thence to Venice. The beginning and progress of the before-mentioned art was told me, by word of mouth, by the worthy man, Master Ulrich Tzell of Hanault, printer at Cologne, in the present year MCCCCXCIX—by whom the fore-mentioned art is come to Cologne."

Schœpflin asserts, that Peter de Olpe, not U. Zell, was the first Cologne printer: Mr. Dibdin satisfactorily answers him, and proves that Zell printed there in 1466, four years prior to Olpe. "Upon the whole," observes Mr. D. "the evidence of Ulric Zell appears to be as honest as it is curious."

Theo. Volchart Coornhert, in his translation of *Cicero's Offices*, which is dedicated to the Burgomasters, Judges, and Senators of Hærlem, 1561, observes, like Junius, that he writes upon the authority of

" Aged persons of the highest respectability and credit, who had repeatedly informed him, not only of the family of the inventor, and of his name and surname, but also concerning the rude manner of printing which he at first practised, and the place of his residence, which they had often pointed out to him with their fingers."

Ludovico Guicciardini, by birth an Italian, in his *Descrisione di tutti i Paesi Bassi*, written 1565, and printed at Antwerp, in the year 1567, gives the following, in support of the claims of Hærlem:

" According to the common tradition of the inhabitants, and the assertion of other natives of Holland, as well as the testimony of certain authors and other records, it appears that the art of printing and stamping letters and characters on paper, in the manner now used, was first invented in this place: but the author of the invention happening to die before the art was brought to perfection, and had required repute, his servant, they say, went to reside at Mentz; where, giving proofs of his knowledge in that science, he was joyfully received; and where, having applied himself to the business with unremitting diligence, it became at length generally known, and was brought to entire perfection; in consequence of which, the fame afterwards spread abroad and became general, that the art and science of printing originated in that city. What is really the truth, I am not able, nor will I take upon me to decide; it sufficing me to have said these few words, that I might not be guilty of injustice towards this town and this country."

That Laurentius Coster carried the art no farther than separate wooden types, appears from a Dutch poem, intituled *Hertspiegal*, published in the sixteenth century, by Henry Spiechal, who exclaims:

" Thou first, Laurentius, to supply the defect of wooden tablets, adaptedst wooden types, and afterwards didst connect them with a thread, to imitate writing. A treacherous servant surreptitiously obtained the honor of the discovery: but truth itself, though destitute of common and wide-spread fame; truth, I say, still remains."

There is no mention in this poem, of metal types; had he been robbed of these, as well as of wooden ones, such a circumstance could not have been passed over in silence.

That the rough specimens with which Laurentius amused himself, should be discovered, at the distance of three centuries, appears almost improbable; yet John Enschedius, a printer, discovered an old parchment *Horarium*, printed on both sides, in eight pages, containing The Alphabet, The Lord's Prayer, The Apostles' Creed, and three short prayers, which he imagines to be the first productions of Laurentius. Mr. Meerman submitted this to artists, (competent judges,) who gave as their opinion that it exactly agreed with the description of Junius: it also corresponds with the first edition of the Dutch *Speculum Salvationis*, and the fragment of the Holland *Donatus*, which are said to have been the productions of Laurentius, and are specimens of his piety and ingenuity, in this essay of his newly invented art. Mr. Meerman has given an exact engraving of this singular curiosity.

Having touched upon the principal arguments in favor of Hærlem, we shall proceed to give those which refer to Mentz:

It is generally affirmed that John Geinfleisch, sen. came to Mentz in 1441, and it is conjectured that he brought with him some of the wooden types, the property of Laurentius Coster of Hærlem, where it is stated that he had been employed, and there learned the art and mystery of printing. In the following year, 1442, we are informed that he gave strong proofs of his industry, by the production of two small works, intituled, *Alexandri Galli Doctrinale*, and *Petri Hispani Tractatus*:—these being books much used in schools, he had every reason to expect that they would meet with a profitable sale, together with a future prospect of success in his new enterprise.

In 1443, he engaged the house *Zum Jungen*, when he was joined by Faust: soon after, J. Meidenbachius and others were admitted partners; but their names are not transmitted to our times. In 1444, they were joined by Guttemberg, who is said to have made ineffectual attempts, for several years, to perfect the art at Strazburg. These ingenious men at length discovered that the wooden types were not sufficiently durable, and not altogether answering their expectation in other respects, the two brothers commenced cutting metal types; while these were preparing, they printed several books of frequent use, such as, the *Tabula Alphabetica*, the *Catholicon*, the *Donati Grammatica*, and the *Confessionalia :* these were printed with separate wooden types and wooden blocks.

To commence printing an edition of THE BIBLE in this early stage of the art, must be acknowledged by all as a most astonishing and wonderful undertaking; it was printed with large cut metal types, and published in 1450: if we consider the immense labor of this work, it is no wonder that it should be seven or eight years in completing. This year the partnership was dissolved; in August, Faust and Guttemberg entered into a new agreement, the former supplying money, the latter skill, for their mutual benefit. Various difficulties arising, occasioned a law-suit for the money which Faust had advanced; the cause was decided against Guttemberg. A dissolution of partnership ensued in 1455; in 1457, a magnificent edition of the *Psalter* was published by Faust and Schœffer, with a singular commendation, in which they assumed to themselves the merit of a new invention, (viz. of metal types,) *ad inventionem artificiosam imprimendi ae characterizandi.* This book was in some measure the work of Guttemberg, and at that time considered uncommonly elegant; it was four years in the press, and came out but eighteen months after the partnership was dissolved between him and Faust.

John Fust, or Faust, a goldsmith of Mentz, was one of the three artists considered as the inventors of printing; it is not certain that he did more than supply the money for carrying on the concern. In 1462, Faust carried a number of Bibles to Paris, which he and his partner Schœffer had printed, and disposed of them as manuscripts; at this time the discovery of the art was not known in France. At first he sold them at the high price of 500 or 600 crowns, the sum usually obtained by the scribes; he afterwards lowered his price to sixty, which created universal astonishment; but when he produced them according to the demand, and even reduced the price to thirty, all Paris became agitated. The uniformity of the copies increased their wonder, the Parisians considering it a task beyond human invention; informations were given to the police against him as a magician; his lodgings were searched, a great number of Bibles were found, and seized; the red ink with which they were embellished was said to be his blood; it was seriously adjudged that he was in league with the devil; whereupon he was cast into prison, and would most probably have shared the fate of such, whom ignorant and superstitious judges condemned in those days for witchcraft. He now found it necessary, in order to gain his liberty, to make known the discovery of the art. This circumstance gave rise to the tradition of "The Devil and Dr. Faustus," which is handed down to the present time. It is uncertain when Faust died, he was at Paris in 1466, and it is strongly conjectured that he fell a victim to the plague, which then raged in that capital.

Naude, in his *Mascurat*, contends that Faust was the first printer in Europe, and that he took in Guttemberg as a partner. He grounds his argument on the impressions bearing the name of Faust, and not the other partners; whereas, if Guttemberg and Coster had had an equal share in the invention, they would not have permitted him and his son-in-law to enjoy the honor, without offering to do the like, or even asserting their own right.

J. Trithemius, in his history of the year 1450, gives the following particulars relative to the invention, which he states to have received from the mouth of Peter Schœffer, the inventor of cast metal types:

"About this time that wonderful and almost incredible Art of printing and characterizing books, was thought of and invented at Mentz, by John Guttemberg, a citizen of Mentz, who have expended almost all his substance in the invention of this art, and struggling with great difficulties, both respecting his circumstances and the impediments which arose, was upon the brink of relinquishing the attempt; but he completed the undertaking through the advice and pecuniary assistance of John Faust, also a citizen of Mentz. They first printed a vocabulary, called the *Catholicon*, with the characters of letters carved in wooden tablets, in a series, and composed in forms. But as these could not serve for any other purpose, since the characters were not moveable from the tablets, but carved, they afterwards contrived better methods, and invented a manner of casting the forms of all the letters in the Latin alphabet, which they called matrices, from which they again cast brass and iron characters capable of sustaining any pressure, which they first cut with the hand."

The person who discovered the method of casting the types and completed the art as it now remains, was Peter Schœffer, the first servant of Guttemberg and Faust, who became son-in-law to the latter; these three kept the art a secret for some time, till at length it was divulged by their servants, whose assistance was required in the concern.

A great majority of German, French, and Italian authors, are decidedly of opinion that the discovery was made in Germany. That printing was exercised at Mentz at an early period, is an incontrovertible fact; and was practised there by several persons, to one or other of whom this invention has been attributed. It is strange, while Mentz is priding herself upon this high honor, the citizens are not agreed to whom the merit is due.

Naude observes, that the person is not yet born who can say that he has seen books printed by either Coster, Guttemberg, or Mentil, before, or as early as those of Faust, all that can be urged on their behalf being founded on reports, conjectures, probabilities, forged authorities, and the jealousies of cities against one another.

Salmuth cites a public act, which states Faust to be the inventor; and, after sustaining it for some time, he at length took in Guttemberg as a partner, to contribute towards the expense, which was great, in consequence of the books being printed on vellum, after the Chinese method.

The most ample testimony in favor of Schœffer is given by Jo. Frid. Faustus of Aschaffenburg, from papers preserved in his family:

"Peter Schœffer of Gernsheim, perceiving his master Faust's design, and being himself ardently desirous to improve the art, found out (by the good providence of God) the method of cutting (*incidendi*) the characters in a *matrix*, that the letters might easily be singly *cast*, instead of being *cut*. He privately *cut matrices* for the whole alphabet; and when he showed his master the letters cast from those matrices, Faust was so pleased with the contrivance, that he promised Peter to give him his only daughter Christina in marriage, a promise which he soon after performed. But there were as many difficulties at first with these letters, as there had been before with wooden ones; the metal being too soft to support the force of the impression; but this defect was soon remedied, by mixing the metal with a substance which sufficiently hardened it."

The first book printed with the improved types was *Durandi Rationale*, in 1459; however, they seem to have had only one size of cast letters, all the larger characters which occur being cut types, as it plainly appears by an inspection of the book. Faust and Schœffer continued to print a considerable number of works till 1466: particularly two famous editions of *Tully's Offices*. They took more impressions on vellum than on paper in their earliest works, which was the case with their *Bibles* and *Tully's Offices*. This was soon inverted; for paper being introduced, they took but few impressions on vellum, which were more for curiosities than for general use. How long Faust lived is uncertain; but, in 1471, we find that Schœffer was in partnership with Conrad Henlif and a kinsman of his master Faust. He printed several books after the death of his father-in-law; the last of which that can be discovered is a third edition of the *Psalter*, in 1490, in which the old cut metal types were used.

We are informed that the Mentz printers, in order that the art might not be divulged, administered an oath of secrecy to all whom they employed; this appears to have been strictly adhered to until the year 1462, at which period the city was sacked and plundered by Archbishop Adolphus, its former rights and franchises were also abolished: amid the consternation occasioned by this extraordinary event, the workmen of the Mentz press, considering their oath of fidelity no longer binding, now became free agents, and spread themselves in different directions; by this circumstance, the hitherto great mystery was rapidly carried through a considerable portion of Europe: the places which received it early, after some time, commenced a contention for the merit of the discovery of this important Art, which has given rise to the numerous disputes we are now endeavoring to reconcile.

Having given the most material points respecting the claims of Hærlem and Mentz, we shall now proceed to state those in favor of Strazburg:

It is asserted by J. Wimphelingius, the oldest writer in favor of the latter city, that Guttemberg was the inventor of " a new art of writing," *ars impressoria*, which he happily completed at Mentz; but he does not mention one work of his printing; in another book he observes, " the art of printing was found out by *Guttemberg, incomplete*."

Richard Bartoline published a work in favor of Mentilius, and states the period to be 1441. Gebwiler, (born 1473,) contends that the art was first discovered at Strazburg, by Mentilius, and that Faust, of Mentz, afterwards imitated him.

Trithemius informs us, that Guttemberg spent all his substance in quest of this art, and met with insuperable difficulties; that, in despair, he had nearly given up all hopes of success, till he was assisted by the liberality of Faust, and by his brother's skill, in the city of Mentz. It is evident that his endeavors at Strazburg were unsuccessful; as appears by the documents of a judicial decree of that Senate, in 1439; after the death of Andrew Drizehen, or Drizenius, whom Guttemberg, (a man of great talent and ingenuity) had engaged to instruct in the art of polishing stones; he afterwards employed one John Riff in the art of making mirrors, or looking glasses, as practised at Aix-la-Chapelle, and also in other arts, in which the said Drizehen, and also Anthony Heilman, wished to be initiated: certain conditions were then agreed upon. These two individuals paid an unexpected visit to Guttemberg, who lived in the suburbs, when they found him busily employed in another mystery, which had been concealed from them. After a short dispute, Guttemberg proposed to instruct them on certain conditions; one of which was, that a portion of the sum advanced by the parties be refunded to their heirs if they should die within the space of five years; Drizehen did not survive the term, when his heirs insisted on the conditions of the engagement; to which Guttemberg, who appears to have been a litigious man, strenuously refused; a legal process was the consequence. From the evidence given by the different workmen, carpenters, servants, &c. it is evident that this mystery was the invention of printing. Immediately after the demise of Drize-hen, Guttemberg gave orders to his servants to convey from his house certain implements in the most secret manner; which afterwards appeared to be a printing-press, and a quantity of letters cut in wood. This discovery was made December 26, 1438.

In 1439, John Dunnius declared before the magistrates, that he had received one hundred florins for work done at a press three years before; this brings the epoch of the first attempt to 1436.

In 1438, the unfortunate Drizehen lamented to his Confessor, the great expense which he had incurred, without having been reimbursed a single *obolus*. Nor did Guttemberg himself, who persisted in his unsuccessful attempts, reap any advantage from them; for on quitting Strazburg, he was overwhelmed in debt, and under the necessity of parting with the greater portion of his property.

John Mentilius, a physician at Paris, has strenuously de-fended the cause of his namesake of Strazburg: but his endeavors have not advanced the cause of Mentilius one tittle beyond what had been done by his predecessors.

The principal argument which the defenders of Mentilius have set forth, is the title of nobility conferred upon him by the Emperor Frederick III. This circumstance was handed down by the grand-daughter of Mentilius, who married J. Schottien; and he gave it publicity in the *Ptolemaic Geography*, printed at Strazburg, 1520. It has been asserted, that he was induced to make this boast, from the conduct of John Schœffer, of Mentz, who had previously announced in his *Colophus*, that the dis-covery was made by John Faust, his grandfather by his mother's side.

This rivalship between Schœffer and Schottus was carried to a considerable height; the former gained many advocates in favor of Faust, without allowing Guttemberg the least merit; amongst the number was the Emperor Maximilian, who, in 1518, granted him an exclusive privilege of printing *Livy*. During the life of this Emperor, the latter remained silent: but it is said that (immediately after his death) he endeavored to persuade his successor, Charles V. and the literati, that Faust had no real claim to the merit of the invention, as the credit of it justly belonged to Mentilius. In consequence of the above-mentioned grant of the title of nobility, we are informed that, in 1520, he began to prefix his family arms to all the books which he afterwards printed : adding,

" That they were granted to John Mentilius, the first inventor of printing."

It appears that coat-armour had been previously conferred on the inventors to perpetuate the discovery, but the grant to Mentilius was merely to gratify his ambition, as the diploma contained not a syllable about the invention of printing.

A variety of evidence might be adduced in favor of Mentilius, had it not been superceded by Schœpflin's discovery of the document of the law-suit; from which it appears, that Guttemberg was the first who attempted printing at Strazburg, although his endeavors proved unsuccessful. We are informed by Jacob Wimphelingius, that Mentilius acquired a fortune by printing his works in a correct and elegant manner: therefore, if Guttemberg claims the honor of the invention, the profitable harvest was reaped by Mentilius.

Two Strazburg Chronologers, (Dan. Speklinus, the other Anonymous) expressly inform us, that John Geinsfleisch, sen. (whom they distinguished from Guttemberg) when he had learned the art from its first inventor, carried it by theft to his native city, Mentz.

They make Strazburg the place of the invention, and Mentilius the inventor, from whom the types were stolen. These writers are completely in error, because Geinsfleisch was a resident at Mentz, in 1441, and Mentilius, according to their account, did not begin to print before 1440; therefore, it is improbable that he could have been a servant to the latter: other authorities state, that Mentilius did not practise prior to 1444 or 1448 ; neither will their narrative agree better with Guttemberg, who certainly printed before Mentilius, as, from the evidence produced in the law-suit, 1439, we have no mention of any servant, except Laurentius Beildek.

We have endeavored in the foregoing pages, to reduce the subject into as small a focus as possible: this we have done by bringing it to one simple question, which in our opinion will settle this long contested point: viz. *Had the Mentz printers any rival prior to* 1462 ? Certainly not. Then we can have no hesitation in decorating their brows with the laurel wreath, as a just reward for their ingenuity and exertion, which others have vainly endeavored to deprive them of.

The medallion in the following page contains the portraits of the individuals generally acknowledged in Germany as the first printers; the subject from which this was copied is supposed to have been engraved by the famous Gubitz, of Berlin, from an old German painting.

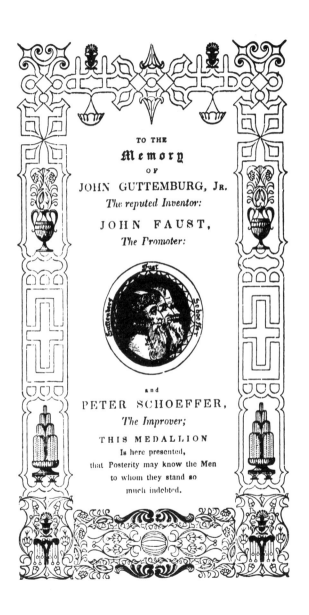

TO THE

Memory

OF

JOHN GUTTEMBURG, Jr.

The reputed Inventor:

JOHN FAUST,

The Promoter:

and

PETER SCHOEFFER,

The Improver;

THIS MEDALLION

Is here presented,

that Posterity may know the **Men**

to whom they stand so

much indebted.

The Art of Printing, from the best authorities, appears to have been introduced into England, at Westminster, in 1474, by William Caxton, mercer, who gained his knowledge of the Art while travelling in Germany as agent for the Company of Mercers, who, in those days, amongst other commodities, dealt in books, which they either purchased in manuscript or caused to be printed. In 1474 appeared the "Game of Chess," considered to be the first book printed in that kingdom. Caxton must have been at that time at least sixty-two years of age, and was remarkable for his habits of industry. He died about six years after the introduction of the Art, having, it is said, in addition to the working of his press, translated not fewer than five thousand folio pages.

Chevellier mentions a book printed at Goa, in 1577; and that Prester John was very anxious, in 1581, to introduce it into Abyssinia; and that it actually passed from Spain into Morocco in that country. S. Olon, the French Ambassador to Morocco, assures us, that there is scarcely a printing-office in the whole territory; and that it is a part of their religion not to suffer corn, horses, or books, to be exported; their fondness for the latter is increased by reason of their scarcity.

Some Danish missionaries are said to have sent a printing-press and workmen to Tranquebar; where they printed the New Testament (in quarto), Prayer Books, Catechisms, &c., in Portuguese, and several Eastern languages, for promoting their pious designs.

A Russian merchant, in 1560, conveyed printing materials into that state, and had several works printed there; but, being a superstitious people, and fearful lest it might tend to alter their religious notions, some persons were employed to destroy the press, &c. which circumstance passed by unnoticed, as no attempt was ever made to discover the perpetrators. Early in the next century, several works were printed at Moscow and St. Petersburg; since which, the art has gradually advanced in that extensive territory. The Arts and Sciences are now improving.

The Art was extended early, by means of Europeans, but more particularly by the Spanish missionaries, into Africa and

America. Mr. Thomas in his *History of Printing in America,* asserts that a press was established at Mexico some years before 1569.

The earliest production from the Peruvian Press was printed at Lima, by Father Pablo Jos. de Arriago, in 1621. Mr. Thomas states its introduction about 1590: most of their works, prior to the last fifty years, are said to have been upon religious subjects. About the beginning of the seventeenth century, a press is said to have been introduced into the Spanish part of St. Domingo; as well as into the Isle of Cuba; the government principally employed these presses.

The first press in North America, is stated to have been at Cambridge, (Mass.) in 1639.

In the accomplishment of what we have here undertaken, we shall be much indebted to *Thomas' History of Printing,* for facts and dates respecting the periodicals published here, previous to the termination of the American revolution. In fact, there is no person to whom the public is more indebted for a correct history of printing, than the late venerable ISAIAH THOMAS, of Worcester, whose vigorous intellect raised him to distinction, and secured those blessings which are the never failing rewards of industry and perseverance. Mr. Thomas was not only the patron of every enterprize which promised utility to the rising generation, but, in a particular manner, in his old age, devoted his honestly acquired wealth in bringing into existence the " American Antiquarian Society," which, in future ages, will tell the story of our country's origin and growth.

Among the first settlers of New England were many pious as well as learned men. They emigrated from a country where the press had more license than in other parts of Europe, and they were acquainted with the usefulness of it. As soon as they had made those provisions that were necessary for their existence in this land, which was then a rude wilderness, their next objects were, the establishment of schools, and a printing press; the latter of which was not tolerated, till many years afterward, by the elder colony of Virginia.

The founders of the colony of Massachusetts consisted of but a small number of persons, who arrived at Salem in 1628. A few more joined them in 1629; and governor Winthrop, with the addition of fifteen hundred settlers, arrived in 1630. These last landed at the place since called Charlestown, opposite to Boston, where they pitched their tents, and built a few huts for shelter. In 1631, they began to settle Cambridge, four miles from the place where they landed. They also began a settlement on the identical spot where Boston now stands. In 1638, they built an academy at Cambridge, which in process of time was increased to a college; and, in the same year, they opened a printing house in that place. In January, 1639, printing was first performed in that part of North America, which extends from the gulf of Mexico to the frozen ocean.

For this press our country is chiefly indebted to the Rev. Mr. Glover, a non-conformist minister, who possessed a considerable estate, and had left his native country with a determination to settle among his friends, who had emigrated to Massachusetts; because in this wilderness, he could freely enjoy, with them, those opinions which were not countenanced by the government and a majority of the people in England.

Very little more than the name of this Father of the American press is known among us. So far as our researches have extended, we can only find that his name has been barely mentioned by two respectable journalists, Governor Winthrop, and Captain Johnson, who were among the first settlers that emigrated here. This was, probably, owing to his having died on his passage to Massachusetts.

Another press, with types, and another printer, were, in 1660, sent over from England by the corporation for propagating the gospel among the Indians in New England. This press, &c. was designed solely for the purpose of printing the Bible, and other books, in the Indian language. On their arrival they were carried to Cambridge, and employed in the printing house already established in that place.

Notwithstanding printing continued to be performed in Cambridge, from a variety of causes it happened that many original works were sent from New England, Massachusetts in particular, to London, to be printed. Among these causes the principal were—first, the press at Cambridge had, generally, full employment, secondly, the printing done there was executed in an inferior style; and, thirdly, many works on controverted points of religion, were not allowed to be printed in this country. Hence it happened that for more than eighty years after printing was first practised in the colony, manuscripts were occasionally sent to England for publication.

The fathers of Massachusetts kept a watchful eye on the press; and, in neither a religious or civil point of view, were they disposed to give it much liberty. Both the civil and ecclesiastical rulers were fearful that if it was not under wholesome restraints, contentions and heresies would arise among the people. In 1662, the government of Massachusetts appointed licensers of the press; and afterward, in 1664, passed a law that "no printing should be allowed in any town within the jurisdiction, except in Cambridge"—nor should any thing be printed there but what the government permitted through the agency of those persons who were empowered for the purpose.— Offenders against this regulation were to forfeit their presses to the country, and to be disfranchised of the privilege of printing thereafter. In a short time, this law was so far repealed, as to permit the use of a press at Boston, and a person was authorized to conduct it; subject, however, to the licensers who were appointed for the purpose of inspecting it.

It does not appear that the press, in Massachusetts, was free from legal restraints till about the year 1755. Holyoke's Almanac, for 1715, has, in the title page, "Imprimatur, J. Dudley."

Boston has the credit of issuing the first newspaper in North America, which was commenced on Monday, April 24, 1704, by John Campbell, Esq. under the title of the *Boston News Letter.* It was discontinued, (1776) after being regularly published for nearly seventy-two years.

The second newspaper which appeared in America, as well as the first, was published in Boston; it was called *The Boston Gazette;* the first number was published December 21, 1719, on a half-sheet foolscap size.

The *American Weekly Mercury,* was commenced the day following at Philadelphia, which made the third paper issued in the United States.

The third newspaper which appeared in Boston was the *New England Courant*, established by James Franklin, August 17, 1721, and was printed on a half sheet crown paper. On Mr. Musgrave's becoming proprietor of the Gazette, the printing was taken from Franklin, which circumstance probably led to the establishment of the *Courant;* for he warmly attacked Musgrave and endeavored to have him turned out of office. A society of gentlemen furnished essays for this paper, which were evidently written by men of talents, attacking persons in office, the clergy and the prevailing religious opinions; and opposed rather rudely the introduction of inoculation for the small pox. These essays attracted general notice, and the paper soon had warm advocates and zealous opposers; and finally roused the attention and interference of the government. Dr. Increase Mather openly denounced the Courant, by an address to the public, which appeared in the Boston Gazette. Before the Courant had been printed a year, Franklin was imprisoned by order of the government in the common jail, where he remained four weeks. After his release from prison, the club was encouraged to proceed with increased boldness, which led to a further interference of the government; and it was "thereupon ordered that James Franklin, the printer and publisher, be strictly forbidden by this Court to print or publish the New England Courant, or any pamphlet or paper of the like nature, except it be first supervised by the Secretary of this Province; and the Justices of his Majesty's Sessions of the Peace, for the county of Suffolk, at their next adjournment, be directed to take sufficient bonds of said Franklin, for his good behaviour for twelve month's time."

Franklin published the Courant, notwithstanding, on the following Monday, without submitting its contents to the Secretary. For this neglect, a bill of indictment was preferred to the grand jury against him for contempt of an order of the Court. The jury returned "*Ignoramus*" on the bill, and he was put under bonds for his good behavior pursuant to the order of the General Court. In consequence of things being thus situated, it was determined to alter the imprint by leaving out the word *James*, and inserting that of *Benjamin*, in order to evade the act.

3*

This was carried into immediate effect, and the Courant purported to be "printed and sold by BENJAMIN FRANKLIN, in Queen street;" although he was a minor, and an apprentice to his brother. The paper continued to be published in the name of Benjamin Franklin for some time after he left his brother; and for any thing that appears, until its publication was discontinued in 1727.

The British Colonies in America, and the West India Islands, first received the art in 1751: their productions were chiefly confined to colonial gazettes, &c.

Port-au-Prince is said to have received a press in 1750, at which an account of a great earthquake (experienced in that Island,) was printed, in 1751: the presses under the dominion of France are chiefly confined to the use of the government.

Cicero, in his *De Natura Deorum*, has a passage, from which Toland supposes the moderns took the hint of printing. That author orders the types to be made of metal, and calls them *formæ literarum*, the very words used by the first printers to express them. In Virgil's time, brands, with letters, were used for marking cattle, &c. with the owner's name.

In the second book, he gives a hint of separate cast letters, when he speaks of some ingenious man's throwing the twenty-four letters of the alphabet, (made either of gold or other metal) by chance together, and thus producing *The Annals of Ennius*. He makes this observation, in opposition to the atheistical argument of the creation of the world by chance.

In the *Philos. Trans.* we find the emperor Justin could not write, in consequence, a similar expedient to the printing of playing cards was resorted to; namely, a smooth piece of board with holes cut through it, in the form of the letters of his name; and when he had occasion to sign anything, this was laid on the paper, and he marked the letters with a pin, or stylus dipped in red ink, and directed through the holes.

The following particulars, relative to the first productions of the art (though well known to the curious,) will, we trust, be deemed acceptable to our readers:—

With respect to their forms, they were generally either large or small folios, or at least quartos: the lesser sizes were not in use. The leaves were without running title, direction-word, number of pages, or divisions into paragraphs. The character itself was a rude old Gothic mixed with Secretary, designed on purpose to imitate the hand-writing of those times; the words were printed so close to one another, that it was difficult and tedious to be read, even by those who were used to manuscripts, and to this method; and often lead the inattentive reader into mistakes. Their orthography was various, and often arbitrary, disregarding method. They had very frequent abbreviations, which in time grew so numerous and difficult to be understood, that there was a necessity of writing a book to teach the manner of reading them. Their periods were distinguished by no other point than the double or single one, that is, the colon or full point; but they a little after, introduced an oblique stroke, thus, /, which answered the purpose of our comma. They used no capital letters to begin a sentence, or for proper names of men or places. They left blanks for the places of titles, initial letters, and other ornaments, in order to have them supplied by illuminators, whose ingenious art, though in vogue before, and at that time, did not long survive the masterly improvements made by the printers in this branch of their art. Those ornaments were exquisitely fine, and curiously variegated with the most beautiful colors, and even with gold and silver; the margins, likewise, were frequently charged with a variety of figures, of saints, birds, beasts, monsters, flowers, &c. which had sometimes relation to the contents of the page, though often none at all: these embellishments were very costly; but for those that could not afford a great price, there were more inferior ornaments, which could be done at a much easier rate. The name of the printer, place of his residence, &c. &c. where either wholly neglected, or put at the end of the book, not without some pious ejaculation or doxology. The date was likewise omitted, or involved in some crampt circumstantial period, or else printed either at full length, or by numerical letters, and sometimes partly one and partly the other; thus, One Thousand CCCC and lxxiiii, &c. but all of them at the end of the book. There were no variety of characters, no intermixture of Roman and Italic; they are of later invention; but their pages were continued in a Gothic letter of the same size throughout. They printed but few copies at once, for 200 or 300 were then esteemed a large impression; though, upon the encouragements received from the learned, they increased their numbers in proportion.

About 1469–70, alphabetical tables of the first words of each chapter were introduced, as a guide to the binder. Catch-words (now generally abolished) were first used at Venice, by Vinde line de Spire. The name and place of the inventor of signatures is obscured by a dark cloud.

———

STEREOTYPING seems to have been invented in Scotland, and first practised by William Ged, of Edinburg, in the year 1725, and when properly made known, was hailed with acclamation by the printing and publishing world. When the types are set with high quadrats and spaces, they are plastered over with liquid stucco to the thickness of about half an inch, so that a level cake is formed on the surface of the types. As soon as the stucco hardens, which it does almost immediately, the cake is separated from the types, and, on being turned up, shows a complete hollow or mould-like representation of the faces of the types and every thing else in the page. There being no longer any use for the types, they are carried off and distributed. As for the cake, it is put into an oven and baked to a certain degree of heat and hardness, like a piece of pottery. It is next laid in a square iron pan, having a lid of the same metal, with holes at the corners. The pan is now immersed in a pot of molten metal, and being allowed to fill by means of the holes, it is at length taken out and put aside till it is cool. On opening the pan, a curious appearance is presented. The metal has run into the mould side of the cake, and formed a thin plate all over, exhibiting the perfect appearance of the faces of the types on which the stucco was plastered. Thus is procured a fictitious page of types, not thicker than the sixth of an inch, and which can be printed from in the same manner as in the case of a real page. Such is the process of stereotyping, or making *fixed*, or *stationary types ;*—and now for the utility of the invention :

In all cases of book work where a small edition only will be required, it is best to print from types, and then distribute them · but in most cases of standard works or books published in parts, or numbers, stereotyping becomes absolutely necessary. It is easy to perceive the reason for this. When books are published in numbers, it often happens that many more copies are sold of one number than of another, and unless the the types be kept up to complete sets in the hands of the publisher, or to print copies according to the increased demand, a serious loss is sustained. The manufacture of stereotype plates is, therefore, simply a means of keeping up fictitious types to answer future demands, at an expense infinitely inferior to that of keeping the actual pages standing.

LITHOGRAPHY is the art of printing from stone. It is only of recent invention, and differs very considerably in principle, from the art of printing from moveable types, wooden blocks or copper or other plates. The process consists in writing on a particular kind of stone, and from thence working off, by a press, any number of copies, the writing thus standing in relief on the stone like raised letters. The peculiar value of this ingenious art is in the cheapness and ease with which it accomplishes impressions of pictorial delineations or manuscript. The discovery of the Lithographic art was made upwards of thirty years since by Senefelder, a native of Germany—a country to which the human race is also indebted for the more noble art of printing from types; but since that period very great improvements have been made upon it.

The history of the origin of lithography is instructive, and affords to the young an additional instance of the triumph of genius over poverty and its attendant disadvantages. Like every new invention, when first attempted to be brought into notice, it met with all the obstacles which ignorance or prejudice could throw in its way; and it was not till after years of laborious perseverance, accompanied with all the evils attendant on very limited means, that the inventor succeeded in establishing his reputation, and gaining for the new art its due degree of admiration.

Senefelder relates with the greatest candor, that having become an author and at the same time being so poor that he could not raise the necessary funds for the printing of his work with a view to publication, he endeavored to devise some method by which his object might be attained, and, after much anxious consideration, he resolved on attempting to accomplish it with his own hands. With this view, his attention was first directed to several original curious modes of stereotype, some of which he considerably matured, and had his circumstances at this period been such as to admit of his devoting a sufficient time to the perfecting of this first part of his undertaking, it is questionable whether his talents would have ever been *forced* into that particular line of study, which, in the end, acquired for his name so great a celebrity. The same remark is applicable to some of the other ingenious attempts which preceded his great discovery. For a time, however, plan succeeded plan, each being abandoned in turn, as new and more plausible theories struck his fancy, and in this way did he persevere, for many months, with various degrees of success, but without the necessary results; and he at last relinquished this course of experiments altogether, as presenting too many obstacles to be overcome by an individual in his circumstances.

Disappointed, but not disheartened, in not having been so successful in his operations as he had anticipated, we next find him attempting to realize his hopes by substituting plates of copper and tin for his metal and composition blocks; but this second course of experiments was attended with little better success than the former; for, after much labor, and numerous trials with the etching needle, and by writing on the copper with different chemical inks of his own composition, this medium was found to be liable to all the objections which had deterred him from prosecuting the stereotype plan. Being, however, still of the opinion that his object was to be accomplished by *art* alone, and having laid aside his copper plates for a time, as too expensive, he began to look around for a substitute which would supply their place for all the purposes of practice, and at a much less cost. He was not long in determining this point; for, being aware that certain kinds of stone had often been used for similar purposes, he converted the slab on which he ground his colors into a plate for exercising in writing, and found it answered his expectations completely. Experiments now followed each other in rapid succession, all tending to encourage him in the prosecution of his design; and, when at length these stone plates were rendered fit for undergoing the operations of the printing press, he was greatly pleased to find that numerous impressions might be taken on paper, without materially injuring the original.

We shall now at once advert to the time when circumstances conspired to force upon his attention those properties of the art, which, on their first unfolding themselves, so astonished and delighted him. "I had (says he) just succeeded in my little laboratory in polishing a stone plate which I intended to cover with etching ground, in order to continue my exercises in writing backwards, when my mother entered the room, and desired me to write her a bill for the washer-woman, who was waiting for the linen. I happened not to have even the smallest slip of paper at hand, as my little stock of paper had been entirely exhausted by taking proof impressions from the stones; nor was there even a drop of ink in the inkstand. As the matter would not admit of delay, and we had nobody in the house to send for a supply of the deficient materials, I resolved to write the list with my chemical ink, on the stone which I had just polished, and from which I could copy it at leisure."

When about to remove this writing from the stone, some time afterwards, the idea struck him, that, by submitting its surface to the action of acquafortis, such an elevation might be given to the writing as would render it suitable, in the same way as wood-engravings, for receiving printing ink. The experiment exceeded his most sanguine hopes, and he lost no time in following up his success with others, all tending to convince him that he had discovered a new and important art.

Thus it will be seen, that, to a very simple occurrence in itself, Senefelder was indebted for the *hint* on which hinged all his succeeding improvements.

Having now briefly adverted to some of the leading incidents which ultimately led to the discovery of chemical lithography, we shall next proceed to the notice of such particulars concerning the progress of the new art under the fostering care of its author, as may be thought generally interesting.

Let it not be imagined that Senefelder's difficulties ceased with this discovery : the fact is otherwise; for, in addition to the many obstacles which he had to combat from lacking the necessary funds for the prosecution of his labors, others were not wanting of a nature equally serious, and which were to him the source of long and painful anxiety. Among the rest, it was not a little annoying to know that others were beginning to lay claim to the merit of a new discovery.

For a series of years, Senefelder's patience and perseverance, under the most disadvantageous circumstances, were truly astonishing; and we shall now proceed briefly to detail such other particulars in further illustration of the preceding remarks, as may be deemed necessary for completing this part of our subject.

Satisfied as to the originality of his new discovery, Senefelder became anxious to turn it to account, by laying it before the world; and in order to raise the necessary funds for at once effecting this object, we find him, when all other means had failed, offering himself as a substitute for a friend who was then a soldier in the service of the elector of Bavaria, but with his usual want of success; for, on presenting himself at Ingolstadt for the purpose of being enrolled, it was discovered that he was not a native of the electorate, and, consequently, inadmissible to its army. His last hope seemed now to have failed him, and he describes his feelings as being at this time in a state "bordering on despair." However, it was not long ere his prospects began again to brighten a little; and he at length succeeded in publishing, in conjunction with the composer, a collection of music, the execution of which was greatly admired, and which obtained for him the patronage of the elector, and a promise of an exclusive privilege.

About this time another candidate for the honor of having discovered the new art came forward in the person of M. Schmidt, professor of the Royal College; and although, for a time, the station which this gentleman filled helped to support his pretensions against his less fortunate rival, public opinion by degrees became less divided, and ultimately there prevailed but one belief on the subject.

It was not till after having labored a considerable time in his new profession, and experiencing innumerable inconveniences from being compelled to execute all his writings on the stone backwards, that he commenced another series. of experiments, the object of which, was to obviate the necessity of *writing* on the stone, by previously doing it on paper, and then transferring it from the paper to the stone, *reversed.* Some thousands of experiments were made before he was enabled to produce a composition for preparing the surface of the paper suited for all the purposes which he had in view, and it was this property of the new art which more particularly attracted public notice, from the incalculable benefits which it was foreseen would be conferred on all kinds of business when fairly brought into general practice. It was about this time also that he invented the lever press, which added greatly to the comfort and certainty of the operations in the printing department of lithography.

Having at length obtained an exclusive privilege for exercising his art in Bavaria, he did not consider it any longer necessary to keep the process a secret, and it soon spread over the greater part of Germany; but his experience enabled him for several years to outstrip all his competitors in so far as the execution of his work was concerned, although, in every other respect, he seemed to be almost the only one in whose hands the art did not give ample returns both for money and labor. In no other way can this uniform want of success be accounted for, than by supposing, that, while others were making the most of what he had already discovered, he was devoting much of his time to the *experimental* part of the business. This in fact was the case.

About the year 1800, Senefelder went to London for the purpose of establishing himself there as a lithographer, but a few months sufficed to convince him that he had little chance of succeeding in his undertaking; and he returned to his own country, where, on his arrival, he found that many attempts had been made in his absence to deprive him of the benefit of

4

his privilege. Among the most forward in this scheme were two of his brothers, to whom he had communicated all the secrets of the art, and it took some time to counteract the bad effects of their ungenerous conduct. Finding that, in his native place (Munich,) others were reaping many of the advantages which by right should have been the reward of his own industry, he was induced to go to Vienna, for the purpose of superintending a calico printing establishment, the operations of which were to be conducted on the principles of the new art; and here, for the space of several years, his talents were entirely devoted to this new undertaking; but, at the end of which time, from a variety of causes over which he had no control, he was again thrown upon the world, destitute of every thing save the resources of his own genius. It was not till about the year 1809 that Senefelder was extricated from the difficulties of his situation, by being appointed inspector of the royal lithographic establishment of Munich, which at once placed him above the necessity of exercising his profession as a means for gaining his daily subsistence, and enabled him to devote a portion of his time to the improvement of such branches of the art, as, in his former circumstances, he had never found it possible to effect.

In conclusion, it may not be out of place to remark, that, in the case of Senefelder, we have another instance to the many recorded facts in the lives of eminent men, of the successful pursuit of knowledge under extraordinary difficulties—presenting an example worthy of our highest admiration and respect.

———————

Hopeless would be our task, were we to endeavor to trace the subject of ENGRAVING to its original source : after we have explored one path, we find ourselves bewildered in a second, and so in a third, till at length we finally lose ourselves in the endless mazes of despair.

It has been contended by some writers, that the *art of impression* was well known to the ancients; in confirmation of this, they instance the stamps of iron and other metals, with which bales of goods and various articles of their manufacture were marked, throughout Italy and other parts of Europe, during the low ages: and that the art of taking impressions from engraved blocks of wood is nothing more than a principle familiarly known to the ancients from time immemorial; consequently, it is not worthy the appellation of a discovery; even Typography itself is considered by them as scarcely deserving the name of an invention. It appears that the ancient artists used separate letters (similar to our bookbinder's tools) for the purpose of stamping the inscriptions, &c. upon their lamps, their vases, and their bassi-relievi of clay; which being first cast, were afterwards finished by the hand of the modeller. The mode of indentation here noticed, being that of pressing one body against another body of a softer texture, thereby occasioning a change of form in its surface: the impression from engraved blocks or letters, primed with ink, is not merely that of indention upon the paper, but a change of color, from the black tint with which the projecting parts were charged, previous to the operation of printing. We have little proof that the ancients had a knowledge of this latter mode of impression; one instance has been adduced: this is an account of a sigillum of a very rare kind in the Duke of Richmond's collection, the letters of which are raised, as well as the rim, after the manner of our printing types. This stamp is of true ancient brass; it is nearly two inches long, and one in breadth; on the back is a ring, for the purpose of holding it when the impression is made. The letters are in Roman capitals, standing in two rows. It contains

CAIUS JULIUS

CÆCILIUS HERMIAS.

which must have been the name of some private man, no account of such person being found upon record. The ground of this seal being uneven, proves that it was intended to make an impression on a thin substance, whereas, if it were stamped on any thing soft, the unevenness of the ground would be visible, which must destroy its appearance. This signet was found near Rome, and is allowed to be the most ancient sample of printing known: from the appearance of the metal, it is judged to be of the Higher Empire.

Impressions have been taken from it on paper, with modern printing ink, which proves the use it was intended for; the mark performs its office as well as any set of letters could do in a similar manner. From this circumstance we may conclude, that the Romans were acquainted with the essence of printing, nothing more being required to form a page, than to increase the length and number of the lines, which would have been similar to the first printer's rude productions.

It must appear evident, that the impressions of the first printers were made from *wooden blocks,* after the method practised by the Chinese. Mr. Bagford thinks that the hint was taken from ancient medals and seals.

According to Vasari, the important discovery of Chalcography was made by Thomas Finiguerra, a Florentine goldsmith of the fifteenth century, who lived from 1400 to 1460. The manner in which he made this discovery, is thus given by the Rev. T. F. Dibdin.

" Of engraving upon copper the earliest known impression is that executed by one Thomaso Finiguerra, a goldsmith of Florence, with the date of 1460 upon it. One of the following circumstances is supposed to have given rise to the discovery. Finiguerra chanced to cast, or let fall a piece of copper, engraved and filled with ink, into melted sulphur: and observing that the exact impression of his work was left on the sulphur, he repeated the experiment on moistened paper, rolling it gently with a roller. This origin has been admitted by Lord Walpole and Mr. Landseer; but another has been also mentioned by Huber:—" It is reported," says he, " that a washer-woman left some linen upon a plate or dish on which Finiguerra had just been engraving; and that an impression of the subject engraved, however imperfect, came off upon the linen ; occasioned by its weight and moistness."

Of all the discoveries which have been made, we conceive the reflecting mind will acknowledge that none have tended more to the improvements and comforts of society than that of Printing ; in truth, it would almost be impossible to enumerate the advantages derived by all professions from the streams of this invaluable fountain, this main-spring of all our transactions in life. It has been justly remarked by a celebrated writer, that, were the starry heavens deficient of one constellation, the vacuum could not be better supplied, than by the introduction of a printing press.

The more we reflect, the greater becomes our surprise, till at length we are lost in wonder and astonishment, that the art should have lain dormant for so many generations, (when the principle was so universally known,) without being brought into general use: still we may consider it fortunate in other respects; and was, no doubt, ordered for a wise purpose, because, had it received its birth during the dark ages, before civilization began to dawn, it is not improbable, (considering the opposition it at first met with,) but it would have been strangled in its infancy, and consigned to an early tomb! But Providence has ordained it otherwise. The first printers, as though aware of the consequence of too early an exposure, administered an oath of secrecy to their servants; and these deserving individuals indefatigably labored for the space of twenty years, until the infant, which they had sedulously rocked in the cradle of industry, arrived at full maturity : then it was that this noble invention filled Europe with amazement and consternation, the powerful blaze of which has proved too much for the whole phalanx of priests, scribes, and their adherents, to extinguish. On finding all their efforts vain, they artfully pretended to turn in its favor, and reported it to be a divine gift, fit only to be exercised in monasteries, chapels, and religious houses; and the printers were courted to fall into their views, several of whom accepted the invitation : but this narrow policy was of short duration, the art spread with too rapid strides to be confined within such circumscribed limits; for as fast as individuals gained a knowledge of the mystery, they commenced the undertaking in different places ; by which means, those who had till then remained in ignorance, gained a true sense of religion, and the chicanery of the priests, from that period, gradually became more apparent, and has sunk into comparative insignificance, during the progress of the glorious reformation.

4*

Viewing the subject in its proper light, can we too highly prize that art, which has, and ever must continue (in opposition to all attempts to shackle it) not only to amuse and instruct the young; but also to cheer and console the aged, while journeying to the close of this vale of tears? It is much to be regretted, that many of those on whom Providence has so profusely lavished her bounty, should withhold their assistance to the laborers in this vineyard: in short, this art, above all others, justly deserves to be encouraged; because, from it we derive almost every intellectual comfort, which man can boast on this side the grave.

TYPOGRAPHIA:

OR

THE PRINTER'S INSTRUCTOR.

Though hard's our task, we fearless tread this ground,
Hope whispers us, " *No work is perfect found :*"
Embolden'd thus, we now proceed to state,
For others use, what to our Art relate :
Should the fastidious Critic vainly try,
Our best endeavors with his jaundic'd eye,
These questions let us ask, to set him right,
That he may view us in a favor'd light :
Has thy eye yet a perfect work e'er seen ?
Look not from us, for what has never been !
How can imperfect man expect to find,
That which is not within the human mind ?
Such being the case, our work we humbly trust
T' the Reader's candor —Americans are just :
To serve the Art, and men's good will attain,
Should we succeed, Ambition's height we gain.

In performing this part of our duty, we shall endeavor, to the utmost of our humble ability, to explain every thing in as concise and clear a manner as possible; at the same time we shall omit nothing, however trivial, that may be connected with this important subject. In doing this, we are fully aware that some will condemn such minutiæ as unnecessary : but, let us ask, is it requisite, because a few are acquainted with it, that the information should be withheld from others ? It is a subject which cannot fail to interest the general reader, and particularly so all the admirers of the Typographic Art.

When any one pronounces a printing-office as *complete,* it ought to be considered as a mere compliment, because, in a strict and literal sense, no office can deserve this epithet, unless it is furnished with all the fusil metal types for both modern and ancient languages : we believe that scarcely any office can boast the appellation. In truth, to supply these almost unnecessary fonts would only waste a man's property; it is sufficient for a printer to have suitable types for the language of the country where he resides.

––––––––

PROPERTIES AND SHAPES OF TYPES.

THE Types or Letters, most generally used for printing in Europe and America, are termed *Roman, Italic,* and *Old English,* or *Black Letter.*

––––––––

ROMAN LETTER.

ROMAN letter has long been held in the highest estimation; and is the national character not only of this country, but also of England, France, Spain, Portugal and Italy. In Germany, and the kingdoms and states which surround the Baltic, letters are used which owe their foundation to the Gothic character; but even in those nations, works are printed in their own language with Roman letters. The reason why the Germans, and those who patronise the Gothic characters, have not altogether rejected them for the Roman, has been chiefly owing to their apprehensions of sharing the fate of the primitive printers, who suffered greatly in their attempt, from the dislike then evinced by the learned to works which had been printed in that character. This compelled them to return to their old mode of using the Gothic, to which men of literature were more accustomed, from its resemblance to the writings of the monks, which at that time were held in great veneration. From the superstition of the age, the lower classes were easily prevailed on to reject whatever had the least appearance of infringing on monastic influence.

The same reason may be assigned why the Dutch still adhere to the black letter in printing their books of devotion and religious treatises, while they make use of the Roman in their curious and learned works.

In Sweden much greater improvements have been made, which is principally owing to the countenance and support of men of authority, learning, and taste. We may reasonably hope, from the pleasing aspect of the present age, when mankind have dared to burst the fetters of prejudice and superstition, being determined to exercise their better judgment, and adopt plans more congenial to true taste, that the Roman character will be universally employed in all civilized states.

The Roman letter, it may be concluded, owes its origin to the nation whence it derives its name; though the face of the present and ancient Roman letters materially differ, from the improvements they have undergone at various times.

That good Roman makes the best figure in a specimen of typography, cannot be disputed; and this superiority is greatly improved by the founders of the present day. A printer, in his choice of type, should not only attend to the cut of the letter, but also observe that its shape be perfectly true, and that it lines or ranges with accuracy. The quality of the metal of which it is composed, and the finish of the letter, demand also his particular attention, as the great competition for low prices among some of the smaller foundries, (which have sprung into existence through the facilities afforded them, of multiplying *matrices* by the Electrotype process,) has induced them to use an inferior metal, and to turn out their letters without due regard to that nicety of finish so necessary for proper justification.

It is equally important that types should have a deep face, which will depend upon the depth of the punches, their hollows being in proportion to the width of the respective letters, and likewise that the letter have a deep nick, which should differ from other founts of that body in the same house.

ITALIC LETTER.

For the invention of this letter we are indebted to Aldus Manutius, by birth a Roman, who erected a printing office in Venice, 1496, where he introduced the Roman types of a neater cut, and gave birth to that beautiful letter which is known to most nations by the name of Italic; though the Germans, and their adherents, show themselves as ungenerous in this respect as they did with the Roman, by calling it Cursiv, *in order to stifle the memory of its original descent, and deprive the Romans of the merit due to their ingenuity.*

In the first instance it was termed Venitian, from Manutius being a resident at Venice, where he brought it to perfection; but not long after, it was dedicated to the state of Italy, to prevent any dispute that might arise from other nations claiming a priority.

Italic was originally designed to distinguish such parts of a book as might be considered not strictly to belong to the body of the work, as *Prefaces, Introductions, Annotations,* &c. all which sub-parts of a work were formerly printed in this character; so that at least two-fifths of a fount was comprised of Italic letter.

At present it is used more sparingly, the necessity being supplied by the more elegant mode of introducing extracts within inverted commas, and poetry and annotations in a smaller sized type. It is often serviceable in distinguishing the head or subject matter of a chapter from the chapter itself, but is too often made use of to emphasize sentences or words without any direct rule.

That this character was not designed to distinguish proper names, nor for several other uses to which it has been applied, can be readily proved, even from works printed in this country. Many have considered it as depriving Roman of its beauty, by loading it with Italic words and terms of common signification and meaning; and have thought it inconsistent to intermix letter of an erect position with that of an oblique inclination.

It destroys in a great measure the beauty of printing, and often confuses the reader where it is improperly applied, who, pausing to consider why such words are more strongly noted, loses the context of the sentence, and has to revert back to regain the sense of his subject.

Italic if justly formed, discovers a particular delicacy, and requires considerable mathematical nicety in the letter-cutter to keep tne slopings within the degree requisite for each body : but this is not always attended to, as a want of uniformity is too often observed in two letters of a particular sort coming together, which require an hair space between them to prevent their riding, and occasions an unpleasant gap; this is too frequently the case where the Italic capitals *F*, *T*, *V*, and *W*, are followed by an ascending letter, as in *Florence*, *Thames*, *Victory*, *Wheresoever*, &c. &c

---

BLACK LETTER.

𝕿his letter which is used in 𝕰ngland and 𝕬merica, descended from the 𝕲othic characters: it is called 𝕲othic by some, and 𝕺ld 𝕰nglish by others; but printers term it 𝕭lack 𝕷etter, on account of its taking a larger compass than either 𝕽oman or 𝕴talic, the full and spreading strokes thereof appearing more black upon paper.

On the introduction of the Roman character, the use of black letter began to decline, and it was seldom used except in Law works, particularly Statute Law; it was at length expelled from these, and only made its appearance in the heads of Law blanks, and as a general display letter.

DIFFERENT SIZES OF PRINTING LETTERS.

THE several bodies to which printing letters are cast in England and America, are twenty in number, viz.

1 Diamond.	11 English.
2 Pearl.	12 Columbian.
3 Agate.	13 Great Primer.
4 Nonpareil.	14 Paragon.
5 Minion.	15 Double Small Pica.
6 Brevier.	16 Double Pica.
7 Bourgeois.	17 Double English.
8 Long Primer.	18 Double Great Primer.
9 Small Pica.	19 Double Paragon.
10 Pica.	20 Canon.

REGULAR BODIED LETTER.

THE class of regular-bodied letter takes in, viz. Great **Primer,** English, Pica, Long Primer, Brevier, Nonpareil, and **Pearl;** and those which go before them, viz. Canon, Double **Great** Primer, Double English, Double Pica, &c. principally used in jobs, to make emphatical words or lines appear conspicuous.

IRREGULAR BODIED LETTER.

THE general sorts of irregular-bodied letters are, Paragon, Columbian, Small Pica, Bourgeois, Minion, and Diamond. We call them irregular, because they are of intermediate sizes to letter of regular bodies; a standard for which, no doubt, was fixed by former printers and founders.

Among the irregular-bodied sorts of letter none has taken so great a run as Small Pica; and very considerable works have been done in that character, &c. It is a letter, indeed, which has now become the favorite character to do voluminous works in; partly, because it is a round and legible letter, and partly because it takes in considerably more matter than Pica.

CHAPTER II.

A FOUNT OF LETTER, AS CONSIDERED BY LETTER FOUNDERS.

A COMPLETE fount of letter is comprised under nine heads, in which is contained the following sorts :—

1. Capitals.

A B C D E F G H I J K L M N O P Q R S T U V W X
Y Z Æ Œ.

---

2. Small Capitals.

A B C D E F G H I J K L M N O P Q R S T U
V W X Y Z Æ Œ.

---

3. Lower Case.

a b c d e f g h i j k l m n o p q r s t u v w x
y z æ œ &.

---

4. Figures.

1 2 3 4 5 6 7 8 9 0,

---

5. Points, etc.

, ; : . ? ! - ' ( ) [ ] * † ‡ § ‖ ¶ .

---

6. Four kinds of spaces.
7. Em and en quadrats.
8. Two, three, and four em quadrats.
9. Accents.

These are the ordinary sorts cast to a fount of letter, and which the founders divide into long, short, ascending, descending, and kerned letters.

5

LONG LETTERS are those which take up the whole depth of their bodies, and are both ascending and descending, such in the Roman, as Q and J, but in the Italic, *f* is a long lower-case letter.

SHORT LETTERS are all such as have their face cast on the middle of their square metal, by founders called shank, as a, c, e, m, n, o, r, s, u, v, w, x, z, all which will admit of being bearded above and below their face, both in Roman and Italic.

ASCENDING LETTERS are all the Roman and Italic capitals; in the lower case, b, d, f, h, i, k, l, t.

DESCENDING LETTERS are g, p, q, y, in Roman and Italic.

KERNED LETTERS are such as have part of their face hanging over either one or both sides of their square metal or shank. In Roman, f and j are the only kerned letters; but in Italic, *d*, *g*, *j*, *l*, *y*, are kerned on one side, and *f* on both sides of its face.

Casting of the above sorts being attended with considerable trouble, accounts for the founders sending so few of them in a fount of letter, when in fact they require a larger number than their casting bill specifies; their beaks being liable to accidents, especially the Roman f, when at the end of a line. Kerned letters of the Italic, especially *f*, *g*, *j*, and *y*, are also subject to the same risk.

Most Italic capitals are kerned on one side of their face; but none ought to be more attended to than *F*, *T*, *V*, *W*, and *Y*, that their angles may not fall upon an ascending letter that may stand next to them.

DOUBLE LETTERS.

DOUBLE LETTERS were originally formed for the convenience of one kerned letter joining with another, as in the instance of a ff, fl, fi, fi, ft, &c., as their beaks would inevitably receive damage unless they were cast in one piece.

Of the number formerly used few now remain, and those permitted only through necessity, as the fi, ff, fl, ffi, and ffl. The introduction of the round s, instead of the long, was looked upon as a valuable improvement in the art of printing, and we see no reason why the beak of the f could not be gracefully thrown back on its own body, and thereby save the founder the inconvenience of kerning it, and the printer the expense and trouble of kerned and double letters.

A BILL OF PICA, ROMAN AND ITALIC.

THIS part of our work might be extended to a considerable length, were we to enter into the minutiæ of the different sorts requisite to form a complete fount for every language printed in the Roman character; but as this would be carrying us beyond our limits, we shall confine ourselves to the improved scale of the present day, calculated for our own language, to which imperfections may be afterwards cast, so as to render the fount serviceable for any other. The Latin and French require more of c, i, l, m, p, q, s, u, and v, than the English: but until such sorts become really necessary, it would be useless to cast them. When a work is completed for which such extra sorts were required, it may then be proper to prevent their remaining inactive, to cast up to them.

It is well known in practice that a great number of imperfections are always wanted in a printing office; and from the construction of language it appears there always will be a great number of particular sorts deficient, whatever the proportions may be at first. In proof of this it may be stated, that a new fount of letter shall be cast for the purpose of printing a work; in composing this letter it shall be found that there is a great deficiency of some letters, and a superabundance of others; to bring the whole fount into use, for the purpose of composing as many pages as possible, the deficient sorts are cast, till the proportions answer to each other. When this work is finished, another author's work is to be printed with the same letter: the disproportion is again felt; those which at the first were deficient are now superabundant, and those which were abundant will be deficient; so that the master printer, to keep the whole of his letter in use is obliged to be continually casting those deficiencies and thus enlarging his founts.

Formerly a fount of letter, weighing 500 pounds, was considered a good sized fount; but now, so much has printing increased, that double that weight would scarcely acquire the appellation.

Upon this subject, we find that a fount of English, at Paris, which formerly set up about twelve sheets of a Surgeon's Case, in quarto, was much admired on account of its extraordinary weight; this observation drew the following remark from an English printer:

" But, how much would their admiration be heightened, were they to see here several founts larger than that: and one in particular of the late Mr. Richardson's, which set up above thirty sheets in folio, of 77 lines long, and 45 m's wide, before imperfections were cast to it, which must be very considerable in course, and have enlarged the fount to several more sheets." ·

Either of the above amazing founts (as then considered) would, at the present day, be thought of a trifling nature. The Messrs. Hansards, proprietors of a celebrated English printing house, have founts of English and Pica, the former of which, we are informed, will set up between three and four hundred sheets of foolscap folio, and that the latter will extend to nearly six hundred sheets of the above: they have also most of the other founts of very considerable extent.

Printers divide a fount of letter into two classes.

1. *The upper case* ⎫
2. *The lower case* ⎬ *sorts.*

The upper case sorts are capitals, small capital letters and references.

The lower case consists of small letters, double letters, figures, points, spaces, quadrats, &c. each of which we shall treat of under distinct heads.

We shall now give what is reckoned by the founders a regular bill, perfect in all its sorts.

A FOUNT OF PICA WEIGHING 800 lbs.

Italic One-tenth of Roman.

a	8500	,	4500	A	600	A	300
b	1600	;	800	B	400	B	200
c	3000	:	600	C	500	C	250
d	4400	.	2000	D	500	D	250
e	12000	-	1000	E	600	E	300
f	2500	?	200	F	400	F	200
g	1700	!	150	G	400	G	200
h	6400	'	700	H	400	H	200
i	8000	(	300	I	800	I	400
j	400	[	150	J	300	J	150
k	800	*	100	K	300	K	150
l	4000	†	100	L	500	L	250
m	3000	‡	100	M	400	M	200
n	8000	§	100	N	400	N	200
o	8000		100	O	400	O	200
p	1700	¶	60	P	400	P	200
q	500			Q	180	Q	90
r	6200	1	1300	R	400	R	200
s	8000	2	1200	S	500	S	250
t	9000	3	1100	T	650	T	326
u	3400	4	1000	U	300	U	150
v	1200	5	1000	V	300	V	150
w	2000	6	1000	W	400	W	200
x	400	7	1000	X	180	X	90
y	2000	8	1000	Y	300	Y	150
z	200	9	1000	Z	80	Z	40
&	200	0	1300	Æ	40	Æ	20
ff	400			Œ	30	Œ	15
fi	500	é	200				
fl	200	à	200				
ffl	100	â	200				
ffi	150	ê	200				
æ	100						
œ	60	All other					
		accents 100					
—	150	each.					
—	90						
—	60						

Spaces.

Thick	18000
Middle	12000
Thin	8000
Hair	3000
em Quads	2500
en Quads	5000
Large Quadrats about 80lbs.	

CAPITALS.

THE use of capitals has been considerably abridged of late years; and the antiquated method of using them with every substantive, and sometimes even with verbs and adverbs, is now discontinued. They are considered, in the present day, as necessary only to distinguish proper names of persons, places, &c. There are, however, some particular works in which authors deem it essential to mark emphatical words with a capital; in such cases, as there can be no general rule to guide the compositor, we would recommend the author always to send his copy properly prepared in this particular, to the printer, or he will become liable to the charge the compositor is allowed to make, for his loss of time in following his alterations. The method of denoting a capital, or words of capital letters in manuscript, is by underscoring it with three distinct lines.

Capitals of whatever body, if they are well proportioned, look well in titles, inscriptions, &c., but it requires both good taste and judgment in the compositor to display them to advantage, either by spacing them or not, as the length of the line may require.

SMALL CAPITALS.

SMALL CAPITALS are in general only cast to Roman founts, but in England often to Italic, and are used for the purpose of giving a stronger emphasis to a word than can be conveyed to it by its being in Italic. They are likewise used for running heads, heads of chapters, &c. instead of Italic, according to the fancy of the printer. The first word of every section or chapter is generally put in small capitals, after a small neat two line letter. They are likewise of considerable service in the display of a title page, particularly in setting the catch lines.

The small capitals c, o, s, v, w, x, z, so closely resemble the same letters in the lower case, as to require particular care to prevent their mixing, as the difference can only be ascertained by their being cast thicker than the others. As a distinguishing feature, however, the nick might be cast somewhat higher on the upper case sorts.

In manuscript, small capitals are denoted by having two lines drawn under them.

ACCENTED LETTERS.

THOSE which are called accented by printers, are the five vowels, marked either with an

Acute	-	-	-	á é í ó ú
Grave	-	-	-	à è ì ò ù
Circumflex	-	-		â ê î ô û
Diæresis		-	-	ä ë ï ö ü
Long	-	-	-	ā ē ī ō ū
Short	-	-	-	ă ĕ ĭ ŏ ŭ

REFERENCES.

REFERENCES are all such marks and signs as are used in matter which has either side or bottom notes, and serve to direct the reader to the observations which are made upon such passages of the text as are distinguished by them, and demand a reference of the same likeness to be put to the notes, by which the matter is illustrated, or otherwise taken notice of.

References which are used in works with notes to them, are variously represented, though oftener by letters than other characters. Accordingly some put common letters between parenthesis; thus (a,) (b,) (c,) &c. Others again, choose to see them between brackets, as [a,] [b,] [c,] and so on to the end of the alphabet; instead of these, some begin the notes of every page with (a,) in which they are as right as the former; and have this advantage besides, that the order of references is not so liable to be interrupted as by going through a whole alphabet. We would recommend, however, literal references to begin with every even page, if it has notes; and to carry them no further than to the last note in the opposite uneven page; by which means the order of the references would appear at one view, and any irregularity in them rectified without much trouble.

Instead of letters, whether capital or lower-case, figures are used in the same manner, and also with equal propriety; for the one as well as the other are of like signification, when used for the same purpose: but the references which look the neatest, besides being the most proper, are superior letters, or else superior figures; for both were originally contrived and intended to be employed in matter that is explained by notes, whether by way of annotations, quotations, citations, or otherwise. Nevertheless, we observe that superior letters are not used upon every occasion, but chiefly in large and lasting works, which have sometimes more than one sort of notes, and therefore require different references; in which case not only superior letters, but also such marks are used as never were designed to serve for references. But, to abide by the title of this article, what are called references by printers are the following:

| Asterisk * | Double Dagger ‡ | Parallel ‖ |
| Dagger † | Section § | Paragraph ¶ |

The above are the names and figures which founders reckon among the points, and are denominated references by printers; these characters were designed to serve for other purposes than those to which they have been applied, as will appear from their respective functions.

1. The Asterisk is the chief of the references, and presents itself most readily to the eye, on account of having its figure on the top, and leaving a blank below, which makes it a superior.

In Roman church-books, the Asterisk divides each verse of a psalm into two parts, and marks where the responses begin, which in our Common Prayer Books is done by placing a colon between the two parts of each verse.

They are sometimes used to supply the name of a person that chooses to pass anonymous. They also denote an omission, or an hiatus, by loss of original copy; in which case the number of asterisks are multiplied according to the largeness of the chasm; and not only whole lines, but frequently whole pages, are left blank, and marked with lines of stars.

In satirising persons in pamphlets and public papers, the asterisk is of great service; for it is but putting the first letter of a person's name, with some asterisks after it, and ill-natured people think they may characterise, and even libel their betters without restriction. Metal rules or dashes, also serve for the above purposes as well as Asterisks.

2. The Dagger, originally termed the Obelisk, or Long Cross, is frequently used in Roman Catholic church-books, prayers of exorcism, at the benediction of bread, water, and fruit, and upon other occasions, where the priest is to make the sign of the cross; but it must be observed, that the long cross is not used in books of the said kind, unless for want of square crosses, (✠,) which are the proper symbols for the before-mentioned purposes; and are used besides in the Pope's briefs, and in mandates of arch-bishops and bishops who put it immediately before the signature of their names. But the square cross is not reckoned among the references of which we are speaking; whereas, the long cross answers several purposes; for besides serving instead of a square cross, it also answers for a signature to matter that has been either omitted, or else added, and which is intercalated after the work is gone beyond the proper place for it. But the chief use which is made of the dagger, is by way of reference, where it serves in a double capacity, viz. the right way, and inverted.

3. The Double Dagger is a mark crowded in to make one of the improper references.

4. The Parallel is another sign which serves for a reference, and is fit to be used either for side or bottom notes.

5. The sign which implies the word Section, is a sort likewise seldom employed, because in a work which is divided into chapters, articles, paragraphs, sections, or any other parts, they are commonly put in lines by themselves, either in large capitals, small capitals, or italic, according to the size of the work. But the sign of section is sometimes used in Latin notes, and particularly such as are collected from foreign books, which generally abound with citations, because the introduction induces the reader to account his author very learned.

6. The Paragraph is a mark which formerly was prefixed to such matter as authors designed to distinguish from the mean contents of their works; and which was to give the reader an item of some particular subject. At present, paragraphs are

seen only in Bibles, where they show the parts into which a chapter is divided, and where its contents change. In common Prayer Books, paragraphs are put before the matter that directs the order of the Service, and which is called the Rubric; because those lines were formerly printed in red. Otherwise it is a useless sort, and unfit to serve for a reference, as long as there are others which have not that antique appearance.

Thus we have shown, that the symbols which are used as references, were designed for quite different purposes. We are therefore of opinion, that it would not have been one of the least improvements, had some other marks been devised which should have appeared in a more becoming shape than the above references, and more perspicuous than superiors of the least size.

LOWER-CASE SORTS.

HAVING already considered the lower case alphabet, we shall merely notice those sorts which have not been already treated on. Those termed lower case-sorts, are, the small letters of the alphabet, double letters, points, the bracket and parenthesis, spaces and quadrats. Of these i, v, x, l, c, are numeral letters, and are generally used in notes; the d, or m, seldom appear in lower-case numerals, though their power is not inferior in calculation to capitals, as they are governed by the same rules.

POINTS.

THEY consist of a comma, semicolon, colon, period or full-point, note of interrogation and note of admiration.

Points are not of equal antiquity with printing, though, not long after its invention, the necessity of introducing stops or pauses in sentences, for the guidance of the reader, brought forward the colon and full-point, the two first invented. In process of time, the comma was added to the infant punctuation, which then had no other figure than a perpendicular line, proportionable to the body of the letter; these three points were the only ones used till the close of the fifteenth century, when

Aldus Manutius, a man eminent for the restoration of learning, among other improvements in the art of printing, corrected and enlarged the punctuation, by giving a better shape to the comma, adding the semicolon, and assigning to the former points a more proper place; the comma denoting the smaller pause, the semi-colon next, then the colon, and the full-point terminating the sentence. The notes of interrogation and admiration were not introduced till many years after.

Perhaps there never existed on any subject, among men of learning, a greater difference of opinion than on the true mode of punctuation, and scarcely can any two people agree in the same method; some making the pause of a semicolon where the sense will only bear a comma; some contending for what is termed stiff pointing, and others altogether the reverse.

The want of an established rule in this particular is much to be regretted. The loss of time to a compositor, occasioned, often through whim or caprice, in altering points unnecessarily, is one of the greatest hardships he has to complain of in the progress of his profession.

Scarcely nine works out of ten are sent properly prepared to the press; either the writing is illegible, the spelling incorrect, or the punctuation defective. The compositor has often to read sentences of his copy more than once before he can ascertain what he conceives the meaning of the author, that he may not deviate from him in the punctuation; this retards him consi-derably. But here it does not end—he, and the corrector of the press, though, perhaps, both intelligent and judicious men, differ in that in which few are found to agree, and the compo-sitor has to follow either his whim or better opinion. The proof goes to the author—he dissents from them both, and makes those alterations in print, which ought to have rendered his manuscript copy correct.

The late Dr. Hunter, in reviewing a work, had occasion to censure it for its improper punctuation. He advises authors to leave the pointing entirely to the printers, as from their constant practice they must have acquired a uniform mode of punctua-tion. We are decidedly of this opinion; for unless the author will take the responsibility of the pointing entirely on himself, it will be to the advantage of the compositor, and attended with less loss of time, not to meet with a single point in his copy, unless to terminate a sentence, than to have his mind confused by commas and semicolons placed indiscriminately, in the hurry of writing, without any regard to propriety. The author may reserve to himself his particular mode of punctuation, by directing the printer to point his work either loosely or not, and still have the opportunity of detecting in his proofs whether a misplaced point injures his sentence. The advantage resulting from this method would ensure uniformity to the work, and remove in part from the compositor, a burthen which has created no small degree of contention.

Having considered it our duty to enter thus fully on a subject that so materially concerns the compositor, we will now proceed to the points themselves.

The comma, which is considered the first, from its requiring the shortest pause, its time being till you can reckon one, is more frequently used and misapplied than any of the other points. Its unnecessary introduction often involves the reader in perplexity; and its omission blends sentences that should be kept distinct—and in unskilful hands may pervert the meaning of the author, and render it ridiculous. The most acceptable mode seems to be what is termed *easy pointing*, which certainly has the advantage of not confusing the reader. All subjects, however, should not be pointed alike; as familiar discourses, or historical and narrative subjects, do not require so many points as explanatory and Law matter.

Commas are used to denote extracts or quotations from other works, in dialogue matter, or any passages or expressions not original, by inverting two of them, and placing them before the passages quoted, and closing such passage with two apostrophes. These are termed inverted commas; and when used, a thin space is sufficient to keep them free from the matter. The method of running them down the sides to the end of the quotation, has been found inconvenient, particularly where a quotation occurs within a quotation, or a speech within a speech; the proper method of distinguishing which, is by placing a single inverted comma, before such extra quotation, and to be concluded with a single apostrophe: or should both quotations close together, put three apostrophes, observing after the first to place a thin space.

Inverted commas owe their origin to Mons. Guillemet, a Frenchman, who, it may be supposed, was no friend to Italic, they being intended to supersede the use of that letter. As an acknowledgment for this improvement, his countrymen call them after his name.

A single comma inverted is used as an abbreviation to the word Mac, as in the instance of M'Gowen.

The semicolon is allowed double the space of time for its pause to the comma, and may be considered an important point of punctuation; it enforces what has been illustrated by the comma, and allows the reader an opportunity to acquire a perfect view of the sentence, before it is terminated by the full-point.

The colon, whose allowed time is till the reader can count three, has been superseded in almost every instance, either by the semicolon, ellipsis line or dash.

The period or full-point is used to terminate a sentence, and 'its pause is double the time allowed to the semicolon. It is also used in abbreviations, but then loses its effect as a full stop in the punctuation, unless at the end of a sentence. Many works have recently been printed, in which this point has been entirely dispensed with as an abbreviation, as in Mr Dr &c., a very convenient, if not an elegant mode.

Full-points are sometimes used as leaders in tables of contents, figure-work, &c., but dotted rules or leaders are much better for this purpose, from their uniform appearance, as they not only supply the place of full-points and quadrats, but save considerable time in the composition.

The sign of interrogation needs not to be explained, for the very appellation tells us, that it is a mark which is used to show where a question is proposed, that gives room for, or demands, an answer.

It is not only proper, but also requisite, that every interrogation or question should begin with a large letter, whether capitals are used in the matter, or not; according to the method which is observed in our Bibles, where, as well interrogatives as responses, besides the beginning of sayings, allocutions, &c. are intimated by a large capital letter.

The sign of admiration, or exclamation, likewise explains itself by its name, and claims a place where surprise, astonishment, rapture, and the like sudden emotions of the mind are expressed, whether upon lamenting or rejoicing occasions.

The sign of exclamation is put after the particles Ah! Alas! O! &c., though the last is not always of that force to be attended by the exclamatory symbol; but is softened by a comma, to enforce what follows, and to make the admiration more complete.

The admirative part of a paragraph, as well as of the interrogatory, is always to begin with a capital letter.

All the points, except the comma and the full-stop, should have a hair space placed between them and the matter, to distinguish them; the comma and full-point not lining with the depth of the face of the letter, do not require any space to bear them off.

Of late years, some founders cast their semicolons, colons, &c. of sufficient thickness to dispense with the hair space between them and the letter, a mode to which we can see no objection, but on the contrary would rather commend.

The m dash, though it cannot be denominated a point, is frequently used in peculiar works, sometimes as a substitute for the comma, at others for the colon, and is found particularly serviceable in rhapsodical writing, where half sentences frequently occur.

HYPHEN, OR DIVISION.

To divide words or syllables with propriety, is an important part of a compositor's business. It will exercise his judgment, and demands particular attention, as authors must leave the use of the hyphen to the discretion of the printer.

The difficulty that formerly existed as to the proper method of dividing syllables, arose from the controversies in which authors were continually engaged on the subject of orthography.—

Without being able to establish a criterion, each arrogated to himself the adoption of his own particular mode, to the subversion of uniformity and propriety.

The Dictionaries of Walker and Johnson are looked up to as the highest authorities, and the labor of these great men appears to have been crowned with complete success. It has silenced those pedantic clamors and divided opinions, which distracted the attention of the compositor, and he is now able to solve any difficulty, by a reference to those excellent standards of English orthography.

Authors of the present day seldom interfere with what is now deemed the province of the printer: they will generally allow him, from his practice, to be a pretty competent judge of orthography, and therefore do not object to his mode of spelling, though it may vary from their own. To the compositor this is an advantage of considerable importance, as it allows him to observe a system in his spelling, and enables him at the same time, to acquire the proper use of the division, in which he should be careful not to suffer a syllable of a single letter to be put at the end of a line, as *a-bide, e-normous, o-bedient,* &c. except in marginal notes, which, from their narrow measure, cannot be governed by this rule. The terminating syllable of a word should not be allowed to begin a line, as *ed, ly,* &c. the hyphen being the thickness of one of the letters, the measure must, therefore, be narrow indeed, or the line very closely spaced, that will not admit the other. A compositor, who studies propriety and neatness in his work, will not suffer an unnecessary division, even in a narrow measure, if he can avoid it by the trouble of over-running two or three lines of his matter.

In large type and narrow measures, the use of the division may admit of an excuse: but, in that case, care should be taken that hyphens do not follow each other. In small type and wide measures, the hyphen may generally be dispensed with, either by driving out or getting in the word, without the least infringement on the regularity of the spacing. The habit once acquired of attending to this essential point, the compositor would find his advantage in the preference given to his work, and the respect attached to his character from his being considered a competent and careful master of his business. The appearance of many divisions down the side of a page, and irregular spacing, are the two greatest defects in composition.

It is proper, if possible, to keep the derivative or radical word entire and undivided; as *occur-rence, gentle-man, respect-ful,* &c. Some printers have adopted the mode of dividing on the vowel, which answers very well in some cases, but will by no means answer as a general rule.

The hyphen, or division, is likewise used to join two or three words together, which are termed compounds, and consist frequently of two substantives, as *bird-cage, love-letter,* &c.; likewise what are termed compound adjectives, as *well-built house, handsome-faced child,* &c. But compounds are sometimes made of words that were never intended for such; therefore, to acquire a competent knowledge of them does not depend upon fancy, but exercises the judgment in discovering the rise and fall of the tone, which is an adjunct: and whether that and the preceding appellative may not be joined into one word, rather than make a compound of it.

The prepositions *after, before, over,* &c. are often connected with other words, but do not always make a proper compound; thus, *before-mentioned* is a compound when it precedes a substantive, as, in the *before-mentioned* place; but when it comes after a noun, as in the place *before mentioned,* it should be two distinct words.

Hyphens are sometimes used in table-work, indexes, or contents; but, like the full-point, they are now generally superseded by leaders or dotted rules.

Hyphens should not be cast of too thick a body; their principal use is in justifying and correcting, therefore they cannot be too thin to be serviceable; they do not require a very bold stroke, except for spelling-books, for which they are generally cast on purpose.

PARENTHESIS AND BRACKET.

THE use of the parenthesis is to enclose such words or sentences of a period as make no part of the subject, yet at the same time strengthen the argument; which, however, would read smoothly on, were the enclosed matter taken away.

Parentheses are not now so generally used as formerly; authors place their intercalations between commas, which make them equally as intelligible as though they were inclosed between parentheses, and look much neater in print; but where parentheses are used, should a point be requisite to mark the sentence, it is placed after the parenthesis, the intercalation not being reckoned any part of that sentence; as, for instance, *My Lord (said I), I will tell your Lordship*, &c.

Brackets are so seldom made use of now, that they require little notice; both parentheses and brackets were formerly used to inclose folios, &c.; but the modern method of putting folios in figures unattended, leaves the bracket scarce a duty to perform.

APOSTROPHE.

THE apostrophe is called a sign of abbreviation, its appearance often ejecting some letter or letters from the word to which it is attached, particularly in poetry, where it often contracts two syllables into one, to give a verse its proper measure; to this the vowel *e* yields oftener than any other letter, as *alledg'd, chang'd,* &c. Sometimes it cuts off a vowel at the beginning of words, as *'bate, 'scape, 'squire,* &c.; sometimes a syllable, as *'prentice;* but these, and many other abbreviations, are common only in poetical works, and are under the arbitration of the author, who best knows where such contractions serve his purpose.

The monosyllables *tho'* and *thro'* are sometimes shortened, but without any appearance of propriety to justify the curtailment, as they retain the same sound, and therefore the use of the apostrophe as an abbreviation cannot in the slightest degree assist the versification.

The genitive case of the singular number is generally known by having *'s* for its termination.

All quotations, which are denoted by beginning with inverted commas, are closed with apostrophes. There is no space required between the apostrophe and the matter.

6*

QUADRATS.

An m quadrat is the square of the letter to whatever fount it may belong; an n quadrat is half that size. In casting m and n quadrats, the utmost exactness is necessary; they also require particular care in dressing, as the most trifling variation will instantly be discovered, when ranged in figure-work, for which purpose they are much used, and unless true in their justification, the arrangement is confused to such a degree, that all the pains and ingenuity of a compositor cannot rectify it. The same observation will hold good with respect to figures.

M quadrats mostly begin paragraphs, by an indention of the first line; but of late years some printers prefer using an m and n for narrow measures, and two, three, or even four m's for wide measures, which certainly must be acknowledged to be an improvement. An m quadrat is likewise the proper space after a full-point, when it terminates a sentence in a paragraph.

N quadrats are generally used after the semicolon, colon, &c., and sometimes after a curved letter; they are also exceedingly useful in spacing.

Two, three, and four m quadrats are likewise cast for break and white lines, but particularly for poetry, on which account it is essentially necessary that they be cast to the exact depth of the letter, otherwise the matter will stand uneven where a number of them come together.

The inconvenience arising from founts of the same body not agreeing in depth, is great, where the quadrats, through necessity, are sometimes mixed. It is a serious evil, and much to be deplored, that some method cannot be adopted to check it; as a particular work will sometimes require more quadrats than were cast to the letter; recourse must then be had to the founder, though there may be other founts in the office of the same body.

Reglets of the same body as the letter of the work, are sometimes used for white lines, instead of quadrats; but, from their being often wet, they are apt to swell, and of course cannot be depended on, and are only fit to be used in jobs, &c. where large type is employed; it would therefore be better for book-work, to use leads, which are cast from four, six, and eight, &c. to a Pica, and from four m's to any length required.

SPACES.

THE use of spaces is to separate one word from another, so that the reading may appear easy and distinct. To enable the compositor to space even, and to justify with nicety, they are cast to various thicknesses.

Five to an m—or five thin spaces; four to an m—or four middle spaces; three to an m—or three thick spaces; and two to an m—or two n quadrats, which may with propriety be reckoned among the number of spaces. Besides these, there are what are called hair spaces, cast remarkably thin, and found particularly useful in justifying lines and assisting uniformity in spacing.

NUMERAL LETTERS.

EVERY letter in the alphabet was used to denote some number by the Greeks and Orientals, and each letter denoted a less or greater number, as it was nearer or more remote from the first letter in their alphabetical order; and no letter, which in the order of the alphabet stands after another, ever denoted a number less than the letter that stands before it. If the Romans, who derived their letters originally from the Greeks, had derived also their numeration by letters, it is in the highest degree probable, that these particulars would have been the same in both; but as not one third of the Roman letters are numerals, so neither is the numeral value of those that are so, more or less, according to their place in alphabetical order; because D and C, which stand among the first letters of the alphabet, and M and L, whose station is in the centre, are of much greater numeral value than X and V which are near the end.

But it has been supposed that the Romans used M to denote 1000, because it is the first letter of Mille, which is Latin for 1000; and C to denote 100, it being the first letter of Centum, the Latin term for 100. Some also suppose, that D being formed by dividing the old M in the middle, was therefore appointed to stand for 500, that is, half as much as the M stood for when it was whole; and that L being half a C, was, for the same reason, used to denominate 50. But upon what just

principle can any person imagine, that 1000 and 100 were the
numbers which letters were first used to express? And what
cause can be assigned why D, the first letter in the Latin word
Decem, 10, should not rather have been chosen for 500, because
it had a rude resemblance to half an M? But if these questions
could be satisfactorily answered, there are other numerical
letters which have never yet been accounted for. We therefore
think these considerations render it probable, that the Romans
did not, in their original intention, use letters to express
numbers at all; the most natural account of the matter appears
to be this—

The Romans probably put down a single stroke I, for one, as
is still the practice of those who score on a slate, or with chalk;
this stroke they doubled, trebled, and quadrupled, to express
two, three, and four, thus, II, III, IIII. So far they could
easily number the minums or strokes with a glance of the eye;
but they found, that if more were added, it would be necessary
to number the strokes one by one; for this reason, when they
came to five, they expressed it by joining two strokes together
in an acute angle, thus V, which will appear the more probable,
if it be considered that the progression of the Roman numbers is
from five to five, that is, from the fingers of one hand to the
fingers of the other. Ovid has touched upon the original of this
in his *Festorum*, lib. iii. and *Vitruv.* lib. iii. c. 1. has made the
same remark.

After they had made this acute angle V, for five, they then
added single strokes to the number of four, thus VI, VII, VIII,
VIIII, and then, as the minums could not be further multiplied
without confusion, they doubled their acute angle by prolonging
the two lines beyond their intersection, thus X, to denote two
fives, or ten. After they had doubled, trebled, and quadrupled
this double acute angle, thus XX, XXX, XXXX, they then,
for the same reason which induced them to make a single angle
first, and then to double it, joined two single strokes in another
form, and instead of an acute angle, made a right angle, L, to
denote fifty. When this was doubled, they then doubled the
right angle, thus, ⊏, to denote one hundred, and having num-
bered this double right angle four times, thus ⊏⊏, ⊏⊏⊏,

ΕΕΕΕ, when they came to the fifth number, as before, they reverted it, and put a single stroke before it, thus I꒳, to denote five hundred; and when this five hundred was doubled, then they also doubled their double right angle, setting two double right angles opposite to each other, with a single stroke between them, thus Ε I꒳, to denote one thousand: when this note for one thousand had been repeated four times, they then put down I꒳꒳, for five thousand; ΕΕI꒳꒳, for ten thousand; and I꒳꒳꒳, for fifty thousand.

That the Romans did not originally write M for one thousand, and C for one hundred, but square characters, as before shown, we are expressly informed by Paulus Manutius; but the corners of the angles being cut off by transcribers for despatch, these figures were gradually brought into what are now called numerical letters. When the corners of Ε I꒳ were made round, it stood thus, ϹIϽ, which is so near the Gothic ⌒, that it soon deviated into that character: so that I꒳ having the corners made round, stood thus IϽ, and then easily deviated into D. Ε also became a plain C by the same means; the single rectangle which denoted fifty, was, without any alteration, a capital L; the double acute angle was an X; the single acute angle a V consonant; and a plain single stroke, the letter I. And thus these seven letters, M, D, C, L, X, V, I, became numerals. As a further proof of this assertion, let it be considered, that ϹIϽ is still used for one thousand, and IϽ for five hundred, instead of M and D; and this mark, ⌒, is sometimes used to denote one thousand, which may easily be derived from this figure, Ε I꒳, but cannot be deviations from, or corruptions of, the Roman letter M. The Romans also expressed any number of thousands by a line drawn over any numeral less than one thousand; thus, $\overline{V}$ denotes five thousand, $\overline{LX}$, sixty thousand: so likewise $\overline{M}$ is one million, $\overline{MM}$ two millions, &c.

Upon the discovery of printing, and before capitals were invented, small letters served for numerals, which they have done ever since; not only when the Gothic characters were in their perfection, but even after they ceased, and Roman was become the prevailing character. Thus, in the time of printing in Gothic characters, i ʋ ϫ l c ꝺ m were, and are still, of the same signification with capitals, when used as numerals. But here it should be observed, that the capital J is no numeral letter, though the lower case j is as often and as significantly used as the vowel i, especially where the former is used as a closing letter, in ij iij vj vij viij dcij, &c., though it is as right not to use j's at all, unless it were out of respect to antiquity; for in Roman lower-case numerals, which are of modern date, the j is not regarded, but the i stands for a figure of 1, wherever it is used numerically.

ARITHMETICAL FIGURES.

ARITHMETICAL or Arabic figures are nine in number, besides the cipher, or nought.

Figures require a founder's particular care to cast them exactly n-thick, and to a true parallel, as the least deviation where a number of them come together in table-work, destroys their arrangement, and causes an inconvenience in the justification which the ingenuity of a compositor cannot, without considerable loss of time, rectify.

Printers at one time thought it a great impropriety to use erect figures in italic matter, judging that the obliquity of that character would be intercepted by them, and therefore had figures cast of the same inclination; this peculiarity is but partially attended to, though it still prevails in some parts abroad.

CHAPTER III.

RULES.

Rules are of two descriptions, viz. brass, and metal, or space rules; the former are cut from sheet brass, and the latter are cast by type-founders.

Brass rules ought to be exactly letter high; if, therefore, founts differ in height to paper, from the regular standard, those rules, accurately made, are rendered useless; for if they are higher than the letter, they come off black and broad; and, besides hindering the adjoining letters from appearing, they cut both paper and tympan. On the other hand, if they are lower than the letter, they do not appear at all, especially if they are thin, and stand between matter without leads at their sides; which (in particular cases) may be left out in Roman letter· yet in mixed matter, or Italic, a lead at least is required before and after a thin brass rule, to prevent its touching upon $d, f, l,$ at the fore-side, and upon $f, g, j, p, y,$ at the hind-side; they are made of various thicknesses for column rules of Magazines and Newspapers, and when required for the latter purpose great care should be taken to procure those made of the very hardest and stiffest material.

The face of the rules ought to be attended to, that they may be of an equal bold, or else tender look, according to the size of the letter or figures with which they are used. But a great difference appears in this particular, when we find it necessary to piece them; a compositor, therefore, when he is driven to this necessity, should endeavor to dress the shorter pieces, in order that they may appear as one length.

The thickness of rules for table-work should be proportionable to their face, without so much shoulder as shall hinder a cross rule from joining a perpendicular line; since it is a maxim, "That rules (in table-work) shall fall upon and touch rules;" which, if followed, has a good effect.

METAL RULES OR DASHES.

METAL RULES or dashes, like quadrats, are cast to m's from the size of one to four, sometimes to six m's, and are used in schemes of accounts, to direct and connect each article with its summary contents, where they stand opposite, and distant from each other.

Sometimes dashes stand for *noughts*, in columns of figures, where the dash should not exceed the extent which figures require. Thus, in a column of four n's, a two-m dash is answerable to them; and where the numeral contents of a column do not amount to above hundreds, an m dash will answer.

Dashes made to line and join accurately, are very useful, as they serve not only for rectilinear, but perpendicular progressions, where no other rules are to touch them. But though they have shouldering sufficient to bear them from the matter, they require, nevertheless, a lead or reglet before and after them, that they may keep in line.

Sometimes a dash stands for a sign of repetition, in catalogues of goods, where it implies *ditto;* and in catalogues of books, where a dash signifies *ejusdem*, instead of repeating an author's name, with the title of every separate treatise of his writing: but it must be observed, that no sign of repetition must be at the top of a page; but that the name of the author, or merchandise, must be set out again at length; and if their series continues, to denote the continuation thereof, at every article, by a dash of three or four m's, so as to range, instead of extending the dash to the different lengths of names.

A dash likewise stands for *to* or *till;* as, chap. xvi. 3—17. that is, from the third to the seventeenth verse. At other times, it serves for an index, to give notice, that what follows it is a corollary of what has preceded; or otherwise matter of import and consequence. N dashes are generally cast, which are very convenient in justifying lines of dashes, and in the arrangement of braces where middles and corners are used.

Dotted metal rules are now cast by some founders to their founts of script, and are exceedingly useful for lines to write upon in Blanks, &c.

SPACE RULES.

Space rules are not always of the same thickness, though two of them generally answer to the depth of a Pearl body. But this is not of so much moment as their being of a neat look, and made to join well; when this is the case they may be considered valuable sorts. These lines are cast to various widths, from one m to six, and are, in intricate rule work, from their joining more exact, neater than brass rule, less expensive, and more convenient to the compositor.

BRACES.

Braces are chiefly used in tables of accounts, and similar matter, that consists of a variety of articles, which would require much circumlocution, were it not for the method of tabular writing now practised.

Braces stand *before*, and keep together, such articles as are of the same import, and are the sub-divisions of the preceding articles. They sometimes stand *after*, and keep together, such articles as make above one line, and have either pecuniary, mercantile, or other posts after them, which are justified to answer to the middle of the brace.

The bracing side of a brace is always turned to that part of an article which makes the most lines.

Braces are sometimes used horizontally in the margin to cut off a chronological or other series from the proper notes, or marginal references of the work. They are generally cast to two, three and four m's of each fount, but can be had larger if desired. When there is occasion for them larger, *middles* and *corners* are cast, and used with dashes, so that the brace may include any space required; but the middles and corners, as well as the dashes, require to be cast with great exactness, that, when joined, they may appear as one piece; their shoulders in dressing should be planed away, so that the beard may not prevent the face from meeting. The difficulty of nicely effecting this has caused some printers, most eminent for their skill and experience in table-work, to form their braces out of brass rule

7

to the exact lengths required for each occurring instance; but, latterly, metal braces have been cast of considerable length entire.

Middles and corners are convenient in genealogical works, where they are used the flat way; and where the directing point is not always in the middle, but has its place under the name of the parent, whose offspring stands between corner and corner of the brace inside, in order of primogeniture: but this may be superseded to advantage by the use of brass rule.

SUPERIORS.

As we have already treated of superior letters and figures under the head of references, it will not be necessary to take further notice of them here, than to observe that they should contain no more than the bare alphabet, without any double letters. Neither ought the j to be used as a reference, on account of its being a descending letter. A larger number should be cast of the first eight sorts; a less of the second, a still less quantity of the third eight sorts; because it often happens that references begin with a in every page; though sometimes they are continued to the end of a chapter, or other division of a work; in which case they may run the length of the alphabet.

The same rule may be observed in respect to superior figures, more of the first five being used than the others, except the nullo, which may be used as a degree in geometrical works.

FRACTIONS.

Fractions, or broken numbers in arithmetic, were formerly seldom cast to any other bodies than those of Pica, Small Pica, Long Primer, Bourgeois, and Brevier, but since the use of small type has become so general they are cast to almost every sized body. A great improvement has recently been introduced by casting them with the separatrix to run obliquely between the numerator and denominator, rendering their appearance much more clear and conspicuous.

Where a fraction happens with large-bodied figures, such as Great Primer and upwards, it is usually set out at length, unless small figures can be conveniently had, which may be justified with the same neatness as fractions cast to the body.

QUOTATIONS.

QUOTATIONS are cast to two sizes, and are called broad and narrow. They should be cast lower than quadrats and require to be dressed and finished with as much care as any other sort, that they may stand true upon all occasions. They vary in size according to the standard of the foundry where they are cast, which is highly improper; as they should be governed by a regular standard as well as every other sort, and to that standard press-joiners ought to cut their furniture; but we are sorry to observe so little attention paid to this important part of the joiner's business, who follow too much in the steps of the letter-founder, and cannot decide on, and adhere to, a standard guage for their furniture. This want of uniformity gives the compositor much trouble in making margin, and, with all his care, a form will sometimes go to press imperfect in this respect, which is immediately discovered on laying on the reiteration. The pressman has then to unlock the form in order to make register; from this, a dispute will too frequently arise between him and the compositor; and, what is still worse, from frequent unlocking on the press, the pages will suffer some derangement, so that the most skillful corrector's endeavors to send a work perfect to press, will thereby be frustrated.

In order to obviate the above difficulties, metal furniture of various widths is now cast by some founders, which can be relied upon for its accuracy, not being liable to warp or expand by heat or moisture, and most of the respectable printing houses are supplied with it. The outlay is considerable at first, but it will ultimately be found more economical than wooden furniture.

Justifiers are cast for broad and narrow quotations, to all sizes, from Double Pica to Pearl inclusive, for the purpose of ranging the side note with its proper text; in doing which, great care is requisite, especially where there are many in a page.

TWO-LINE LETTERS.

They are now cut to the following bodies, Diamond, Pearl, Nonpareil, Minion, Brevier, Bourgeois, Long Primer, Small Pica, Pica, English, Great Primer, &c. and are found extremely useful in titles, beginning of chapters, advertisements, jobs, &c.

FLOWERS.

At one period flowers were held in the greatest estimation, and the skill and ingenuity of the compositor was often put to the test in forming faces and devices to grace the head pages of his work.

The variety and richness of the designs recently introduced by some of our founders, seems to have occasioned a desire on the part of several printers to introduce the old mode of ornamenting.

A few years since, so great was the rage for novelty and alteration, that some printers were not content with merely the exclusion of flowers, but they stripped their works of every article which had the least appearance of ornament; even rules of every description were banished from their proper stations in title-pages, heads, &c.; but this new-fangled rage did not long continue, and it was with some reluctance that they would consent to the re-introduction of them in certain cases, and thus, by degrees, rules have again resumed their necessary functions.

LEADS.

Leads form a very important part of a printer's stock in trade, since it is scarcely possible to set up a single page in which they may not be usefully employed; but their chief use is for opening the lines to a regular distance from each other. They are usually cast by letter-founders in a long mould, and then cut to the required lengths. The bodies are regulated by pica standard, and they are usually cast four, six, or eight to pica; but are occasionally varied from one down to fourteen to pica. The lengths also vary, twenty m's pica being about the average, though they are cut to almost every length, in order that, by being combined, they may suit every measure.

They are almost indispensably necessary in regulating the blanks between displayed lines in titles and other pages. They are also used in newspapers to designate editorial matter from communicated and selected.

NAMES OF LETTERS, AND THEIR BEARINGS TO EACH OTHER.

HAVING already treated upon the properties and shapes of types, and of all the sorts contained in a complete fount of letter, with some observations on the use and proper application of them, we shall now endeavor to explain the origin of the names of the various sized letters.

Canon is confessed to have been first produced by some artizan, of the French nation, and employed in some work relating to the canons of the church; to which the German title, Missal, likewise alludes.

Two-lines Double Pica, Two-lines Great Primer, Two-lines English, Two-lines Pica, and Double Pica, have their names from the respective bodies of which the depth of two m quadrats answers to one of the double sizes. But we must here take notice, that our Double Pica falls in with what the Germans call Secunda, from which it follows, that there should be a Prima; but because we have met with no letter of that name, we conclude that Prima, being a size larger than Secunda, and happening to answer afterwards to two lines of English, Prima lost its first name, and was turned into that of Roman. Besides, that Double Pica goes in Germany by the name of Secunda, that letter is also called Text; as we cannot assign the reason for it, we shall leave it to connoisseurs to observe which of the primitive books has its text printed in that character.

Paragon is the only letter that has preserved its name, being called so by all the printing nations. Its appellation shows, that it was first cut in France; and at the same time gives us room to suppose, that the state of well-shaped letter there, was at that time but indifferent; because, when Paragon happened to turn out a letter of better shape than the rest, it received the name of *perfect pattern*, which the word Paragon implies.

7*

Great Primer, in Germany, is called Tertia, and is therefore one of the major sizes of letter which, in the infancy of the Art, served for printing several works of consideration, and particularly the Bible; on which account it is by some called Bible Text.

English is called Mittel by the Germans, and St. Augustin by the French and Dutch; both which names might be productive of considerable argument; the word Mittel bearing the same meaning with Middle, intimates, that the former sizes of letter were seven in number, the centre of which being English, with Prima, Secunda, and Tertia, ranging on one side, and Pica, Long Primer, and Brevier, occupying the other. As to the name of St. Augustin, as it is designated by the French and Dutch, we understand that the writings of that Father were the first works done in that sized letter.

Pica is another letter that admits of having particular notice taken of it, on account of its being called Cicero by the French and Germans;

for as the preceding size was distinguished by the name of St. Augustin, so has this been honored with that of Cicero, on account of the Epistles of that writer having been first done in letter of this size, and the only point now to decide is, whether the Germans or the French were the first who dedicated the letter of this body to the name of Cicero on the before-mentioned account.

Small Pica, being of an irregular body, takes its name here from its inferiority to Pica. But in France they assign the invention of this body of letter to Philosophie; for which, indeed, they may have their reason, considering that their Cicero and Philosophie are of one and the same face; from which, we conclude, that they did not consider Small Pica worth cutting with a face proportionable to its body; and that the cramping of Cicero to Philosophie, was done with no other view than to get in upon the former. This we venture to suggest, though we can form no idea why the Germans give this letter the name of Brevier.

Long Primer. Upon the same supposition, that some bodies of letter took their names from works in which they were first employed, we are induced to believe that the Germans gave the name of Corpus to this character, on account of their Corpus Juris being first done in this size, as it is still continued in that letter; but whether *Garmond* is the name of the author, or what signification else it bears, we have no items of. In contradistinction of the *French Gros Romain*, they call this size letter Petit Romain, conformable to the distinction that is made between Great Primer and Long Primer, in England.

Bourgeois is a letter of an irregular body, and has hitherto been received accordingly. By its name it seems to have first come from France, having been dedicated to the master printers there. *Gaillarde* is a letter of the same body, but has the face of Petit Romain. Two lines of this letter are equivalent to a Great Primer body ; and one line to two of Diamond.

Brevier takes its name from being first used for the Breviary, a Roman Catholic Church-book, which is commonly printed in this character. It is called Petit; and Jungfer, or Maiden Letter, by the Germans, on account of its comeliness.

Minion. Why this letter was denominated Minion, we have not yet been informed ; probably it was held in great estimation on its first introduction, and consequently received the title of (Darling) Minion.

Nonpareil. Little can be observed with respect to this character: why it received the name of Nonpareil no one has yet ventured to investigate, it is therefore most probable that the appellation was given on account of its extraordinary smallness in proportion to those letters at that time in general use.

Pearl. With respect to this size we are left in the same situation as the last-mentioned, consequently we shall again venture at a suggestion for the name which it has ventured: it is probable that the success of the foregoing induced the founders to attempt cutting another letter, upon a smaller body; and as this was, undoubtedly, a greater advance to perfection, it, of course was designated Pearl.

Even the minuteness of the type just mentioned, did not deter the founders from attempting one upon a still smaller scale, in which they have succeeded even beyond the most sanguine expectation, for which they are justly entitled to great credit; thus, having gained the summit of perfection, they bestowed upon it the name of Diamond. as most suitable to its extraordinary neatness and consequent value. We are of opinion that their efforts at farther minutiae must now cease, unless they will undertake to furnish mankind with eyes possessing all the qualities of a magnifying glass.

In the type last mentioned, so minute is each character, that of the lower case i about 2,800 go to a single pound, and the thinnest space about 5,000!

It is necessary to observe that the foregoing gradation of types, from Great Primer to Diamond inclusive, were not cast by one and the same founder; still this is not of the least consequence, when it is considered that the founders have various faces to the same body, consequently it would have not only been improper to have made a selection of those which might agree as to the regular gradation, but it would also have been attended with a waste of time, and an unnecessary expense; therefore, we thought proper to take those which were immediately at our command.

Independently of the letters which are cast upon these bodies, the founders cast a Nonpareil face on a Minion body, and a Minion on a Nonpareil: a Small Pica on a Pica, and all the other sizes, either in ascending or descending order.

We shall now give the proportion which one size of type bears to another in *width*; but it is necessary to observe that it must be taken with certain limitations, because each founder has letter of every size, that will either drive out or get in with others of the same body; therefore it is impossible for us to present our readers with a *regular* gradation of the different sizes from *Great Primer* to *Diamond* inclusive; the limitation of each line is marked by an inverted full-point.

GRADATION OF TYPES.

Does not this 'divine Art,' which has   28

Does not this 'divine Art,' which has enlightened   39

Does not this 'divine Art,' which has· enlightened the   42

Does not this 'divine Art,' which has· enlightened the world, ju   51

Does not this 'divine Art,' which has· enlightened the world, justly deser   58

Does not this 'divine Art,' which has· enlightened the world, justly deserve   60

Does not this 'divine Art,' which has· enlightened the world, justly deserve our en   65

Does not this 'divine Art,' which has· enlightened the world, justly deserve our encoura   70

Does not this 'divine Art,' which has· enlightened the world, justly deserve our encouragement, in pre   81

Does not this 'divine Art,' which has· enlightened the world, justly deserve our encouragement, in preference to all other   98

Does not this 'divine Art,' which has enlightened the world, justly deserve our encouragement, in preference to all other inventions ?   108

   1   2   3   4   5

The length of the line is divided into six parts, five four m's and one of two m's Pica, and the number of letters contained in each is given at the end.

It is a point of the utmost importance that a printer should be well acquainted with the exact proportion which one body of letter bears to another; without a possession of this knowledge, he is unable to form an accurate judgment as to the size of the type most suitable for a work that is intended to be confined within a given number of sheets; neither can he form a correct opinion as to the extent of a work, unless he possess a rule whereby to guide his calculation as to the quantity of copy which the proposed type may either take in, or otherwise drive out.

A scale has been introduced in England for measuring the depth of letter from Great Primer to Nonpareil; we should have inserted a similar one, had we not been convinced of its inutility; because, as we have before observed, not only do respective founders vary, but as great a difference exists in each individual foundry. If letter were cast, as it ought to be, to a mathematical standard, such a scale would be of the greatest consequence: a certain number of m's unquestionably, should be allowed to a foot, as three barley-corns to an inch; viz. Pica 72 m's, and all others in the same proportion; whereas, we now have halves and quarters included: from such a system, what can we expect but confusion? They may vary the face of the letter as they please; but, as to height to paper and depth of body, the printers should insist upon their keeping to a true mathematical standard.

In order to show the variations in the depth of type, we shall give an example, by inserting two lines of Long Primer m's

$$\text{mm mm mm mm mm mm mm mm mm mm mm mm}$$

The great difference in body here exhibited, not only applies to Long Primer, but also to every other size.

CASTING OFF COPY.

To cast off manuscript with accuracy and precision, is a task of a disagreeable nature, which requires great attention and mature deliberation. The trouble and difficulty is much increased, when the copy is not only irregularly written (which is too frequently the case), but also abounds with interlineations, erasures, and variations in the sizes of paper. To surmount these defects the closest application and attention is required; yet, at times, so numerous are the alterations and additions, that they not unfrequently baffle the skill and judgment of the most experienced calculators of copy. Such an imperfect and slovenly mode of sending works to the press (which is generally attended with unpleasant consequences to all parties) cannot be too strongly deprecated by all admirers of the art.

The first thing necessary is to take a comprehensive view of the copy, and to notice whether it is written even, if it has many interlineations, &c. also the number of break-lines, and whether divided into chapters and sub-heads, in order that allowance may be made for them in the calculation, so that the plan of the work may not afterwards be infringed on. These observations should be entered as a memorandum, on a separate piece of paper, to assist the memory, and save the trouble of re-examining the manuscript.

This preparation being made, we then take that part of the copy for calculation which comes nearest to the general tendency of the writing, and reckon the number of words contained in one line, previously counting a number of separate lines, so that the one we adopt may be a fair average; we then take the number of lines in a page, and multiply the one by the other, which we again multiply by the quantity of folios the manuscript copy may contain, and thus we are put in possession of the amount of the words contained in the work, with as little loss of time, and as much accuracy as circumstances will admit; the necessary allowances should then be made for break-lines, chapters, insertions, &c. according to the observations previously made on the memorandum.

If the information has been furnished, what size letter the work is to be done in, and what the width of the page, we make our measure accordingly, and after composing a few lines of the manuscript copy, are enabled to form an opinion what number of words come into each printed line; we then take the length of our page, generally to double the number of m's contained in a single line, or less, and multiply the one by the other, which produces the information we had previously gained from the

adoption of the same mode on the manuscript page; we compare
their results, and if the manuscript drives out, we multiply the
print by a larger number than the last folio of the writing, and
so *vice versa;* if the print drives out, we multiply it by a less,
until we bring the number of words to agree; the multiplier on
the printed calculation will show what will be the last folio of
the printed volume, which we divide into sheets according to
the given size of the work, and we are then in full possession,
whether it will bear to be leaded, or the chapters begin pages,
&c., or whether it must be made up close, the measure widened,
the page lengthened, or the size of the letter reduced.

Should the size of the page and letter be left to the opinion of
the printer, with no other order than the number of sheets the
work is intended to make, from following the above mode he
will be enabled pretty accurately to give his directions;—but as
it is necessary, on a subject like the present, to be as clear in our
observations as possible, we will exemplify what has been laid
down. We are supposed to have made our remarks upon the
manner of the writing as directed, and we take the number of
words in a line of manuscript at 20, the lines in a page at 50;
we multiply 50 by 20, which will produce 1000 words in a page;
we then multiply 1000 by 422, which are supposed to be the
number of folios in the manuscript, and we shall find it contain
422,000 words.—The work being printed in Pica 8vo. 20 m's
measure, and each line containing 10 words, each page 40
lines—the case will stand thus :—

MANUSCRIPT.		PRINTED.
50	40	
20	10	
1000	400 $\}$	1055
422		400
2000		422000 words.
2000		
4000		Divide
422000 words in MS.		16 | 1055 | 65 sheets,
		15 pages.

Having ascertained the number of sheets the work will make,
and that number being sufficient for two volumes, they are

divided accordingly. But should the author wish to have his work comprised in one volume, it is requisite to be prepared with the sized type and measure which may accord with his inclination.

As there are two methods of casting off copy, we shall conclude this article with the one laid down in former grammars:

" After having made the measure for the work, we set a line of the letter that is designed for it, and take notice how much copy will come into the line in the stick, whether less or more than a line of manuscript. And as it is seldom that neither one nor the other happens, we make a mark in the copy where the line in the stick ends, and number the words that it contains. But as this is not the safest way for casting off close, we count not only the syllables but even the letters that are in a line in the stick, of which we make a memorandum, and proceed to set off a second, third, or fourth line, till a line of copy falls even with a line in the stick. And as we did to the first line in the stick, so we do to the other, marking on the manuscript the end of each line in the stick, and telling the letters in each, to see how they balance against each other. This being carefully done, we begin counting off, each time, as many lines of copy as we know will make even lines in the stick. For example, if 2 lines of copy make 3 lines in print, then 4 make 6, 6 make 9, 8 make 12, and so on, calling every two lines of copy three in print.

" In like manner we say, if 4 lines make 5, then 8 make 10, and so on, comparing every four lines of copy to five lines in print.

" And in this manner we carry our calculation on as far as we have occasion, either for pages, forms, or sheets.

" The foregoing calculations are intended to serve where a line of print takes in less than a line of copy, and therefore where a line of print takes in more than a line of copy, the problem is reversed, and instead of saying, if 2 lines make 3, we say, in this case, if 3 lines of copy make 2 lines in print, then 6 lines make 4, 9 make 6, 12 make 8, and so on, counting three lines of copy to make two lines in print. In this manner we may carry our calculation to what number of pages, forms, or sheets we will, remembering always to count off as many lines

8

of copy at once, as we have found they will make even lines in the stick. Thus, for example, if 5 lines make 7, the progression of 5 is 10, 15, 20, &c. and the progression of 7 will be 14, 21, 28, &c.

"In counting off copy, we take notice of the breaks; and where we judge that one will drive out, we intimate it by a mark of this [shape; and again, where we find that a break will get in, we invert it thus]. And to render these marks conspicuous to the compositor, we write them in the margin, that he may take timely notice of, and keep his matter arcordingly. We also take care to make proper allowance for heads to chapters, sections, paragraphs, &c.

"In examining the state of the copy, we must observe whether it has abbreviations, that we may guard against them in casting off, and allow for them according to the extent of the respective words, when written out at length."

We trust that the foregoing observations upon this subject, will convey a sufficient idea as to the best mode of casting off copy; still these remarks more properly apply to regular written, as well as thoroughly revised copy. Upon this subject Smith justly observes—

"But how often one or more of these requisites are wanting, compositors can best tell; though very few will imagine, that among men of learning there should be some, who write after such a manner, that even those who live by transcribing, rather shun than crave to be employed by them: no wonder, therefore, if compositors express not the best wishes to such promoters of printing. But it is not always the capacious genius that ought to be excused for writing in too great a hurry; for sometimes those of no exuberant brains affect uncouth writing, on purpose to strengthen the common notion, that *the more learned the man, the worse is his* (hand) *writing;* which shows, that writing *well,* or *bad,* is but a habit with those that *can* write."

CHAPTER IV.

COMPOSING.

HAVING arrived at that portion of our work which more immediately concerns the young practitioner, we deem it highly requisite to offer a few remarks on the attitude or position which it is necessary that he should acquire upon his first introduction to the department of composing.

There are many persons now employed in the art, who frequently, with great justice, inveigh in strong terms against the conduct of those unto whose care they were first entrusted, for suffering them to contract those ill-becoming postures which are productive of knock knees, round shoulders, and other deformities. It is deeply to be regretted, that those who undertake so important a charge, are not better qualified to fulfil that duty: instead of suffering the tender shoot to grow wild and uncultivated, when the pruning-knife, in a gentle hand, with a little admonition, would have checked its improper growth, and trained it in a right course.

What to a learner may appear fatiguing, time and habit will render easy and familiar; and though to work with his cases on a level with his breast, may at first tire his arms, yet use will so inure him to it, that it will become afterwards equally unpleasant to work at a low frame. This method will likewise keep the body in an erect position, and prevent those effects which result from pressure on the stomach.

The standing position of a compositor should be perfectly upright, without stiffness or restraint; the shoulders thrown back, the feet firm on the floor, heels nearly closed, and toes turned out to form an angle of about 45 degrees. The head and body should be kept perfectly steady, except when moving from the roman to the italic case, the operations of distributing and composing being performed by the various motions of the arm, from the shoulder joint alone; and if, to reach a box placed in the further part of the cases, to put in, or take out a letter, he should incline the body by a slight motion, he should immediately resume his erect position. The height of a compositor and his frame should be so adjusted, that his right elbow may just clear the front of the lower case by the a and r boxes, without the smallest elevation of the shoulder joint; his breast will then be opposite the space, h, and e boxes. Sitting to his work should only be permitted on particular occasions, and then his stool should be a small piece of board, fastened to a single leg: resting the whole weight of the body upon one leg, while the other foot is on the bottom of the frame, must be strictly avoided, as a deformity of the legs will be the certain consequence; if fatigued by walking previous to beginning work, he should rather take the stool for a short time, than resort to the means above mentioned for relief. There are, undoubtedly, circumstances under which it may be necessary for a compositor to be much on his stool,—lameness, weakness, old age, or other infirmity; but, in the absence of these excuses, an habitual sitter I should call an habitual idler: that which at first going to case may appear fatiguing to the novice, habit will render familiar and easy; a perseverance in conquering a little fatigue will be amply repaid by the reflection that it will prevent all the evils of knock knees, round shoulders, obstructed circulation of the blood, and respiration of the lungs, and though last, not least, habits of idleness.

The question still remains undecided with many masters, as to the most proper part of the business that should first engage the attention of the learner without confusing his ideas; various methods are adopted, each following the mode he thinks best. Sorting pi is generally the first employment, and afterwards to set it up, which unquestionably gives the youth a strong insight into the nature of the business, makes him acquainted with the different sizes of type and the method of composing, and prepares his understanding for the comprehension of whatever direction may be given him when he is put to the case. The next duty is that of teaching him the nature of the cases, a knowledge easily acquired by paying proper attention to that part of the profession.

In presenting the cases to the notice of the beginner, we shall first give those generally used in the United States; secondly, the late Lord Stanhope's plan; and lastly, those which we have adopted.

The schemes of cases in the following pages, are given as those generally in use in the United States, or at least those which we have found to be most numerous; but it is here necessary to observe that in some offices slight deviations will be found, such as the transposition of the comma and w, y, and p, &c. In the upper case several empty boxes will be found, which are usually filled with fractions or useful sorts employed in the work in hand, but not unfrequently with *pi*.

8*

UPPER CASE GENERALLY USED IN THE UNITED STATES.

Œ	Æ	&	— (3 em)	(rule)	(rule)	☞
[	⟨	⌊	{ (3 em)	{	—	¶
G	F	E	D	C	B	A
O	N	M	L	K	I	H
W	V	T	S	R	Q	P
ffl		U	J	Z	Y	X
☞		Œ	G	O	W	)
¶		&	F	N	V	]
=		Œ	E	M	T	U
§		Æ	D	L	S	J
‡†			C	K	R	Z
†			B	I	Q	Y
*			A	H	P	X

LOWER CASE GENERALLY USED IN THE UNITED STATES.

8	7	6	5	4	3	2	1						
9	ff	g	f	s		i	e	k ,	d	c	b	j ?	ffi
0	fi	w	,	p	y	o	h	t	n	m	l	– z	. ;
m quadrats.	n quadrats.	: '	; .	r	a	Spaces.	t	u	v	x ç			
quadrats.							4 em spaces / 5 em spaces						

We beg to call the reader's attention to the cases upon the late Earl Stanhope's plan, and also to his remarks on the same:

" I have deemed it advisable to contrive a new pair of composing cases, making a new arrangement of the types in the boxes, introducing a new set of double letters, which I denominate logotypes; and rejecting altogether the double letters ff, fi, fl, ffi, ffl, formerly occupying room in the cases, but used so seldom that they might rather be considered as retarding than forwarding the work of the compositor.

" My object, in this matter, has been, to afford the best means for the compositor's comfort in composing, combining therewith the greatest attainable expedition. Upon first looking into this part of the business, which naturally fell under my observation, I was forcibly struck with the result of some examinations which I caused to be made, in order to ascertain correctly the frequency of the occurrence of the several different types in composition. Those examinations pointed out, that the double letters ff, fi, fl, ffi, ffl, Æ, Œ, æ, œ, were so little used in composition as to occupy room in the composing cases unnecessarily ; I therefore resolved on getting rid of them; and resorted to the adoption of a slight change in the shape of the letter f, to keep the dot which forms its top from overhanging and being broken off by ascending letters. Man is so much the child of custom, and so much the implicit admirer of fancied beauty, that I believe if the human body generally was very round shouldered, and if the head projected considerably beyond the chest, it would, in such a case, be deemed a deformity to see a man with an upright body, and carrying his head erect. Having this opinion upon so weighty a subject, I was not surprised to meet with objectors to the proposed alteration in the shape of so humble a servant of literature as the letter f: readers had been so long accustomed to meet her with a downcast head, apparently too weighty to be supported by her feeble neck, that she failed in meeting with a welcome reception in assuming the appearance of strength, by carrying her head upright. Let us put the two together. Now I do not say that though the beauty of the letter be diminished by the change, yet that, in consideration of the advantage attendant upon the change, we should reconcile ourselves to it;

but I say that, independent of every other view of the matter, the f which I introduce is of a preferable shape, in look alone, to the f which I discard. I can easily conceive that many fantastical flourishes which are given to some letters in old printed books, had their admirers when these books were first published; but it would be difficult for any person now to succeed, if he were to undertake to show their superior beauty, and insist upon their restoration to use. I shall not hesitate in being for once a prophet, and foretel that when the f which I insist upon introducing, has become common in books, the f now admired will be condemned solely because of its comparatively inelegant shape.

" I have said thus much on the f, because it has stood in the way of the improvement which I planned, by occupying with its numerous relatives, considerable portions of the composing cases.

" Although I condemn all the above double letters, as inelegant and useless, as occupying, to the inconvenience of the compositor, a considerable part of the area of composing cases, as loading founts with sorts which sometimes remain new when the fount is generally worn out; as burthening the type-founder with the expenses of punches and matrices from which he might be entirely exonorated; yet I am led to view another sort of double letters in just as favorable a light as those appear the reverse.

" *First.* The nine logotypes now in use are omitted. They are proposed to be printed with separate types, thus: ff, fi, fl, ffi, ffl, &c. And the Italic thus: *ff, fl,* &c. instead of *ff, fi, fl,* &c. In 20 pages of Enfield's Speaker, (namely, from page 71 to 90, both inclusive,) those logotypes occur only 95 times, viz.

PRESENT LOGOTYPES.

ff	fi	fl	ffi	ffl	Æ	Œ	æ	œ	} Total
28	51	10	4	2	0	0	0	0	} 95.

" *Secondly.* Eight new logotypes are introduced. Their regular and frequent occurrence expedite the process of composition in a very considerable degree; for, in those same 20

UPPER CASE UPON THE LATE EARL STANHOPE'S PLAN.

X	Y	Z				U	†	‡	=	X	Y	Z	—	|	J	U
P	Q	R				J	§	¶	☞	P	Q	R	s	T	V	W
H	I	K	L	M		*em* ~				H	I	K	L	M	N	o
A	B	C	D	E		~ *galley*				A	B	C	D	E	F	G

				LEDGER			
3	6	9	□	on	—	&	?
2	5	8	◇	of	—	&	?
1	4	7	0	to	—	—	—

LOWER CASE UPON THE LATE EARL STANHOPE'S PLAN.

v	in	g	f	e	an	re	x	z
w	se	h	th		d	c	k	j
m quadrats	: ;	s	o	i	n	m	b	
n quadrats	,	r	a	thick and middling Spaces	t	u	l p y	
quadrats	5 em space / hair spaces	—					q	'

pages, the new logotypes would save to the compositor no less than 3073 lifts, viz.

STANHOPE LOGOTYPES.

th	in	an	re	se	to	of	on	Total,
771	441	413	385	291	279	264	229	3073.

" *Thirdly.* The introduction of the new logotypes and the great imperfection of the various existing arrangements of composing cases, have caused the above new and very superior arrangement to be adopted.

" *Fourthly.* The front side of each box of the lower case is made sloping, instead of upright; which shape is convenient both to the view and to the hand of the compositor, and it enables him to lift the types with the same rapidity and ease when the boxes are nearly empty as when they are full. The types are much better preserved from wear, by means of this shape. It also allows the lower case to be made deeper than usual; so that, two of them contain as much as three lower cases on the old construction. At the bottom of each box of the upper case, the internal front arras is filled up.

" The saving of time is of immense importance, especially in all cases where despatch is particularly required. The new cases are, by experience, found to save full *one day* out of *six* to the compositor.

" Fifteen boxes on the left-hand side of the upper case are represented empty. They are intended for the sorts which are sometimes used for particular works; such as, accented letters, mathematical marks, &c.

" As the asterisk, or star, (*) is very liable to be filled with ink at press, it is intentionally excluded from among the reference marks.

" In the upper case I have put a galley ledge over the third row of boxes. I do not propose putting the galley, as usual, towards the right-hand end of the case, for I occupy that neighborhood with useful sorts, that is, sorts which may be often wanted in composition; but I propose placing the galley on the left-hand side of the case, which I therefore represent as empty boxes, leaving them to be filled when occasion requires, with accented letters, or other unusual sorts. This quarter of the case is evidently that which requires the most awkward motion of the compositor, if he has occasion to go there to take types out of the boxes, and therefore the most proper to be generally left unoccupied with types. I consider the figures to be fully as well arranged as formerly, easily to be remembered, and better placed in being so compactly together. The small capitals undergo the least change as to arrangement: this is, however, clearly improved, inasmuch as their first row, that most used, is entitled to be brought nearer to the compositor than the last three letters of the alphabet, which are, in comparison so little used."

This logo system, we are informed, was once attempted at the London Times office, but soon after abandoned; it was found that the hands could get through much more work by the old process, than by the proposed improvement. It was also tried at Boston, Mass., some ten or twelve years since, under our own observation, and found to be ineffectual.

We must certainly coincide with his Lordship in his arguments in favor of discarding the double letters, as we consider them quite as inelegant and useless as was the long s, long since discarded.

UPPER CASE UPON T. F. ADAMS' PLAN.

♣	℔	@	3em		:	:	☞	¶	=	§	‡	†	*
⌐	‹	⌐	3em {	{	|	❦	7/8	5/8	3/8	1/8	3/4	1/2	1/4
&	Œ	Æ	3em	|	|	–	℀	œ	ẞ	Œ	Æ		1/3
G	F	E	D	C	B	A	G	F	E	D	C	B	A
N	M	L	K	J	I	H	N	M	L	K.	J	I	H
U	T	S	R	Q	P	O	U	T	s	R	Q	P	O
]	)	Z	Y	X	W	V	hair space		Z	Y	X	W	V

LOWER CASE UPON T. F. ADAMS' PLAN.

1	2	3	4	5	6	7	8
	i	s	s	f	g	? !	9
	o	y	p	,	; :	• ‚	0
n quadrats.				,	.	•• -	m quadrats.

e		k	j	fi	ffi	ff	fl
		d		c		b	ffl
h		n		m		l	z
							x
							q
Spaces.	W	r	a	n quadrats.			
5 em space / 4 em space							
u	t						
v							

It has always been a matter of surprise to us, that so little attention has been paid to the improvement of this important branch of the compositor's business, while there seems to have been so much care and expense lavished upon the other branches of the Art. Presuming to be aware of the defects of the cases upon the old plan, we have endeavored to furnish the trade with what we deem to be an essential improvement.

In presenting our plan of cases to the trade, we are aware of the many objections that will, at first sight, be brought against them; but we are induced to believe, that after an impartial and unprejudiced examination of them, their superiority over those of the old plan, will be readily acknowledged; in short, they have met the decided approbation of all practical printers, to whom they have been submitted, who have expressed their entire willingness to adopt them.

We shall now endeavor to point out some of the advantages, on which our claims to a preference, are founded.

The principal improvement at which we have aimed, is that of bringing all the spaces immediately under the hand, without removing the *a*, *t*, and other letters, but half a box from their original places, or curtailing the capacity of any of the principal boxes. The advantage gained by this arrangement must be obvious, when it is considered, that in spacing out a line, the hand is frequently extended to the remotest parts of the case, to the n quadrat and thin space boxes, causing much unnecessary delay in the progress of composition; for it not unfrequently occurs, that the time occupied in spacing out a line, is greater than that employed in composing it; nor is this immense loss of time confined to composing alone, for in distributing, the thin spaces almost invariably accompany the thick, which in the old plan, must be dropped some distance from each other, consequently, much time and labor is saved by the proximity of their situation. It has been satisfactorily ascertained, by counting the n quadrats and thin spaces in 1000 m's of matter, that the distance which the hand has to traverse unnecessarily, to reach those sorts in their old position, is 600 feet in 1000 m's, or in the same ratio, 4,200 feet in a day's work of 7000 m's, and the same distance again traversed over in distributing.

It will be perceived by referring to the schemes in the pre-ceding pages, that we have not only brought the spaces together, but also the points, figures, and double letters, and by curtailing the ? and ! boxes, have brought all the double letters into the lower case; these alterations, though seemingly of minor im-portance, nevertheless render the position of those sorts more consistent in their arrangement.

We have thought it quite unnecessary to enter into a minute detail respecting the particular position which each letter occupies, believing that the members of the profession generally, are possessed of sufficient penetration to discover why those letters most used, are placed nearest the hand.

In the arrangement of our upper case, we also beg leave to differ from the customary plan, by transposing the capitals and small capitals, and by introducing the J and U or V, in their regular order in the alphabet, with some few alterations of little consequence. Our reason for transposing the capitals and small capitals, must be apparent to every practical printer, upon a moment's reflection, their old position requiring one of the most awkward movements of the body, to reach them. We can see no reason why the J and U or V, should not occupy their respective situations in the alphabet, since their admission into general use. This arrangement would prevent considerable confusion in regard to the position of the U and V, as some offices leave out the U, and others the V, consequently, those boxes are frequently found to contain a mixture of both letters.

Our object in offering these few remarks, is more particularly to call attention to the improvement of the lower case, as many printers consider the arrangement of an upper case as a matter of but little importance; to such, we would only recommend the lower case, believing that the alterations are of sufficient conse-quence to receive their notice.

LAYING OF CASES.

This process consists in filling the cases with the respective sorts contained in a new fount of letter.

After having ascertained the weight of the fount, and pro-vided ourselves with a sufficient number of cases, (say one pair of cases to about every fifty or sixty lbs. of letter,) and a fount case, we begin to lay the letter, filling each box moderately with its proper sort; after which we deposit the remainder in the fount case, which is put in some convenient place till wanted.

As new letter is very liable to stick, after having been wetted, it would be advisable to sprinkle it with a little strong soap water, which would greatly tend to prevent such unpleasant consequences.

DISTRIBUTING.

DISTRIBUTING, or conveying the different sorts of letter to their respective compartments, is generally the first of a compositor's practical exercise; though it would be found more advantageous both to employer and employed, were this custom sometimes reversed, and composing made antecedent to distributing, which depends upon a perfect knowledge of what is contained in each of the different boxes in a pair of cases. But as the arrangement of sorts differ, in some degree, in almost every printing-office, it follows, that such irregularities must have their effects accordingly; of which we do not want for instances. The first that offers itself to our observation, is the loss which a compositor sustains every time he changes his place of work; for, being unacquainted with the situation of each sort, he is hindered, for some time, in his quick and ready way of distributing, which might be easily prevented, were establishers of new houses to follow one uniform method.

Other evils result from this want of uniformity, which, as we have before observed, equally affect both the employer and the employed. Some compositors, rather than charge their memory with the different situations of particular sorts, transpose them into such boxes as contained them at their last place of work, consequently the situation of the letters, in that Roman case, at least, is destroyed, and the transposed sorts not being replaced, the boxes become receptacles for pi, for the right sorts being distributed at the top, the undermost are rendered useless, because they are not expected to lodge in quarters that were not assigned them; therefore, if the hidden sorts happen to run short, they must be re-cast.

It would be the means of preserving a clean pair of cases were they filled and provided with letter for a new compositor to begin his work upon, that by composing first, he might become acquainted with the contents of his boxes, and be better prepared for distribution; but as few compositors feel inclined to quit the beaten track, and as a difficulty would occur in compelling them to leave the cases as they found them, or if they did leave them full of letter, might distribute it carelessly, knowing they would not have to set it out again, the evil might be still far from being remedied.

To make a young apprentice the sooner fit for distributing, he should be informed that there are some letters that resemble others, and at the same time be shown how to distinguish one from another; viz. *b* from *q*, *d* from *p*, *l* from *I*, *n* from *u*, &c. And in order to prove whether he has acquired a perfect knowledge of the distinction between such letters as have a similarity to each other, let the young compositor distribute a handful of broken matter into an empty case, and if, upon examination, the before mentioned sorts are found in their proper boxes, he may be trusted to distribute for himself. But before he proceeds, he should be cautioned not to take up too much matter at a time, for, should he break his handful, he will have the less pi to clear. Even to those who are not likely often to meet with this accident, the caution is not unnecessary, as too great a weight weakens the wrist, and it is a mistaken notion that it saves time, for if one handful falls into the case, it will be more than equivalent to the time gained.

In taking up a handful, the head of the page should be towards the distributor, which prevents the trouble as well as danger of turning it round, in order to have the nick uppermost. So much matter only should be taken at a time, as can be conveniently held in the left hand, and not to be higher than the thumb, which guards the ends of the lines from falling.

He should be careful not to throw the letters into the case with their face downwards, as it batters them; neither should he distribute his case too full, for it invariably creates pi.

He should not be impatient to acquire a quick method at first; his principal study should be propriety, though his progress be slow; that attained, expedition will follow from practice, and he will find his advantage in composing from a clean case, though he may be longer in distributing it. A man loses double the time in correcting, that he imagines he saves from quick distribution.

With many compositors much time is unnecessarily lost in looking at the word before they distribute it. By proper attention, the learner may avoid this, and become, without the appearance of hurry, an expeditious as well as a clean distributor. To attain which, we would recommend him never to take more letters between the fingers than he can conveniently hold, and if possible, always to take an entire word; to keep his handful on an inclining position, so that the face of the letter may come more immediately under his eye. By proper attention and practice he will become so completely acquainted with the beard or shoulder of the type, as to recognize the word he takes from his handful, with the cursory view he may have of it while in the act of lifting.

It is to this method that so many in the business are indebted for their expedition and cleanness in distribution; though to an observer the movements of their hands appear but slow. It is not to velocity of movement that compositors are indebted for their expedition, either in composing or distributing—it is to *system*, without which their attempts may have the appearance of expedition, but produce only fatigue from anxiety and false motion. Therefore, to system we would particularly call their attention, and as clean distribution produces clean composition, which not only saves time at the stone, but acquires them a respectable name, they can not be too attentive to that part of their business.

Another material point, before distributing, is the well laying up of the form. In this particular many compositors are shamefully remiss, and from this negligence arise inconveniences that lose more time than if they had taken the first trouble, besides the unpleasantness of working with dirty letter.

The letter-board should always be kept clean, and the bottom as well as the face of the form well washed before it is laid on the board and unlocked, for if any of the dirt remain from the lie brush after it is unlocked, it will sink into the matter instead of running off. This precaution taken, the pages should be well opened, and the whole form washed till the water appears to run from it in a clean state. A form can not be well laid up without plenty of water. If the form appears particularly dirty, it is best to lock it up again, which works out the filth; then rinse the bottom of it, and proceed as before.

Many compositors keep a piece of allum in their cases, in order to contract the grain of the skin of their fingers when distributing slippery letter; this is a declaration of their want of cleanliness, for had they washed their letter properly, it would not be slippery.

It is sometimes necessary to dry the letter at the fire after distributing; it is particularly recommended not to use the letter after it is dried in this way, until it is perfectly cold, as very pernicious effects arise from the antimony, which the heat of the fire brings into action, when joined to the tender particles of the skin; nor to stand near the case, either while at the fire, or until completely cool. The noxious vapor which arises is so easy to be perceived that it must alone be sufficient warning of the effects: it is the only part of the business that has any thing injurious to health, and being entirely at the choice of the compositor, he, for his own sake, ought always to avoid it as a pestilence, which will equally effect his respiration and his sinews, by the former instantly affecting his lungs, and the latter causing contractions of the fingers. It is always better, where it can be conveniently managed, to distribute at night, or before meals, so that the letter may dry without artificial heat.

OBSERVATIONS ON COMPOSING.

Composing is a term which includes several exercises, as well of the mind as the body; for when we are said to compose, we are at the same time engaged in reading and spelling what we are composing, as well as in taking care to space and to justify our matter. But that we may observe some method in our remarks, we will begin with what immediately precedes the composition.

When the copy of a work is put into the hands of the compositor, he should receive directions respecting the width and length of the page; whether it is to be leaded, and with white lines between the breaks; and whether any particular method is to be followed in the punctuation and in the adoption of capitals. These instructions being given, the compositor will make his measure to the number of m's directed, which is done by laying them flat-ways in the composing stick, and then screwing it up, not too tight, as it is apt to strain it, nor so slack as to allow the measure to give. He then fits a setting-rule to the measure, and his case being supplied with letter, he is prepared for composing.

If the copy he is to begin on be a re-print, he will observe whether there be any difference between the type he is about to use and the copy, so that his spacing may not be effected, against which he must take the necessary precautions at the time, by widening or lessening his measure, if solid matter, or driving out or getting in each paragraph, if leaded. He should select a close spaced line from the copy, which will at once prove if there be any variation.

Being now provided with a case of letter, and all the requisites for composing, we examine the copy, to ascertain if it be written fair and legible, and spelled and pointed according to the modern way. Upon this subject Smith thus remarks:—

" If therefore it happens that the copy turns out to our liking, we wish the work to last long; whereas if it proves otherwise. we are glad to have done with it, especially if the author should chance to be a humorous gentleman, and unacquainted with the nature of printing; for then a compositor is obliged to conform to the fancy of his author, and sometimes to huddle his work up in such a manner as exposes both him and his employer; whereas the gentleman that pursues the elaboration of his plan, and leaves the gracing of his work to the judgment of the printer, seldom finds room to be dissatisfied upon that score.

" By the laws of printing, indeed, a compositor should abide by his copy, and not vary from it, that he may clear himself, in case he should be charged with having made a fault. But this good law is now looked upon as obsolete, and most authors expect the printer to spell, point, and digest their copy, that it may be intelligible and significant to the reader; which is what a compositor and the corrector jointly have regard to, in works of their own language, else many good books would be laid aside, because it would require as much patience to read them, as books did when no points or notations were used; and when nothing but a close attention to the sense made the subject intelligible."

Having taken particular notice of the state of the copy, and received directions respecting the method to be adopted in the execution of it, he then commences his work. It will not be improper to point out in this place, what we have before observed, that an ill habit once acquired, is with great difficulty shaken off—truly ludicrous are the attitudes and motions exhibited by some compositors, while performing the operation of composing; such as nodding the head, agitating the body, throwing out the arm, ticking the letter against the case or the setting-rule, with numerous other false movements, which not only lose time, but fatigue the mind and exhaust the body. The swift movement of the hand is not always a just criterion of the quick progress of a compositor. In proof of which, the following anecdote is given:—

" A gentleman, some few years back, not a professed printer, though the proprietor of an extensive concern, gave orders to his overseer to discharge a compositor who had not the appearance of moving his arm so quick as others in the office with him; but his overseer was able to convince him that this man was not only the neatest, but the most expeditious, and consequently the most valuable man in his employ."

The left hand, which contains the composing stick, should always follow the right, which takes up the letters. If the former be kept stationary, considerable time is lost in bringing each letter to the stick, because the latter would, consequently, have to traverse a much greater space than is necessary: the eye should instantly precede the hand, being steadily fixed upon that particular letter, which lies with the nick from you, which should be taken up by the upper part; this would effectually prevent any false motion, and preclude the necessity of turning the letters when in the hand. A sentence of the copy should be taken, if possible, at one time, and while putting in the point and space which concludes the sentence, the eye is at full liberty to revert again to the copy, for a fresh one. It is to perfection in this particular, that those compositors who are so much admired in the profession, are indebted for their swiftness. The time thus gained is very considerable, without the least appearance of bustle or fatigue. By their taking a sentence into the memory at one time, they preserve the connexion of the subject, which renders the punctuation less difficult.

The compositor, from habit, becomes so well acquainted with the peculiar feel of each type, that he can generally detect a wrong letter without looking at the face. Those who are careful in their distribution, find the advantage of it in composition. What greater disgrace can be attached to a compositor, than being denominated a foul or slovenly workman? To avoid this stigma, he should use his earnest endeavor; it would even be better that he should read every line as he composed it, than to lose so much of his time at the stone, independent of the disgrace just mentioned. If he accustom himself to glance his eye over each line, as he justifies it, he will find it turn greatly to his account, without the least impediment to his progress.

Uniformity in spacing, unquestionably, is a most important part of the compositor's occupation; this requires both care and judgment, and, therefore, cannot be too strongly impressed upon the mind of the young beginner. Close spacing is equally unpleasant to the sight as wide spacing, and ought never to be permitted, except in very narrow measures; and frequently, even then, with care, it might partly be prevented. What is commonly called the composing space, is the best and proper separation between each word; though this rule cannot always be adhered to in narrow measures, when large type is used. It is not merely necessary to have a line here and there uniformly spaced—a careful compositor evinces an anxiety to give every page that uniformity of appearance, in which consists one of its chiefest excellencies. Careless and foul compositors will never preserve this most desirable uniformity; because, when their proof is crowded with corrections, the utmost possible care in rectifying those blunders, will not make the spacing regular. Therefore, we wish to impress this important maxim upon the mind of the young beginner: that it is better to do little, and be determined to do that little *well*, than to be anxious to put together a great number of letters, without any regard to accuracy and uniformity. Authors, certainly, should send their copy *finally* corrected to the press; for when alterations and additions are made in the proof sheet, it becomes difficult, where there are few paragraphs, to make the spacing equal.

In correcting, many compositors do not over-run the matter, through the stick, as they ought to do, but prefer doing it on the stone, in which case they not unfrequently hair space, or treble space, in order either to get in or drive out a word; when, by over-running a line or two forward or backward, they would not only preserve uniformity, but also save considerable labor.

In a late work upon this subject, we find a mixture of all the spaces (except the hair space and n quadrat) strongly recommended, in which it is urged that it would expedite the compositor in his justification—in this instance we must differ, and shall ever contend against any advantage being derived from so slovenly a practice. For how many compositors are there, who would, upon finding their line to justify without an alteration of the spaces, take the trouble to examine whether the thin spaces were not between perpendicular and the thick ones between sloping letters; which would be in direct violation of the only true rule for even spacing—and should there be any that would even condescend to take that trouble, what advantage would they gain by mixing their spaces in distributing and assorting them from their stick while composing?

Where a line is even spaced, and yet requires justification, the additional spaces should be put between those words in the line where it will be least observable, *viz.* a *d* and an *h* being perpendicular letters, will admit an addition, but not more than a middle and thin space to a thick spaced line; or, after a kerned letter, the beak of which may bear upon the top of an ascending letter, as the *f* and the *h, i, l,* &c., but not always after a kerned letter, as the *f* and the *w,* where the distance would in some cases be too conspicuous.

10

The same rule should be observed where it may be necessary to reduce the spacing of a line; less space being required after a sloping letter than a perpendicular one, the comma requires only a thick space, but the other points should have a hair space before, and an n quadrat after them, except the full point, which should have an m quadrat, as terminating a sentence. Still this rule will not always hold good, it must depend entirely upon circumstances, for, should it be necessary to reduce the spacing, those spaces after the points must also be altered in the same proportion. Spaces are now cast to such regular gradations, that the compositor can urge no reasonable excuse either for bad justification or improper spacing.

Having made these preliminary and most essential remarks, we shall now proceed:—Should the length of the page be left to the compositor's discretion, he then sets such a number of lines as he conceives to be a proportioned page, this is generally taken at nearly double the width; he next puts in the head and direction (if any,) and cuts an exact guage as follows:—after having marked off the length of the page, we then, with a sharp penknife, make a light mark at the bottom of each line, commencing after the first: these marks are of the greatest service to a neat compositor, he is thereby enabled to make up his work with greater certainty and less trouble, particularly when the work consists of light matter, heads, sub-heads, quotations, &c. This is done before he makes up the first page, as that will vary according to the different founts which are necessarily introduced.

Head lines are generally set in small capitals of the same fount, or in italic, and sometimes in capitals. Capitals of letter about three sizes smaller than the body of the work, with folios of a proportionable size, have a much neater appearance than either of the foregoing. If only folios are placed at the top of the page, it is better to make use of figures of rather a bold appearance, without parentheses or brackets.

Direction-words at the bottom of the page are not now generally used; the omission of them does not injure the appearance of the work, but saves time and expense where overrunning occurs in the proof; nevertheless, in making up the page it is necessary to substitute a white line for the signature, volume, &c.

Much trouble and loss of time was formerly experienced by compositors, in making up the first page of a work, when they had to introduce head-pieces and facs, formed with flowers of different bodies. This taste for flowery decorations is now exploded, and it is only necessary to set the title of the work in a neat type. The setting of titles must depend on the fancy and ingenuity of the compositor, and the fashion of the day, (which varies materially from year to year,) under general directions from the employer, as no fixed or certain rule can be laid down for this purpose.

The compositor will also receive directions, when there are notes, what letter they are to be set in. The usual rule is for the notes to be two sizes less than the text of the work: thus, to Pica work, Long Primer; Small Pica, Bourgeois; Long Primer, Brevier. Side notes are usually smaller in proportion; and when the work is of the nature of bibles, law-books, &c., in which the side notes or references, frequently drive down more than the lines of the text to which they refer, the expedient of cut-in-notes must be resorted to. This is a difficult part of a compositor's business, and requires much skill and patience to adjust all parts, so that every line of note and text may have proper and equal bearing. The reglet, scaleboard, or lead, which is placed between the lines of matter and the side-note must be cut with as much nicety as possible to the length of the text, as far as where the note is to run under; and having accurately adjusted, by means of the quotations and justifiers, the situation of the first line of the note, such lead or scaleboard, is added to the text as will make it precisely correspond in depth with the lines of note that stand on the side before turning: the remainder of the note is then set in a long measure, to correspond in width with the text, reglet, and side-note; and the page is made up with note, or the text begun again after the note is finished. In bibles with notes and annotations, in law books, some classics, and other works, it frequently happens that a page exhibits several of these alternate frame-works of note and text, which, if done well, display a workman's skill to the best advantage; but if done at all ill, nothing exhibits a more vile appearance.

On beginning a work, the compositor should be informed what number of volumes it is intended to be comprised in, in order that he may place the number of the volume in the left hand corner of the signature line, in the first page of every sheet. The above and the signature are generally put in small capitals; and where they extend to more than one alphabet, the second one should begin, 2A, 2B, and so on. In our opinion the signature is much better both in appearance, and for collating, when placed within about six m's from the end of the line, than in the centre, according to the old custom.

The title, preface, &c., of a volume is always left till the body of the work is finished, as many circumstances may arise in the course of its progress through the press, which may induce the author to alter his original preface, date, &c. or the work may conclude in such a manner as to admit of their being brought in at the end, in order to complete a sheet, which may save both paper and press work. For this reason it is customary to begin the first sheet of every work with signature B, leaving A for the title sheet. To a sheet of octavo, two signatures only are necessary, which are placed to the first and third pages; to a sheet of twelves three signatures, to the first, third and ninth pages, thus, B, B2, B3.

In works printed in half sheets, figures are generally used instead of letters. This plan is considered to cause less confusion with the binder, particularly in works of five or six hundred pages.

Instead of beginning the work with a two-line letter, according to the old custom, capital letters have a much neater appearance; the remainder of the word may be put either in capitals or small capitals, the latter is most preferable.

We now proceed to the second page, and set the running title in a neat letter proportioned to the size of the page; but this must be governed by the quantity of matter necessary to be introduced at the head of the page. A full line, as a running title, has a very clumsy appearance, and should, if possible be avoided. To a solid page, two leads make the usual space after the head, to a single leaded page, three leads or a Long Primer white; and to a double leaded page, a Pica white.

It has long been, and still is a practice too prevalent among compositors, to drive out a word at the close of a paragraph, or even to divide it, in order to reap the advantage of a break line. Part of a word, or a complete word in a break line, if it contain no more than three or four letters, is improper. It should be the business of the proof-reader, at all times, to notice this encroachment. The last line of a paragraph should not on any account begin a page, neither should the first line of a paragraph come at the bottom of a page, if the work has white lines between the breaks. To obviate which, the compositor makes his page either long or short, as most convenient, always taking care that the corresponding pages back, by which means the long or short appearance of the page escapes observation.

If the work is very open, consisting of heads, whites, &c. the compositor must be particularly attentive to their depth; so that though the white may be composed of different sized quadrats, yet that their ultimate depth shall be equal to the regular body of the type the work is done in; for unless care is taken in this particular, the register of the work must be incomplete. The pressman cannot make the lines back if the compositor is not careful in making up his matter.

The first line of a new paragraph is indented an m quadrat, of whatever sized letter the work may be; though we prefer an m and an n in small measures, and two or even three m's when the measure runs very long, by which means the paragraph is more strongly marked; the mere indention of an m being scarcely perceptible in a long line. Authors vary materially in the mode of making paragraphs; some carry the argument of a position to a great length, before they relieve the attention of the reader; while others break off at almost every place that will admit only of a full point. But in this case we follow the author's plan, unless, upon particular occasions, it may be necessary to multiply or reduce the breaks in the copy, if it can be done with propriety, in order to make the work look uniform. Authors should always make the beginning of a new paragraph conspicuous to the compositor, by indenting the first line of it far enough to distinguish it from the preceding line, in case it should be quite full.

10*

Many hints, in addition to what have already been dropped, relative to composing, might be added for the information of learners, were we not persuaded that practice, and a close attention to the mode of doing business by good workmen, will be of more service to them than a multiplicity of rules. It is the duty of the person under whose tuition an apprentice is placed, to discharge that trust with fidelity. The youth's future prospects in life, depend in a great measure on the principles on which his first instructions are formed; and it is the duty of every man to correct those habits in youth which may be improper, whether arising from carelessness or any other cause. When a youth makes choice of a profession, and is aware that his future support and prospects in life must depend on a correct knowledge of that profession, he should be anxious to attain that knowledge; but to withhold it from him, or allow the practice of improper habits, is, in his preceptor, a neglect highly reprehensible, and unjust.

After the body of the volume is completed, the contents sometimes follow next, though they belong more properly to the beginning of the work; and for this reason we shall defer speaking of them here, but introduce them in their proper place. The index is generally placed at the end of the volume, and set in letter two sizes less than that of the work; it is always begun upon an uneven page. Running titles may be set to an index, but folios are seldom put to them, unless it is to recommend the book for its extraordinary number of pages; for as an index does not refer to its own matter by figures, they are needless in this case. The signatures, however, are always carried on regularly to the last whole, or half sheet of the work.

It was formerly the plan to set the subject word of each article in Italic, and all the rest in Roman, indenting all the matter an m quadrat that makes above one line, what is technically termed—to run out and indent; but the Italic is now in a great measure exploded, it being attended with extra trouble, and at the same time destroys the uniformity of the page.

Care should be taken that the subject words are ranged alphabetically, as it is not expected that the compositor will transpose his matter afterwards, without being paid for it.

Where figures have a regular succession, a comma is put after each folio; and where their order breaks off, a full point is used. Thus, for example, after 6, 7, 8, 9, commas are put; and after 12. 16. 19. 24. full points; but to save figures and commas, the succession of the former is noticed, by putting a dash between the first and last figures, thus, 4—8. Again, if an article has been collected from two pages, the folio of the second is supplied by *sq.* or *sequente;* and by *sqq.* or *sequientibus,* when an article is touched upon in succeeding pages. A full point is not put after the last figures, because it is thought that their standing at the end of the line is a sufficient stop. Neither is a comma or a full point placed to the last word of an article, in a wide measure and open matter; but it is not improper to use a comma at the end of every article in narrow columns, or where figures are put after the matter, instead of running them to the end of the line.

At the conclusion of the index, the volume is considered as completed, with the exception of the title, preface, &c. A compositor's first consideration, then, is in what manner the work has ended, what number of pages the titles, &c., will make, and whether he can impose them in such a form as to save paper and presswork. To answer this purpose, a preface may be drove out or got in; or if matter is wanting, it is customary to set a half title.

The method of setting or displaying a title is governed entirely by fancy; and in this country the style of late years is much altered for the better, as a comparison between the title pages of the last and present century fully evince. We concur in the assertion, that no fixed rules can be laid down for instruction, because it depends entirely upon the taste and ingenuity of the compositor; such being the prevalent opinion, we trust that we shall be pardoned for obtruding a few hints, which, in our judgment, may tend to assist the juvenile portion of the profession. 1st. Having divided the title into lines, and decided upon the sized type most suitable for the principal one, we begin by composing those of the second and third class, both in ascending and descending order. 2d. We avoid having two lines of equal length to follow, or come in contact with each other. 3d. Catch words should be set on a very reduced scale, and proportioned according to the strength of the preceding and succeeding lines; because, when catch words are bold, they take from the general effect of the title, it being impossible that it can appear to advantage if the striking lines, which ought to stand forward, are too much crowded by the full appearance of their neighbors' faces. 4th. This knowledge will be best attained by a close attention to those title pages which are considered, by those who are judges, to be displayed with true taste and judgment.

Authors should endeavor to make their title pages as short and concise as possible; for a crowded title never can be displayed with elegance or taste.

The dedication generally follows the title, and seldom exceeds one page. It should be set in capitals and small capitals, displayed in the manner of a title; but where it extends to a considerable length, it is generally set in a letter two sizes larger than the work. There is neither folio nor direction line required to it, where it does not exceed a page; but if it happens to be the third page of the sheet, the signature must be inserted. The French Manual gives very particular directions upon this head : "When a book is divided by several different titles, we must give to each division its suitable type. Thus, if we set the word 'Part' in Pica, we should set 'Chapter' in Long Primer, 'Article' in Bourgeois, and 'Section' in Brevier."—In English works this does not often occur, but the principle laid down is very proper. "In Epistles Dedicatory, the name of the person to whom the work is dedicated, should always be in capitals, and the terms, Your very humble and very obedient, &c. should be set in a smaller type, and the signature, or name of the author, in capitals of a less fount than that in which the name of the personage to whom dedicated, has been set."

Formerly, the preface was uniformly set in Italic; at present this plan is seldom adopted, and Roman is used in its stead, of one size larger than the body of the work. The running title to the preface is commonly set in the same manner as those of the body of the work, at the same time the folios are put in numeral letters, beginning with ii over the second page, and continuing the rest in the usual manner. If the work itself was printed with folios only, then the preface should have them also in the middle of the line.

The title, dedication, preface, introduction, &c., form what is called the title sheet, viz. signature A, which makes the printer's alphabet, consisting of twenty-three letters, complete; provided that the body of the work begins with B. To ascertain more readily how many sheets a book consists of, more than are marked with signatures in capitals or small capitals, a lower case Roman a is put to the first sheet, and thus carried on till the beginning of the body of the work.

What has been observed concerning prefaces, relates equally to introductions, drawn up and intended to elucidate their respective works.

The contents follow the preface or introduction, and are either set in Roman or Italic, generally two sizes smaller than the body of the work; the first line of each summary full, and the rest indented an m quadrat, with the referring figures justified at the ends of the respective lines.

The errata are put immediately before the body of the work, or at the end of it, and should consist only of such corrections as are *indispensably necessary*, without noticing any defects in the punctuation, unless where the sense is perverted.

It is most devoutly to be wished, that works could issue from the press perfectly free from errors, which would more likely be the case were authors to endeavor to render their copy more legible, before they place it into the hands of the printer. It can hardly be expected that the corrector, under whose inspection such a variety of subjects are continually passing, should be able to enter thoroughly into every one of them, and to guess so nicely at the author's meaning when the copy is obscure, and unable to afford him any assistance: besides every form is exposed to accidents which can seldom be detected as it passes through the hands of the printer; so that every additional proof may be productive of fresh error.

CHAPTER V.

IMPOSING.

Having sufficiently treated, in the preceding chapter, upon the principal subjects connected with the department of composing, it next becomes our duty not only to lay schemes of the various impositions before our readers, but also to endeavor to give a general outline for the imposition of whatever odd matter there may be at the conclusion of a work; and likewise to explain, in as clear a manner as possible, every point connected with this important branch of the art.

This article not only comprehends a knowledge of placing the pages so that they may regularly follow each other after they are printed off, and the sheet folded up, but also the mode of dressing chases, and the manner of making the proper margin.

We will suppose that a compositor has got up as many pages as are required for a whole sheet, or such portions of a sheet, of whatever size; he begins to lay them upon the imposing stone, placing the first page with the signature to the left hand facing him, according to the following schemes, which, it is hoped, will be found to contain every necessary imposition; they consist of folios, quartos, octavos, twelves, sixteens, eighteens, twenties, twenty-fours, thirty-twos, thirty-sixes, forties, forty-eights, sixty-fours, seventy-twos, ninety-sixes, and one hundred and twenty-eights. We have also introduced schemes for imposing from the centre, by which means the blank or open pages may be thrown in the centre of the form, leaving the solid pages on the outside to act as bearers for the rollers, as well as for the better regulation of the impression.

Schemes of various other irregular sizes might also be introduced, but they could answer no other purpose than that of pleasing the fancy, by exhibiting the possibility of folding a sheet of paper into so many different forms.

Abstract Title Deeds of Estates.

1

Abstract Title Deeds of Estates are printed with blanks at the back, with all the margin on the left side, and on single leaves, which are stitched together at the corner.

This method of imposing the form is to save press-work and the compositor's charge.

Lock up.   *Lock up.*

ᘔ

A Single Sheet of Folio.

Inner

ᘔ

Form.

Ɛ

1

Outer

A

4

Form.

Two Sheets of Folio, Quired, or lying one in another.*

Outer Form of the Outer Sheet.

Outer Form of the Inner Sheet.

---

* Imposing in quires may be carried to any extent, by observing the following rule :—first, ascertain the number of pages, then divide them into so many sheets of folio, and commence laying down the two first and two last, which form the first sheet, and so on to the centre one, always remembering that the odd pages stand on the left, and the even on the right; the folios of each two forming one more than the number of pages in the work: for example, let us suppose the work to consist of thirty-six pages, which is nine sheets of folio, then they should be laid down according to the scheme at the foot of the opposite page.

Two Sheets of Folio, Quired, or lying one in another.

Inner Form of the Outer Sheet.

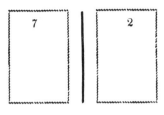

Inner Form of the Inner Sheet.

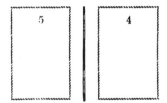

Outer.	Inner.	Sheet.	Outer.	Inner.	Sheet.	Outer.	Inner.	Sheet.
1	36	35	2, *1st*	3	34	33	4, *2d*	5	32	31	6 *3d*
7	30	29	8, *4th*	9	28	27	10, *5th*	11	26	25	12 *6th*
13	24	23	14, *7th*	15	22	21	16, *8th*	17	20	19	18 *9th*

The furniture must be reduced in the backs of the inner sheets, to allow for stitching

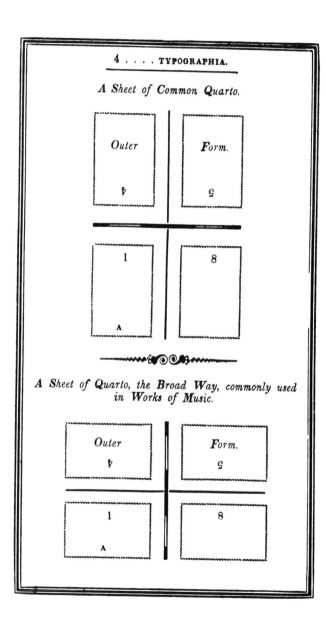

A Sheet of Common Quarto.

A Sheet of Quarto, the Broad Way, commonly used in Works of Music.

A Sheet of Common Quarto.

*I*nner 9	ɀⱯ *Form.* Ɛ
7 Ⱉ	2

A Sheet of Quarto, the Broad Way, commonly used in Works of Music.

*I*nner 9	ɀⱯ *Form.* Ɛ
7	2

Two Half Sheets of Quarto, worked together

Outer	*Form.*
۶*	٤*

1	4
Λ	

Half a Sheet of Common Quarto

ᴄᴏ	4

ᴎ	1
	ᴀ

Two Half Sheets of Quarto, worked together

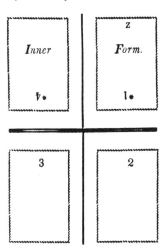

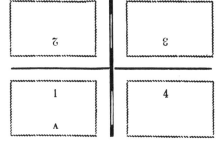

Half a Sheet of Quarto, the Broad Way.

Outer Form of a Sheet of Common Octavo

| 8 | 6 | ᘔ1 | ꓽ |
| 1 | 16 | 13 | 4 |

Outer Form of a Sheet of Octavo, the Broad Way.

| ᘓ1 | 12 | 6 | 16 |
| ᖾ | ꓼ A3 | 8 | 1 A |

Inner Form of a Sheet of Common Octavo.

9	11	01	ㄥ
3 A2	14	15	2

Inner Form of a Sheet of Octavo, the Broad Way.

15	01	11	14
2	ㄥ　A4	6	3　A2

Two Half Sheets of Common Octavo worked together.

Half a Sheet of Common Octavo.

Inner Form of Two Half Sheets of Octavo.

2	7	6	3 A 2
3 B 2	6	7	2

Two Quarters of a Sheet of Octavo, worked together.

2	3	4	1 B
1 A	4	3	2

Sheet of Octavo, 12 of the Work, and 4 other Matter.

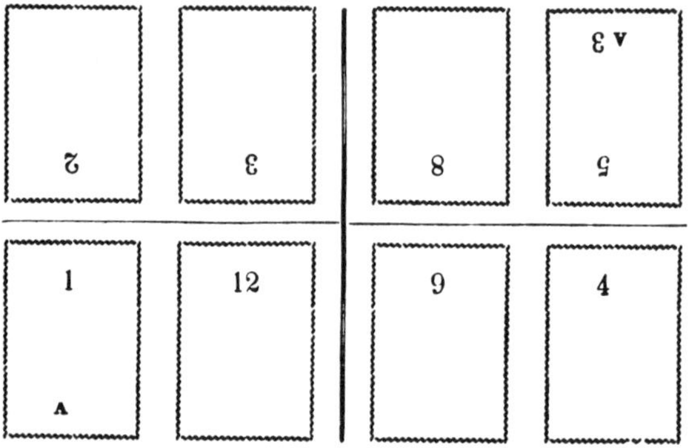

Outer Form of a Sheet of Octavo, of Hebrew Work.

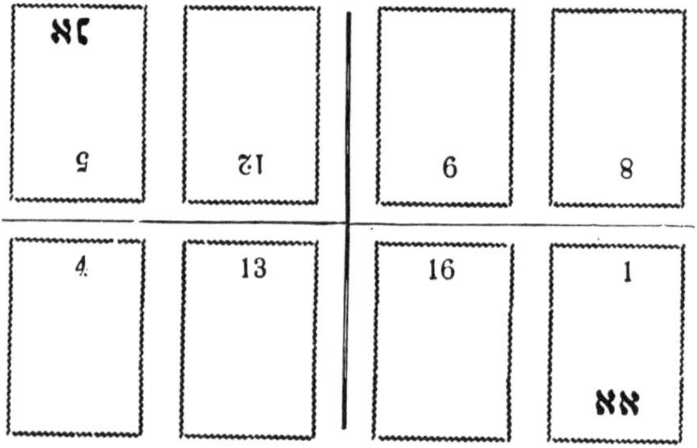

Inner Form of Octavo, 12 of the Work, and 4 other Matter.

			Z
9	7	4	1
3	10	11	2
A2			

Inner Form of a Sheet of Octavo, of Hebrew Work.

אל			
7	10	11	9
2	15	14	3
			אב

Outer Form of a Sheet of Octavo, Imposed from the Centre.

12	5	8	9
13	4	1	16
		A	

A Half Sheet of Octavo, Imposed from the Centre.

6	3	4	5
7	2	1	8
		A	

Inner Form of a Sheet of Octavo, Imposed from the Centre.

| 61 | 7 | 9 | 11 |
| 15 | 2 | 3 | 14 |

A

Two Quarters of a Sheet of Octavo, Imposed from the Centre.

| 4 | 1 | 5 | 8 |
| 3 | 2 | 1 | 4 |

A

Outer Form of a Sheet of Twelves.

A	1	8	12
24	17	13
21	20	16
4	5	9 A3

Inner Form of a Sheet of Twelves.

A2	3	9	10
22	19	15
23	18	14
6	7	11

A Sheet of Twelves without cutting.

1 A	4	5. A3
24	12	20 Outer
13	16	17 Form.
12	9	8
11	10	7
14	15	18 Inner
23	22	19 Form.
2	3 A2	6

A Sheet of Twelves with Two Signatures.

A 1	8	20
Outer 16	6	21
Form. 13	21	24
4	5 3A	17 B
A2 3	9	81
Inner 14	11	33
Form. 15	01	22
2	7	61 B2

A Common Half Sheet of Twelves.

Half Sheet of Twelves without cutting.

Different methods of **Imposing** *Half Sheets of Twelves, from the Centre.*

21 20 16

4 5 6 2v

▲ 1 8 12

24 17 13

23 18 14

2 7 11

3 9 10

22 19 15

A Sheet of Twelves, Imposed from the Centre.

Outer Form of a Sheet of Long Twelves.

1 ∧	4
16	13
9	12
8	5
17	20
24	21

One third, or 8 pages of a Sheet of Twelves.
To be imposed as a Slip, or in the Off-cross.

1 ∧	8 Outer	5 Form.	4

Inner Form of a Sheet of Long Twelves.

A2 3	2
14	15
11	10
6	7
19	18
22	23

One third, or 8 pages of a Sheet of Twelves.
To be imposed as a Slip, or in the Off-cross.

3	6	7	2
A2	Inner	Form.	

Two Half Sheets of Twelves worked together.

A 1	4	9
12	6 Outer	7
B 1	4 Form.	9
12	6	7

11	10	8
2	3 Inner	5 B2
11	10 Form	8
2	3	5 A2

Half Sheet of Twelves with 2 Signatures.
4 pages of other matter.

A 1	4	2
8	5	3
7	6	4
2	3	1 B

A Half Sheet of Sixteens.

A 1	8	7	2
16	9	10	15
13	12	11	14
4	5	6	3 A2

A 1	16	13	4
Outer 32	17	20	29
Form 25	24	21	28
8	9	12	5 A3
7	10	11	9
Inner 26	33	22	27
Form 31	18	19	30
2	15	14	3 A2

A Sheet of Sixteens with One* Signature.

* A Sheet of Sixteens, with Two Signatures, is imposed as two sheets of common octavo, putting the first signature for the one half sheet where A stands, (folio 1), and the first page of the other half sheet in the place of A 3 (folio 5.)

A Half Sheet of Eighteens.*
Containing 16 pages.

144	43 4			6	11
4	13	8	9	14	2 4
1 ^	16	7	10	15	2

A Half Sheet of Eighteens.†

14	43 4	10	6	9	13
4	15	12	7	16	2 4
1 ^	18	11	8	17	2

* The white paper of this half sheet being worked off, the centre pages to be transposed; viz. seven and ten in the room of eight and nine, and pages eight and nine in the place of seven and ten: when this is done your imposition will be true.

† The white paper of this form being now worked off, the four lowermost pages in the centre must be transposed; viz. pages eight and eleven in the room of seven and twelve, and pages seven and twelve in the place of eight and eleven; this being done, the sheet will then fold up right.

Outer Form of a Sheet of Eighteens, to be folded together.

5 A3	32	29	8	17	20
4	33	28	9 A2	16	21
1 A	36	25	12	13	24

Outer Form of a Sheet of Eighteens, with One Signature.

10	27	26	11 A6	20	17
8	29	32	5 A3	22	15
1 A	36	33	4	23	14

Inner Form of a Sheet of **Eighteens,** *to be folded together.*

19	18	7 A4	30	31	6
22	15	01	27	34	3 A2
23	14	11	26	35	2

Inner Form of a Sheet of **Eighteens,** *with* **One Signature.**

18	19	12	25	28	9 A5
16	21	9	31	30	7 A4
13	24	3 A2	34	35	2

Outer Form of a Sheet of Eighteens, with Two Signatures.

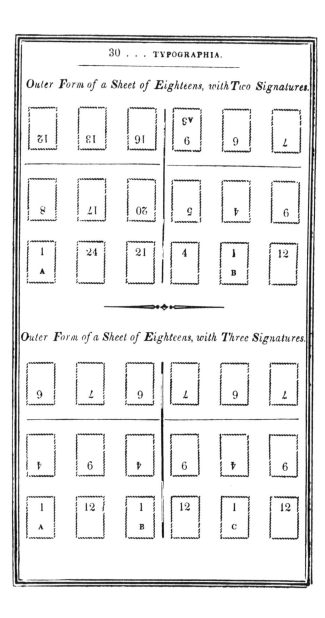

Outer Form of a Sheet of Eighteens, with Three Signatures.

Inner Form of a Sheet of Eighteens, with Two Signatures.

8	B2 5	10	15	14	11
10	3	6	19	18	7
11	2	3 A2	22	23	2

Inner Form of a Sheet of Eighteens, with Three Signatures.

8	C2 5	8	B2 5	8	A2 5
10	3	10	3	10	3
11	2	11	2	11	2

*Half Sheet of Eighteens, without Transposition.**

Half Sheet of Twenties, with Two Signatures.

* To print a half sheet of eighteens without transposition, has long been considered as impossible; at last a wiseacre made this discovery; it is here given with a view of showing its absurdity! Is three single leaves preferable to the transposition of four pages?

Inner Form of a Sheet of Twenties.

19	6		15	10	2
22	35		26	31	39

23	34		27	30	38
18	7 A4		14	11 A6	3 A2

Outer Form of a Sheet of Twenties.

17	8		A7 13	12	4
24	33		28	29	37

21	36		25	32	40
20	5 A3		16	9 A5	1 A

A Half Sheet of Twenty-fours.

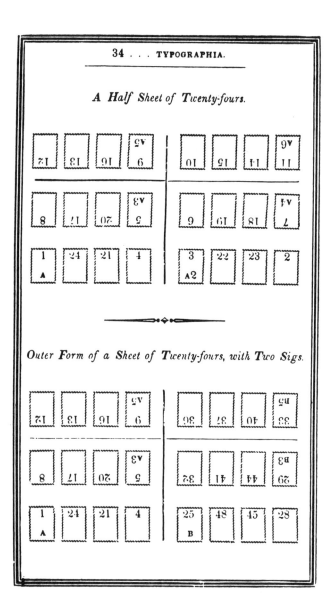

Outer Form of a Sheet of Twenty-fours, with Two Sigs.

A Half Sheet of Twenty-fours, the Sixteen-way.

Inner Form of a Sheet of Twenty-fours, with Two Sigs.

A Half Sheet of long Twenty-fours.

A Half Sheet of Twenty-fours, with Two Signatures.

A Half Sheet of Twenty-fours, without Cutting.

5 A3	20	17	8		7 A4	18	19	6
⊅	1Z	9I	9 A5		0I	9I	ZZ	3 A2
1 A	24	13	12		11 A6	14	23	2

A Half Sheet of Thirty-twos.

⊅	6Z	8Z	9 A3		9	⌊Z	0E	3 A2
13	20	21	12		11 A6	22	19	14
9I	⌊I	⅂Z	6 A5		0I	3Z	8I	9I
1 A	32	25	8		7 A4	26	31	2

Outer Form of a Sheet of Thirty-twos.

4	61	36	29	28	37	60	5 ᴬ3
13 ᴀ7	52	45	20	21	44	53	12
16	49	48	17	24	41	56	6 ᴬ5
1 ᴀ	64	33	32	25	40	57	8

Outer Form of a Sheet of Thirty-twos, with Four Sigs.

50	63	62	51 ᴅ2	36	45	48	33 c
55 ᴅ4	58	59	54	37 c3	44	41	40
8	9	12	5 ᴬ3	22	27	26	23 ʙ4
1 ᴀ	16	13	4	19 ʙ2	30	31	18

Inner Form of a Sheet of Thirty-twos.

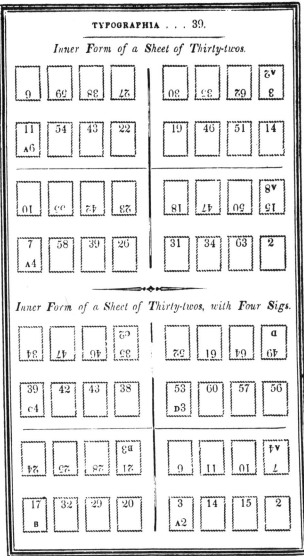

Inner Form of a Sheet of Thirty-twos, with Four Sigs.

A Half Sheet of Thirty-twos, with Two Signatures.

18	31	30	19 / B2		20	29	32	17 / B
23 / B4	26	27	22		21 / B3	28	25	24
8	9	12	5 / A3		9	11	10	7 / A4
1 / A	16	13	4		3 / A2	14	15	2

A Half Sheet of Thirty-twos, 20 pages of the Work, 4 pages of Title, &c. and 8 of other Matter.

18	19	24	24		18	14 / b	20	17 / a
1 / a	1*	3† / b2	6†		5†	4†	3*	2*
8	9	12	5 / A3		9	11	10	7 / A2
1 / A	16	13	4		3 / A2	14	15	2

A Half Sheet of Thirty-sixes.

A 1	8	10	A5 9	A4 7	2
36	29	27	28	30	35
33	32	26	25	31	34

4	A3 5	A6 11	12	6	A2 3
23	22	20	19	21	24
14	15	17	18	16	13

A Half Sheet of Thirty-sixes, without Cutting.

A 1	4	A3 5	6	A2 3	2
36	33	32	18	31	35
25	28	29	30	27	26

12	A5 9	8	A1 7	10	A6 11
13	16	17	18	15	14
24	21	20	19	22	23

A Half Sheet of Thirty-sixes, with Two Signatures.

A 1	8	26	B 25	A4 7	2
24	17	35	36	18	23
21	20	34	33	19	22

4	A3 5	B2 27	28	6	A2 3
15	14	32	31	13	16
10	11	B3 29	30	12	A5 9

A Half Sheet of Forties.

| 20 | 21 | 24 | 17 | 18 | 23 | 22 | 19 |
| 5 A3 | 36 | 33 | 8 | 7 A4 | 34 | 35 | 6 |

16	25	28	A7 13	14	27	26	A8 15
9 A5	32	29	12	11 A6	30	31	10
1 A	40	37	4	3 A2	38	39	2

A Quarter Sheet of Forty-eights, with Two Signatures.

			7.2				Z
18	23	22	19	20	21	24	17

			A3				A4
8	9	12	5	6	11	10	7

| 1 A | 16 | 13 | 4 | 3 A2 | 14 | 15 | 2 |

A Half Sheet of Forty-eights, with Two Signatures.

			A2				B2
2	23	22	3	26	47	46	27

| 7 A1 | 18 | 19 | 6 | 31 B4 | 42 | 43 | 30 |

| 11 A6 | 14 | 15 | 10 | 35 B6 | 38 | 39 | 34 |

			A5				B5
12	13	16	9	36	37	40	33

			A3				B3
8	17	20	5	32	41	44	29

| 1 A | 24 | 21 | 4 | 25 B | 48 | 45 | 28 |

A Quarter Sheet of Forty-eights, without Cutting.

5 A3	20	17	8		7 A4	18	19	6
4	21	16	9 A5		10	15	22	3 A2
1 A	24	13	12		11 A6	14	23	2

A Half Sheet of Forty-eights, with Three Signatures.

45	47	46	35 c2		36	45	48	33
39	42	43	38		37 c3	44	41	40
18	31	30	19 B2		20	29	28	17 B

23	26	27	22		21 B3	28	25	24
8	9	12	5 A3		9	11	10	7
1 A	16	13	4		3 A2	14	15	2

A Common Quarter Sheet of Forty-eights.

7ᴉ	13	16	6		10	15	14	11
8	17	20	ꜱ A3		9	19	18	ꜱ A4
1 A	24	21	4		3 A2	22	23	2

A Quarter Sheet of Sixty-fours, with Two Signatures.

18	31	30	19 B2		20	29	32	17 B
23 B4	26	27	22		21 B3	28	25	24
8	9	12	ꜱ A3		9	11	10	ꜱ A4
1 A	16	13	4		3 A2	14	15	2

A Common Quarter Sheet of Sixty-fours.

| 4 | 29 | 28 | A3 / 5 | | 6 | 27 | 30 | A2 / 3 |
| 13 | 20 | 21 | 12 | | 11 A6 | 22 | 19 | 14 |

| 16 | 17 | 24 | A2 / 6 | | 10 | 23 | 18 | 15 |
| 1 A | 32 | 25 | 8 | | 7 A4 | 26 | 31 | 2 |

A Quarter Sheet of Sixty-fours, 20 pages of the Work, 8 of Title, and 4 of other Matter.

| 2* | 7* | 24† | 23† | | 24† Z | 11† | 8* | 1* V |
| 3* | 6* | 17 B | 20 | | 19 | 18 | 5* | 4* |

| 8 | 9 | 21 | A3 / 5 | | 6 | 11 | 10 | A4 / 7 |
| 1 A | 16 | 13 | 4 | | 3 A2 | 14 | 15 | 2 |

A Half Sheet of Sixty-fours.

2	63	34	31	26	39	58	7 (A4)
15 (A8)	50	47	18	23	42	55	10
14	51	46	19	22	43	54	11 (A6)
3 (A2)	62	35	30	27	38	59	6
4	61	36	29	28	37	60	5 (A3)
13 (A7)	52	45	20	21	44	53	12
16	49	48	17	24	41	56	9 (A5)
1 (A)	64	33	32	25	40	57	8

A Half Sheet of Seventy-twos, with Three Signatures.

Half Sheet of Ninety-sixes, with Six Signatures.

1 A	8	55 D2		90	71 E2	99
16	6	58		63	74	62
13	21	59		62	75	78
4	5 A3	54		51 D4	70	67 E3
19 B2	22	37 C3		36	85 F3	48
30	27	44		45	92	93
31	26	41		48	89	96
18	23 B4	40		33 C	88	17 F

17 E	74	39 C4		34	87 F4	82
32	25	42		47	90	95
29	28	43		46	91	94
20	21 E2	38		35 C2	86	83 F2
3 A2	9	53 D3		52	69 E3	68
14	11	60		61	76	77
15	10	57		64	73	80
2	7 A4	56		49 D	72	65 E

Half Sheet of One Hundred and Twenty-eights, with Eight Signatures.

All odd matter, for whatever sized form, should be divided into fours, eights, twelves and sixteens, which is the ground-work of all the impositions, except the eighteens, which differ from all the others; for instance, sixteens, twenty-fours, and thirty-twos, are only octavos and twelves doubled, or twice doubled, and imposed in half sheets: for example, the sixteens are two octavos imposed on one side the short cross; the twenty-fours are two twelves imposed on each side the long cross, and a thirty-two is four octavos imposed in each quarter of the chase. Thus a sheet may be repeatedly doubled. By this division, any form or sheet may be imposed, always bearing in mind, that the first page of each class must stand to the left hand, when the foot of the page is towards you, and to the right when the head of the page is nearest to you. Having set down the first page, then trace the remainder according to the scheme which applies to its number; in proof of which, the standard rule for all other impositions may be adopted; namely, each two pages that come together, will make one more than the number of pages in the class or sheet. The first page of any portion can be placed in the situation of any odd page, where they make even numbers. It is necessary to make a few observations on the method of tying up a page, which is done with a piece of strong pack thread or fine twine, turned four or five times round it, and fastened at the right hand corner, by thrusting a noose of it between the several turnings and the matter, with the rule, and drawing it perfectly tight, taking care always to keep the end of the cord on the face of the page, and while tying it to keep the fore finger of the left hand tight on the corner, to prevent the page from being drawn aside.

The page being tied up, the compositor removes it from the ledges of the galley, to see if the turns of cord lie about the middle of the shank of the letter; if they lie too high, as most commonly they do, he thrusts them lower, and if the page be not too broad, he places the fore and middle finger of his right hand, on the off side of the head of the page, and his thumb on the near; then, bending his other fingers under, presses them firmly against the head of the page; he next places the fingers of his left hand in the same position at the foot of the page, and raising it upright, lays it on a page paper; then, with his right hand he grasps the sides of the page and the paper, which turns up against the sides of the page, and sets it in a convenient spot under his frame, placing it on the left hand, with the foot towards him, that the other pages that are in like manner set down afterwards, may stand by it in an orderly succession until he comes to impose them.

If it be a large folio page, or a broadside, he has tied up, he cannot take that into his hands, because it is too broad for his grasp; therefore he carries his galley and page to the imposing stone, and turns the handle of the galley towards him, and taking hold of the handle with his right hand, he places the ball of the thumb of his left hand against the inside of the head ledge of the galley, to hold it and keep it steady, and by the handle draws the slice with the page upon it, out of the galley, letting the slice rest upon the imposing stone: he then thrusts the head end of the slice so far upon it, that the foot of the page may stand an inch or two within the outer edge of the stone, and placing his left hand against the foot of the page, in the same posture he last placed it against the head ledge of the galley, he then draws the slice from under the bottom of the page. We shall now return to our subject:—

In half sheets, all the pages belonging to the white paper, and reiteration, are imposed in one chase. So that when a sheet of paper is printed on both sides with the same form, that sheet is cut in two in the short cross, if quarto or octavo, and in the short and long cross, if twelves, and folded as octavo, or twelves.

When a compositor proceeds to impose, he carefully takes the pages, which he had previously placed on pieces of paper, in regular succession, from under his frame: in doing this, the paper should be tightly grasped on both sides the page, in order that it may be kept firm to the bottom of the page, whereas if it should be left slack, the letters will be liable to slip out, unless it be particularly well tied up; having conveyed it to the stone, he next places the two last fingers of his right hand under the head of the page, but not under the page paper at the head of it, still grasping the sides with his fore fingers and thumb; he then slips his left hand so that the palm of it may turn towards the bottom; and lifting the page upright on his right hand, he disengages the left to remove the paper: he next grasps th foot end of the page with his left hand, in the same manner as the right holds the head of it, and turning the face of the letter towards him, lays it nimbly down, so that the whole page may come in contact with the face of the stone at one time, thereby preventing any letters from slipping out, which would endanger the breaking, squabbling, or hanging of the page.

As the foregoing method, particularly in inexperienced or careless hands, would frequently endanger a page, because, should it be large, double, or treble columns, or have side notes, it would be much safer to pursue the following plan, which is now adopted by many compositors; namely, to provide good strong, not coarse and rough, page papers, and when the pages are brought to the stone, instead of lifting them up as just noticed, they are slided off the papers in the same manner as before directed respecting a folio page on the slice galley, being careful that no particles of dirt remain under the page.

Being sure that our pages are laid down right, we proceed to dressing of chases, which we will suppose to be for a sheet of octavo. Accordingly we endeavor to come at a good pair of chases, that are fellows, as well in circumference as in other respects; and having laid them over the pages for the two different forms, we consider the largeness of the paper on which the work is to be done, and put such gutter-stick between page and page, and such reglets along the sides of the two crosses, as will give the book proper margins after it is bound.

The pages of a sheet or half sheet being now laid, our next business is to arrange the margin, so that each page may occupy one side of a leaf, and have the proper proportion of white paper left at the sides, as well as at the head and foot thereof. Custom has familiarised us to the printed page being a little higher than the middle of the leaf, and to its having a little more margin on the outside than in the back.

In making margin, some use the following method, for octavos; viz. they measure and mark the width of four pages by compasses, on a sheet of paper designed for the work, beginning to measure at one extremity of the breadth of the sheet. The rest of the paper they divide into four equal parts, allowing two-fourths for the width of two separate gutter-sticks; the remaining two-fourths they divide again into four equal parts, and allow one-fourth for the margin along each side of the short cross, and one-fourth for the margin to each outside page. But because the thickness of the short cross adds considerably to the margin, they reduce the furniture in the back accordingly, and thereby enlarge the outside margin, which requires the greatest share to allow for the unevenness of the paper itself, as well as for pressmen laying sheets uneven, when the fault is not in the paper. Having thus made the margin between the pages to the breadth of the paper, they proportion the margin at the head, in the same manner, to the length, and accordingly measure and mark the length of two pages, dividing the rest into four parts, whereof is allowed one-fourth on each side of the long cross, and one-fourth for the margin that runs along the foot of the two ranges of pages. But though each part is counted equal to another, they do not prove so upon examination; for as in the short cross, so they lessen the furniture on both sides the long one, to enlarge the bottom margin, for the same reasons that were assigned for extending the side margin.

This being the method that is used by some in making margin to octavos, they go the same way to work in twelves, where their chief care is to fix upon a proper size for the head-sticks; and, according to them, allow in the following manner: viz. for the outer margin along the foot of the pages, the amount of two-thirds of the breadth of the head-sticks, and the same for the inner margin, that reaches from the foot of the fifth page to the centre of the groove for the points; and from the centre of that groove to the pages of the quire, or that cut off, they allow half of the breadth of the head-stick. As to the margin along the long cross, it is governed by the gutter-sticks; and it is common to put as much on each side of the long cross as amounts to half the breadth of the gutter-stick, without deducting almost any thing for the long cross, since that makes allowance for the inequality of the outer margin.

Thus much may suffice about making margin the above way; which is laid down in Smith's Grammar, published in 1755. We shall now proceed to give the plan adopted by us, which seems to be much more simple in its arrangement than any we have noticed in the various works upon this subject. Having laid our pages as nearly as possible in their proper places on the stone, with a suitable chase around them, we fold a sheet of paper which has been wetted for the work, or one of the same size, into as many portions as there are pages in the form, and holding the sheet thus folded on the first or left hand page of the form, one edge even with the left hand side of the types, we place the adjoining page so that its left side may be even with the right hand edge of the folded paper, which will leave a sufficient space between the two pages to admit the gutter stick, which should then be selected of a proper width to suit the form in hand, as follows:—In Octavos, about a Great Primer less in width than the space between the pages, as determined by the above rule; in Duodecimos, about a Pica less; in Sixteens, about a Long Primer, and proportionably less as the number of pages are increased. Having thus secured the proper width for the gutter sticks, we cut them according to the rules laid down for that purpose, and holding one of them between the two pages above the page cord, close the pages up to it; we then open our folded sheet so as to cover the two pages, and bringing the fold in the paper exactly in the middle of the gutter stick, we secure it there with the point of a penknife or bodkin; the right hand edge of the paper thus opened, must be brought to the centre of the cross bar, which determines the furniture required between it and the pages. Having thus arranged our margins for the back and fore edge of the book, we proceed in like manner to regulate the head and foot margins, by bringing the near edge of the folded paper even with the bottom of the first page, and so placing the adjoining off page, that its head may be barely covered by the off edge of the folded paper, which will give the required head margin; all other sections of the form must be regulated by the foregoing measurements, when our margins for the whole sheet will be found correct.

15*

In imposing jobs where two or more of the same size, requiring equal margins, are to be worked together, we fold our paper to the size appropriate for each, and so arrange our types, that the distance from the left side of one page to the left side of the adjoining one, shall be exactly equal to the width of the folded paper, as before described.

All that has been said concerning making margin, relates properly to imposing the first sheet of a work; for after that is truly dressed, a second, or more sheets, may be dressed with less trouble; for then we impose from wrought-off forms, where we have nothing else to do but to put the chase and furniture about the pages, in the same manner as we take it off the form we are stripping; after which we untie the pages to make room for the quoins, which we put to each quarter in the same order as we take them off the form we impose from.

Having dressed the inside of our pages, we then place side and foot sticks to their outsides; being thus secured by the furniture, we next untie them, quarter after quarter, the inner page first, and then the outer, at the same time forcing the letter towards the crosses, and using every precaution to prevent the pages from hanging or leaning; and in order to guard against accidents, when the quarter is untied, we secure it with a couple of quoins.

By observing a proper method in cutting up new furniture, the same will be serviceable for other works, as well as the one for which it is intended, even though the size of the page may differ, provided it agrees with the margin of the paper. The gutters should be cut two or three lines longer than the page; the head-sticks wider; the back furniture may run nearly down to the rim of the chase, but must be level with the top of the page, which will admit of the inner head-stick running in; the difference of the outer head-stick may go over the side-stick, and the gutter will then run up between them. The side-stick only need to be cut exact, and the furniture will completely justify.

We then proceed to locking up our forms; first carefully examining whether the pages of each quarter are of an exact length, for even the difference of a lead will cause them to hang. We ascertain their exactness by placing the ball of each thumb against the centre of the foot-stick, raising it a little with the pressure, and if the ends of both pages rise equal with the stick, it is a proof they will not bind; we then fit quoins between the side and foot-stick of each quarter and the chase, till the whole form may be raised. And though locking up a form may be thought a trifling function, it demands our attention, nevertheless, in several instances. When we have pushed the quoins as far as we can, with our fingers, we make use of the mallet and shooting-stick, and gently drive the quoins along the foot-sticks first, and then those along the side-sticks, taking care to use an equal force in our strokes, and to drive the quoins far enough up the shoulders of the side and foot-sticks, that the letter may neither belly out one way nor hang in the other; and as to the lower quoins, they ought to be driven to a station where they may do the office of keeping the letter straight and even. And here we may venture to disprove of the custom of slanting quoins on both sides, and planing their edges and corners off, whereby all the bevelled-off parts are rendered ineffectual to do the office of a quoin or wedge; for the slanted side of a quoin running against the square side of the chase, must needs carry a cavity with it, and consequently be void of binding with equal force in every part. As to the edges that are planed off across the two ends of a quoin, the want of them causes the shooting-stick to fly off the quoin at almost every hard stroke of the mallet, because the quoin end of the shooting-stick is rounded off; for which reason we should choose to have that end cut to suit the angle of the quoin and imposing stone, when the stick is held in a proper position.

It often occurs that the quoins, from having been locked up wet, stick so tight to the furniture as to render it troublesome to unlock them: in such cases the inconvenience is remedied by driving the quoin up instead of down, which immediately loosens it, and it unlocks with ease.

Our form, or forms, being now locked up, and become portable, we remove them to the proof-press, and pull a proof of them; we then rub them over with a wet lie-brush, put them in the rack, and deliver the proof-sheets and copy to the reader.

CHAPTER VI.

CORRECTORS AND CORRECTING.

It has ever been the pursuit of eminent printers to aim at accuracy, by their particular care that the effects of their profession should appear without faults and errors, not only with respect to wrong letters and false spelling, but chiefly in regard to their correcting and illustrating such words and passages as are not fully explained or expressed, or are obscurely written in the copy. The office of corrector is not to be applied to one that has merely a tolerable judgment of his mother tongue, but who has some knowledge of such languages as are in frequent use, viz. Hebrew, Greek, Latin, French, Italian and German, and possesses a quick and discerning eye—these are the accomplishments by which a corrector may raise his own and his employer's credit; for it is a maxim with booksellers to give the first edition of a work to be done by such printers whom they know to be either able correctors themselves, or that employ fit persons, though not of universal learning, and who know the fundamentals of every art and science that may fall under their examination. We say, examination; for in cases where a corrector is not acquainted with the subject before him, he, together with the person that reads to him, can do no more than literally compare and cross-examine the proof by the original, without altering either the spelling or punctuation; since it is an author's province to prevent mistakes in such case, either by delivering his copy very accurate, and fairly written, or by carefully perusing the proof-sheet.

What is chiefly required of a corrector, besides espying literal faults, is to spell and point after the prevailing method and genius of each particular language: but these being two points that never will be reconciled, but always afford employment for pedantic critics, every corrector ought to fix upon a method to spell ambiguous words and compounds always the same way.

And that the compositors may become acquainted with and accustomed to his way of spelling, the best expedient will be to draw out by degrees, a catalogue of such ambiguous words and compounds.

As it is necessary that correctors should understand languages, so it is requisite that they should be acquainted with the nature of printing, else they will be apt to expose themselves in objecting against several things that are done according to method and practice in printing. It is for this reason that correctors, in most printing-offices, are chosen out of compositors that are thought capable of that office, and who know how not only to correct literal faults, but can also discern where improprieties in workmanship are used, which cannot he expected in gentlemen who have not a sufficient knowledge of printing; and it would be very ungenerous in a compositor to swerve from the common rules in practice, because the corrector is not printer enough to find fault with it.

Inaccuracy may proceed either from inattention and carelessness in the printer, or else to his non-acquaintance with all languages, both ancient and modern; also to a deficiency of knowledge in the arts and sciences, and other abstruse subjects, wherein technical phrases and terms often occur, which, unless very distinctly written, may be misunderstood by the most attentive and accurate corrector.

If attention be paid to right spelling of proper names of persons, places, technical terms, &c. the finishing of sentences marked by the period, that the author's ideas may not be misunderstood, and the hand-writing tolerably legible, much time, and a very considerable expense would be saved, and the great object of accuracy gained, by gentlemen who communicate their sentiments to the public through the medium of the press.

[1] *a/* THOUGH a veriety of opinions exist as to
the individual by whom the art of printing was [2] *9*
first discovered; yet all authorities concur in
admitting Peter Schoeffer to be the person [3] *Caps*
who invented *cast metal types*, having learned
[4] *9* the art of of *cutting* the letters from the Gut-
[5] ⊙ tembergs; he is also supposed to have been [7]
[6] # the first whoengraved on copper plates. The */| /—/*
following testimony is preseved in the family, [8] *r/*
[9] ‿ by Jo. Fred. Faustus, of Ascheffenburg: *<# 6*
[10] ⌐‿ 'Peter Schoeffer, of Gernsheim, perceiving *S. Caps*
[11] \/ his master Fausts design, and being himself
[12] *tr* desirous \ardently) to improve the art, found
out (by the good providence of God) the
method of cutting (*incidendi*) the characters [13] *stet.*
in a *matrix*, that the letters might easily be
[5] ,/ singly *cast;* instead of bieng *cut.* He pri- [12] *ei/*
[14] | vately *cut matrices* for the whole alphabet: [15]
Faust was so pleased with the contrivance, [17]
/that he promised Peter to give him his only *wf*
[16] /daughter Christina in marriage a promise [3] *Ital.*
/which he soon after performed)
[19] *as* / 'But there were many difficulties at first [18] *no* ¶
/ with these *letters,* as there had been before [3] *Rom.*
[20] + with wooden ones, the metal being too soft [3] *Ital.*
to support the force of the impression: but
this defect was soon remedied, by mixing [9] */*
a substance with the metal which sufficiently *tr.* [12]
[5] ⊙ /hardened it,'

and when he showed his master the
letters cast from these matrices,

THOUGH a variety of opinions exist as to the individual by whom the art of printing was first discovered; yet all authorities concur in admitting PETER SCHOEFFER to be the person who invented *cast metal types*, having learned the art of *cutting* the letters from the Guttembergs: he is also supposed to have been the first who engraved on copper-plates. The following testimony is preserved in the family, by Jo. Fred. Faustus, of Ascheffenburg:

'PETER SCHOEFFER, of Gernsheim, perceiving his master Faust's design, and being himself ardently desirous to improve the art, found out (by the good providence of God) the method of cutting (*incidendi*) the characters in a *matrix*, that the letters might easily be singly *cast*, instead of being *cut*. He privately *cut matrices* for the whole alphabet: and when he showed his master the letters cast from these matrices, Faust was so pleased with the contrivance, that he promised Peter to give him his only daughter *Christina* in marriage, a promise which he soon after performed. But there were as many difficulties at first with these letters, as there had been before with *wooden ones*, the metal being too soft to support the force of the impression: but this defect was soon remedied, by mixing the metal with a substance which sufficiently hardened it.'

EXPLANATION OF THE CORRECTIONS.

A WRONG letter in a word is noticed by drawing a short perpendicular line through it, and making another short line in the margin, behind which the right letter is placed. (See No. 1.) In this manner whole words are corrected, by drawing a line across the wrong word, and making the right one in the margin, opposite the faulty line.

A turned letter is noticed by drawing a line through it, and the mark No. 2 in the margin. If a corrector is not able to distinguish such turned letters as have a resemblance to others, it is much better to mark such letters in the margin.

If letters or words are to be altered from one character to another, a parallel line or lines should be made underneath the word or letter, viz. for capitals, three lines; small capitals, two lines, and Italic, one line: and write in the margin opposite the line where the alteration occurs, *Caps, Small Caps,* or *Ital.* (See No. 3.)

When letters or words are set double, or are required to be taken out, a line is drawn through the superfluous word or letter, and the mark No. 4, placed opposite in the margin.

Where the punctuation requires to be altered, the colon, and period, if marked in the margin, should be encircled. (See No. 5.)

Where a space is wanting between two words or letters which are to be separated, a caret must be made where the separation ought to be, and the sign, No. 6, placed opposite in the margin.

No. 7 describes the manner in which the hyphen and ellipsis line are marked.

Should a letter have been omitted, a caret is put at the place, and the letter marked as No. 8.

Where words or letters that should join are separated, or when a line is too wide spaced, the mark No. 9, must be placed under it, and the junction signified by that in the margin.

Where a new paragraph is required, a quadrangle is drawn in the margin, and a caret placed at the beginning of the sentence. (See No. 10.)

No. 11 shows the way in which the apostrophe, inverted commas, the star, and other references and superior letters and figures are marked.

Where two words are transposed, the word placed wrong should be encircled, and the mark No. 12 placed in the margin : but where several words require to be transposed, their right order is signified by a figure placed over each word, and the mark, No. 12, in the margin.

Where words have been struck out that have afterwards been approved of, dots should be marked under such words, and in the margin write *Stet*. (See No. 13.)

Where a space sticks up between two words, a horizontal line is drawn under it, and the mark, No. 14, placed opposite, in the margin.

Where several lines or words are added, they should be written at the bottom of the page, and a line drawn from the place where the insertion begins, to those lines or words. (See No. 15.) But if more is added than can be contained at the foot of the page, write in the margin, *Out, see copy*, and enclose the omission between brackets, and insert the word *Out*, in the margin of the copy.

Where letters or lines stand crooked, they are noticed by drawing lines before and after them; but where a page hangs, lines are drawn across the entire part affected. (See No. 16.)

When a smaller or larger letter, of a different fount, is improperly introduced into the page, it is noticed by the mark, No. 17, which signifies wrong fount.

If a paragraph is improperly made, a line should be drawn from the broken-off matter to the next paragraph, and write in the margin, *No ¶*. (See No. 18.)

Where a word or words have been left out, or are to be added, a caret must be made in the place where they are intended to come in, and the word or words written in the margin. (See No. 19.)

Where a faulty letter appears, it is marked by making a cross under it, and placing a similar one in the margin, though some prefer to draw a perpendicular line through it as in the case of a wrong letter. (See No. 20.)

CORRECTING IN THE METAL.

By correcting, we understand the rectifying of such faults, omissions, and repetitions, as are made by the compositor, either through inadvertency or carelessness. And though the term of *corrections* is equally given to the alterations that are made by authors, it would be more proper to distinguish them by the name of *emendations;* notwithstanding it often happens, that after repeatedly mending the matter, the first conceptions are at last recalled: for the truth thereof none can be better vouchers than compositors, who often suffer by fickle authors that know no end to making alterations, and at last doubt whether they are right or wrong; whereby the work is retarded, and the compositor greatly prejudiced in his endeavors; especially where he is not sufficiently satisfied for spending his time in humoring such whimsical gentlemen.

Correcting is the most disagreeable part of a compositor's business, attended not only with loss of time, but great fatigue, from leaning over the stone, and is therefore extremely prejudicial to health. To avoid this we recommend silence, and attention when at work. The noise and confusion which too often prevail in a printing-office, from light and frivolous conversation, not only retard business, but at the same time distract the attention of the compositor from the subject he has in hand, and cause him to run into such mistakes as can only be rectified by loss of time, and fatigue at the imposing stone. Some men, no doubt, are capable of supporting a conversation, and at the same time compose correctly, but their noise must confuse those who are unable to preserve that accuracy but in quiet, and by close attention to their copy. The press-room should, if possible, be separated from the composing-room, as the pressmen are generally discussing some *important topic*, and are less liable to feel the inconvenience of much talking.

The first proof should merely contain the errors of the compositor, but it too frequently happens that the corrector heightens them by his peculiarities; when this is unnecessarily done, it is an act of injustice to the compositor: it is sufficient for him to rectify such mistakes as arise either from inattention or want of judgment. By the term, "want of judgment," we beg not to be understood as including the alteration of points, that being a subject which can never be reconciled: the compositor ought not to suffer from the caprice of a reader, in altering commas and semicolons in the first proof (unless the sense is perverted,) which he not unfrequently re-alters in the second, from a doubt upon his mind which would be the most proper points to be adopted.

We certainly agree, in conjunction with all our contemporaries, with the necessity for the immediate correction of proofs by the compositor; still we consider that we should not have performed our duty, (according to our original intention,) were we to urge an *ex parte* case, when a similar injunction is equally incumbent on both parties. Ought not the reader or overseer to be equally as punctual in despatching the proofs in his department? Can it reasonably be expected that the compositor will feel that inclination to forward his proof, when he knows that the reader will not equally assist him?

Should a compositor have transposed two or more pages, either from a mistake in the folios, or any other cause, he must then unlock such quarter or quarters, and loosening the cross or crosses from the furniture, he next lifts the chase and the remaining quarters off the stone; should he have furniture sufficient round each page, he may move them into their proper stations by pressing the balls of his thumbs and fingers against the furniture at the head, foot, and sides of each page:— if the letter be small, it will be advisable to wet the pages, because few imposing stones are horizontal, or so steady that they will not shake when touched, or by the motion of the floor, occasioned either by persons walking, or the dragging of forms.

Should a compositor find that his pages *hang*, he must unlock that quarter or quarters, and pat the face of the type with the balls of his fingers, and so twist it, until he gets it into a square position.

When a compositor unlocks his form, he should be careful not to leave the unlocked quoins too slack, as the force necessary to loosen the others may either *squabble* the matter, or occasion it to *hang*.

A compositor should possess the following requisites before he begins to correct—

"What is required of a compositor when he goes about correcting a foul proof, is a sharp bodkin and patience, because without them the letter cannot escape suffering by the steel; and hurrying will not permit him to justify the lines true. No wonder, therefore, to see pigeon-holes in one place, and pi in another."*

It is too well known to all compositors, the delay and inconvenience (not to say actual loss,) which they daily suffer from the want of a regular despatch of proofs; it is not for us to say whether it arises from an overpressure of business, or whatever cause; but this we can state, (having not only repeatedly witnessed it, but also greatly suffered from it ourselves,) that there are some overseers who do not give themselves the least concern about reading proofs, (provided the work is not in a particular hurry) as long as the compositor can rake together more letter to make up: at length, being run out of sorts, he is necessitated to press for his proofs, and should the reader then have leisure, he probably receives the whole of them as fast as he can correct, which is very much to his disadvantage in two points of view:—first, he has to perform a disagreeable task, which takes longer time than if he had received them as they were imposed, because much correcting fatigues, and makes a man careless, that would otherwise have done his work more justice: secondly, should his proofs turn out foul, and take up

---

* In proof of the trouble and inconvenience to which compositors are not unfrequently subjected, we present the reader with the following epitaph, which, no doubt, was written by a Typo, while performing the most disagreeable task attendant on his profession:

"No more shall copy bad perplex my brain,
No more shall type's small face my eye-balls strain;
No more the proof's foul page create me troubles,
By errors, transpositions, outs, and doubles:
No more my head shall ache from author's whims,
As overrunnings, driving-outs, and ins;
The surly pressman's frown I now may scoff,
Revised, corrected, finally wrought off."

a considerable time, his bill for that week must be greatly diminished, as few men make allowance from their week's earnings, for the corrections which may occur in the following one. We ever shall contend, be the station of the parties what it may, high or low, rich or poor, for "equal rights, and equal laws."

When the compositor has as many corrections between the thumb and fore-finger of his left hand as he can conveniently hold, or in his composing-stick, beginning at the bottom of the page, in order that they may follow regularly; and an assortment of spaces on a piece of paper, or, what is more convenient, in a small square box, with partitions in it, let him take the bodkin in his right hand, and instead of raising each letter he may have to alter, he should place the point of the bodkin at one end of the line, and with the fore-finger of his left hand against the other, raise the line altogether, sufficiently high to afford him a clear view of the spacing; he may then change the faulty letter, and alter his spacing before he drops the line. By observing this method, he will not injure the type, which must be the case where the bodkin is forced either into their sides or heads; it likewise ensures a greater degree of regularity where there may be occasion to alter the spacing, and will not take up more time than the other method.

In tables, and such like matter, where rules prevent the lines from being raised, as just noticed, the letters must be then drawn up by the bodkin; this is done by the compositor holding the latter fast in his right hand, with the blade between his fore-finger and thumb, within about half an inch or three quarters of the point, thus guiding it steadily to the faulty letter, he sticks the point of the bodkin into the neck of the letter, between the beard and the face, and thus draws it up above the other types, so that he can take it out with the fore-finger and thumb of his left hand. In performing this operation, as small an angle as possible should be made with the blade of the bodkin, viz. it should be kept as flat as possible to the face of the type, but the blade of the bodkin should not touch any of the surrounding neighbors of the faulty letter, as the slightest graze imaginable must injure their face, and consequently they will appear imperfect in the next proof, when he will have the trouble of altering them, and his employer suffers the loss of his type; we are again brought to the union of interest between the parties.

The reason why the bodkin blade should be kept flat to the form is, because a small horizontal entrance of its point into the neck of the letter, will raise it above the face of the form; but should the bodkin be held nearly upright, it would not have sufficient purchase to draw the letter up, because the weight of the type and its close confinement, would have greater power than the sharp point of the steel. By pressing sideways, the bodkin blade acts as a lever, even though it has no other purchase than merely the slight motion of the hand.

The most careful compositor cannot at all times avoid leaving a word or words out, or composing the same word twice; when this happens, he should consider the best mode of rectifying the accident, by driving out or getting in, either above the error or below it; this ascertained, let the matter be taken into a galley, and overrun in the composing-stick: overrunning on the stone is an unsafe, unworkmanlike, and dilatory method, destroys the justification, and renders the spacing uneven.

One of our predecessors gives the following:—

"But a great deal of trouble might be saved in cases of outs and doubles, would correctors try to add as much as will fill up the double, or to shorten the matter, to make room for an out; unless both the one and the other are too considerable for that expedient; which otherwise might be safely ventured, without either castrating or corrupting a writer's meaning. This would be a sure means to secure a neat compositor's workmanship, and care in true spacing his matter; whereas that beauty is lost by alterations and overrunning."

In correcting, care should be taken not to hair-space a line, if it can possibly be prevented, but avoid it by overrunning either back or forward. He should also in overrunning the matter, use the division as little as possible; for though he may carefully follow the instructions laid down in this work, on the subject of spacing and dividing, yet the effect of his attention will be completely destroyed, if not followed up at the stone.

The following observation has been made with respect to the despatch of proofs:—

"The first proof being corrected, a perfect sheet is pulled clean, to be sent to the author, or to the person by him authorised; either of whom, if they understand the nature of printing, will not defer reading the sheet, but return it without any alteration perhaps, to be made ready for the press. But because such good authors are very scarce, compositors are discouraged every time they send a proof away, not knowing when or how it may be returned, and how many times more it will be wanted to be seen again, before the author is tired, or rather ashamed, of *altering*."

Ye Authors list! we must a tale unfold,
Which, doubtless, some of you have oft been told,
You little dream how much poor *Typo's* vex'd,
When with *bad copy* his mind's sore perplex'd;
Nor is this all, he still has cause to dread
The *Reader's gall*, when first his *proof* is read;
Corrected now, to you 'tis strait convey'd,
And in a trice the greatest havoc's made;
The *proof's* return'd—the *Chapel's members* all
Rush to the *stone*, obedient to his call,
Aloud they roar—enough to strike him dead,
" *A mob, a mob, th' riot act must be read!*"
His grief to soothe—they, sympathising ball,
"*Patience and a sharp bodkin cures all!*"
His form, with heavy heart, he then *lays up*,
And *letters* seeks, which fills his bitter cup:
How often, when *correcting* at the *stone*,
He's prayed for you, while *breaking his breast-bone*,
Reflect, when next you wield your potent quills,
And spare the printer all these dreaded ills;
Revise, transcribe, and make your *copy* right,
Thus save his labor and his precious sight!

THE DEPARTMENT OF A READER.

HAVING just given an account of the nature of correcting, and the duties of a corrector, we deem it not improper, considering the vast importance of this branch of our profession, to enter somewhat more minutely into the subject.

When it is considered how much the credit of our art, and the general interest of literature depend on the grammatical accuracy and typographical correctness of our labors, it will readily appear that a careful and steady *Reader* must be indispensable in every printing office. We shall therefore detail the business and qualifications requisite to form such a reader, or corrector of the press, as can alone save the typographic art from degenerating into one of those ordinary occupations that require only the mechanical operation of the fingers, to form a perfect and complete workman.

It is always desirable that a reader should have been previously brought up a compositor. By his practical acquaintance with the mechanical departments of the business, he will be better able to detect those manifold errata which, unperceived by the mere man of learning and science, lie lurking, as it were, in a thousand different forms, in every sheet; and, if overlooked, evince a carelessness and inattention to our labors, that must always offend the just taste and professional discernment of all true lovers of correct and beautiful typography.

Some of the principal imperfections which are most easily observed by the man of practical knowledge in the art of printing, are the following: viz. imperfect and wrong-founted, or inverted letters, particularly the lower-case *n*, *o*, *s*, and the *u;* awkward and irregular spacing; uneven pages or columns; a false disposition of the reference marks; crookedness in words and lines; bad making-up of matter; erroneous indention, &c. These *minutiæ*, which are rather imperfections of workmanship, than literal errors, are apt to be overlooked and neglected by those readers who have no idea of the liability there is, even with the most careful compositor, occasionally to fall into them.

It is desirable that a reader should have been brought up a compositor, because the imperfections above enumerated may not be observed by one who is not practically acquainted with every department of the art. Nevertheless, long and frequent habits of reading proof-sheets for the press, a quick eye, and a steady mind, will certainly enable a person, though not a compositor, to detect those minor deviations from correctness, which the inexperienced and the careless are apt to overlook. But while these habits are acquiring, without which no person can be safely entrusted to read a sheet for press, the labors of the printer are liable to go forth into the world in a manner thàt will reflect discredit on the employed, and give offence to the employer. This observation equally refers to those readers who have previously been compositors. No form, therefore, ought to be put to press, until it has been read and revised by an *experienced* reader.

But even habit itself is not sufficient to form a competent reader, unless he possess those literary qualifications which are obviously necessary in an employment of this nature. No one should undertake this arduous task, until he has made himself a complete master of, at least, his native language.

A reader ought to be well versed in all the peculiarities of the English tongue—its idioms, its true genius, and singular adaptation to that variety of expression in which we embody our thoughts, and portray the human intellect. Instances will frequently occur, particularly in large printing-offices, where a knowledge of this nature and extent will be almost indispensable. Many, even of our first-rate authors, are too apt, in the warmth of discussion, the flights of speculation, and the laborious exercise of the thinking powers, to pass over, unobserved, those deviations from pure diction and strict grammatical accuracy, which they have imperceptibly acquired the habit of falling into, by their ordinary conversation with mankind.

Although no corrector of the press can strictly be required to do otherwise than to *follow his copy*, that is, faithfully to adhere to the original, with all its defects, yet every one must perceive, that it would often be performing a friendly, and perhaps a charitable service, to point out, in proper time, imperfections and mistakes which have escaped the observation of a quick or voluminous writer. This remark will, however, chiefly apply to inaccurate orthography, and glaring instances of erroneous syntax. With the spirit, the opinions, the whims of an author, no corrector of the press has any business to interfere. Some writers, after all the labors of the printer, and the skill of the reader, are doomed to make their appearance before the world with many "imperfections on their heads," are condemned to bear the contumely, and face the broad eye of an unrelenting critic.

We shall conclude this part of our subject by remarking, that a reader ought not to be of a captious or pedantic turn of mind: the one will render his situation and employment extremely unpleasant, and the other will tempt him to habits destructive of that consistency of character in his profession, which he ought ever scrupulously to maintain. It too frequently happens, that when a compositor is called from his frame, and is appointed to fill the situation of a reader, and is admitted into the sanctum,* much less the sanctum sanctorum,† that he considers the importance of his station has placed him above the rank of his former associates: and they, on the other hand, conceive that he still is, (literally) but as one of themselves; because both hold their situations by the same tenure, namely, a supply of business and good conduct: consequently it behoves them so to acquit themselves, that they may retain the esteem of their fellow workmen, lest they should unfortunately be forced into the ranks,‡ when they would be continually upbraided for their improper conduct. Should a compositor have a foul proof, either from inability or carelessness, the reader often taunts him with it: the compositor very aptly replies, "if we could compose without faults, there would be no necessity for proof readers!" We have known instances of such readers, when at case, not possessing half the ability of the compositors whom they wish to hold up to derision; and who committed equally as many errors when composing! Let such men reflect on this, "He that is without fault, let him cast the first stone."

---

* Technical term for the reader's room.
† Do. overseer or employer's room.
‡ Technically applied to compositors in their frames.

We should always preserve a strict uniformity in the use of capitals, in orthography, and punctuation. Nothing can be more vexatious to an author, than to see the words *honour*, *favour*, &c. spelt with, and without the *u*. This is a discrepancy which correctors ought studiously to avoid. The above observations equally apply to the capitaling of noun-substantives, &c. in one place, and the omission of them in another. However the opinions of authors may differ in these respects, still the system of spelling, &c. must not be varied in the same work: but whatever authority is selected should be strictly adhered to, whether it be Walker, or any of his contemporaries.

Such being the qualifications of a reader, it will not be improper to glance at the application of those attainments, by exhibiting the process which proof-sheets ought to undergo before they are put to press.

When a first proof is pulled, the compositor who imposed the sheet, ought to collect and arrange the copy, and deliver both to the reader, who then calls his reading-boy, to read the copy aloud to him. This boy should be able to read any copy put into his hands with ease and distinctness; he should be instructed not to read too fast, but to pay the same attention to the subject, as though he were reading for his amusement or edification. The eye of the reader should not follow, but rather precede the voice of the boy; accustomed to this mode, he will be able to anticipate every single word in the copy; and should a word or sentence happen to have been omitted in the proof, his attention will the more sensibly be arrested by it, when he hears it pronounced by his reading-boy. He ought to be careful lest his eyes advance too far before the words of the boy; because in his attention to the author's meaning, he will be apt to read words in the proof which do not actually appear there, and the accuracy of the reading-boy will but tend to confirm him in the mistake.

The proof being read with the reading-boy, the signatures, head-lines, titles, and folios of each page should be most carefully examined; and the number (if more than one) of the volume, signature, and *prima* of the ensuing sheet, accurately marked on the margin of the copy, and a bracket made between the last word of that and the first of the next sheet, in order that the compositor, should he not have composed beyond the sheet, may know where to begin, without having the trouble of referring, either to the proof or the form, and the reader will be certain that the commencement is right when he gets the succeeding sheets—this prevents unnecessary trouble both to the reader and compositor.

Before the proof is sent to the compositor to be corrected in the metal, an entry should be made in a book, according to the following plan :

Date of reading.	Signa-tures.	Names of Works.	Sent out.	Returned	Read for press.
1844. May 2 4 6 7	11 82 20 2	Decorative Printing, . . . Physiognomical Portraits, Typographia, ... Musical Library, ...	1844. May 2 4 7 8	1844. May 4 5 8 9	1844. May 5 6 8 9

This account being attended to at the different stages of each proof-sheet, will enable the reader to furnish the employer or overseer with an exact account of the state of each work, without trouble or inconvenience.

After the compositors have corrected the errors in the form, a clean proof is pulled, which with the first proof, is again handed to the reader, or overseer; whose duty it is to collate the corrected sheet with the one before read, in order to ascertain if the corrections have been properly made, and that others have not been created in the process; and in the case of a reprint, or where the author is not to examine the proof, he then proceeds to read it very carefully for press.

There are many compositors whose proofs are so foul, that it is almost an impossibility for them to correct all the marks at one time, consequently it is indispensable to have a second proof corrected before it can be sent out; and it not unfrequently happens that compositors, in the course of correcting, either transpose a letter or word, or else alter a letter in a word that is not marked, thereby not only leaving one error uncorrected, but also making another: likewise, when the line is raised to change the spaces, it often happens that some of them get transposed. Consequently it is absolutely necessary, in revising a proof, that the reader should not only look at the word marked, but he ought also to glance his eyes across every line in which an alteration had been made.

In those offices where more than one reader is employed, it is advisable that a proof-sheet should be read over by at least two of them; because the eye, in traversing the same ground, is very liable to be drawn into mistake and oversight. The interest having abated which was excited by the first reading, a certain degree of listlessness imperceptibly steals upon the mind, which greatly endangers the correctness of a proof. Should *outs* or *doubles* occur in a proof, it ought to be again read by copy, to prevent any improper connection in the overrunning, either by the insertion or removal of them.

Although we recommend the propriety of proofs being examined by more than one reader, yet we beg to be understood as not admitting each reader to the privilege of altering the punctuation; this duty should be exclusively confined to one individual, as no two men point alike, nor will a subject always appear to a person in the same light upon a second or third reading; consequently where a compositor is liable, in this particular, to the whim or caprice of several readers, it is neither more nor less than the taking of so much money out of his pocket, because his valuable time is unnecessarily frittered away: nor is this the only evil, the employer not only has the work retarded, but also his types injured, as well as the liability of creating fresh errors, &c.

Stower concludes with these observations:—

" It may not be improper, in this place, just to take notice of the great danger to the correctness of a work which arises from the practice, too common with some authors, of keeping their proof-sheets too long in their hands, before they are returned to the printer. As the pages in the metal get dry, the adhesion of the types to each other is weakened, and the swell or extension of the quoins and furniture, which the moisture had occasioned, is removed; so that there is great danger of letters falling out, when a form is long kept from the press. Nor is the danger which is hereby occasioned to correctness the only inconvenience; the impatience of authors to see their works in a fit state for publication is almost proverbial. The pleasure arising from beholding, as it were, the ' form and texture' of one's thoughts, is a sensation much easier felt than described. That authors, therefore, may partake of this pleasure in a speedy and regular succession, they should make a point of forwarding their proof-sheets to the printer as quick as possible, not only that they may the sooner be got ready for press, but that the work may proceed in a regular manner, without being interrupted by the forwarding of other works in lieu of that, the proof-sheets of which are detained beyond the proper time in the hands of the author.

"Authors are very apt to make alterations, and to correct and amend the style or arguments of their works, when they first see them in print. This is certainly the worst time for this labor, as it is necessarily attended with an expense which in large works will imperceptibly swell to a serious sum; when, however, this method of alteration is adopted by an author, the reader must always be careful to read the whole sheet over once more with very great attention, before it is finally put to press.

" A proof-sheet having duly undergone this routine of purgation, may be supposed to be as free from errata as the nature of the thing will admit, and the word ' Press' may be written at the top of the first page of it. This is an important word to every reader: if he have suffered his attention to be drawn aside from the nature of his proper business, and errors should be discovered when it is too late to have them corrected, this word ' Press' is as the signature of the death-warrant of his reputation. A reader, therefore, should be a man of one business—always upon the alert—all eye—all attention. Possessing a becoming reliance on his own powers, he should never be too confident of success. Imperfection clings to him on every side!—Errors and mistakes assail him from every quarter! His business is of a nature that may render him obnoxious to blame, but can hardly be said to bring him in any very large stock of praise. If errors escape him he is justly to be censured—for perfection is his duty! If his labors are wholly free from mistake—which is, alas! a very rare case—he has done no more than he ought, and consequently can merit only a comparative degree of commendation, in that he had the good fortune to be more successful in his labors after perfection, than some of his brethren in the same employment."

The form being finally laid on the press, and a *Revise* pulled by the pressman, he sends it to the overseer, who carefully casts his eyes along the sides and heads of the respective pages, to observe whether any letter should have fallen out, any crookedness have been occasioned in the locking up of the form, any battered letters, or any *bite* from the frisket. Should the revise prove faultless, he returns it to the pressman with the word Revise written on the margin; if otherwise, to the compositor to whom the form belongs, whose duty it is to see it immediately corrected.

MATHEMATICAL, ALGEBRAICAL, AND GEOMETRICAL CHARACTERS.

$+$ *plus*, or *more*, is the sign of real existence of the quantity it stands before, and is called an affirmative or positive sign. It is also the mark of addition: thus, $a + b$, or $6 + 9$, implies that a is to be added to b, or 6 added to 9.

$-$ *minus*, or *less*, before a single quantity, is the sign of negation, or negative existence, showing the quantity to which it is prefixed to be less than nothing. But between quantities it is the sign of subtraction: thus, $a - b$, or $8 - 4$, implies b subtracted from a, or 8 after 4 has been subtracted.

$=$ *equal.* The sign of equality, though Des Cartes and some others use this mark ∞; thus $a = b$, signifies that a is equal to b. Wolfius and some others use the mark $=$ for the identity of ratios.

$\times$ *into* or *with.* The sign of multiplication, showing that the quantities on each side the same are to be multiplied by one another, as $a \times b$ is to be read, a multiplied into b; 4×8, the product of 4 multiplied into 8. Wolfius and others make the sign of multiplication a dot between the two factors; thus, 7 . 4, signifies the product of 7 and 4. In algebra the sign is commonly omitted, and the two quantities put together; thus, $b d$ expresses the product of b and d. When one or both of the factors are compounded of several letters, they are distinguished by a line drawn over them; thus, the factum of $a + b - c$ into d, is wrote $d \times \overline{a + b - c}$. Leibnitz, Wolfius, and others, distinguished the compound factors, by including them in a parenthesis; thus, $(a + b - c) d$.

$\div$ *by.* The sign of division; thus $a \div b$ denotes the quantity a to be divided by b. Wolfius makes the sign of division two dots; $12 : 4$ denotes the quotient of 12 divided by $4 = 3$. If either the divisor, or dividend, or both, be composed of several letters, for example, $a \cdot\cdot b \div c$, instead of writing the quotient like a fraction.

☭ *involution.* The character of involution

vv *evolution.* The character of evolution, or the extracting of roots.

7 or $\sqsubset$ are signs of majority; thus, $a \; 7 \; b$, expresses that a is greater than b.

$\angle$ or $\sqsupset$ are signs of minority; when we would denote that a is less than b.

∞ is the character of similitude used by Wolfius, Leibnitz, and others. It is used in other authors for the difference between two quantities, while it is unknown which is the greater of the two.

$::$ *so is.* The mark of geometrical proportion disjunct, and is usually placed between two pair of equal ratios, as $3 : 6 :: 4 : 8$, shews that 3 is to 6 as 4 is to 8.

$:$ or $\therefore$ is an arithmetical equal proportion; as, $7 . 3 : 13 . 9$: i. e. 7 is more than 3, as 13 is more than 9.

$\square$ Quadrat, or regular quadrangle, as follows: $\square$ AB $= \square$ BC; i. e. the quadrangle upon the line AB is equal to the quadrangle upon the line BC.

$\triangle$ Triangle; as, $\triangle$ ABC $= \triangle$ ADC.

$\angle$ an Angle; as $\angle$ ABC $= \angle$ ADC.

$\perp$ Perpendicular; as, AB $\perp$ BC.

$\square$ Rectangled Parallelogram, or the product of two lines.

|| The character of parallelism.

∨ equiangular, or similar.

⊥ equilateral.

∟ right angle.

○ denotes a degree; thus 45○ implies 45 degrees.

′ a minute; thus, 50′, is 50 minutes: ″, ‴, ⁗, denotes seconds, thirds, and fourths : and the same characters are used where the progressions are by tens, as it is here by sixties.

∺ the mark of geometrical proportion continued, implies the ratio to be still carried on without interruption, as 2, 4, 8, 16, 32, 64 ∺ are in the same uninterrupted proportion.

√ *irrationality.* The character of a surd root, and shows, according to the index of the power that is set over it, or after it, that the square, cube, or other root, is extracted, or to be extracted; thus, √ 16, or √² 16, or √ (2) 16, is the square root of 16. ∛ 25, the cube root of 25, &c.

—: the differences, or excess.

Q or q, a square.

C or c, a cube.

Q Q, The ratio of a square number to a square number.

These and several other signs and symbols, we meet with in mathematical and algebraical works; though authors do not confine themselves to them, but express their knowledge in different ways, yet so as to be understood by those skilled in the science. In algebraical works, therefore, in particular, gentlemen should be very exact in their copy, and compositors as careful in following it, that no alterations may ensue after it is composed; since changing and altering work of this nature is more troublesome to a compositor than can be imagined by one that has not a tolerable knowledge of printing. Hence it is that very few compositors are fond of algebra, and rather choose to be employed upon plain work, though less profitable to them than the former; because it is disagreeable, and injures the habit of an expeditious compositor besides. In the mean time we venture to say, that the composing of algebra might be made more agreeable were proper cases contrived for the letter and sorts belonging to such work, where it is likely to make a return towards its extraordinary charges.

CELESTIAL AND ASTRONOMICAL SIGNS.

The twelve Signs of the Zodiac.

♈ Aries,	♌ Leo,	♐ Sagittarius,
♉ Taurus,	♍ Virgo,	♑ Capricorn,
♊ Gemini,	♎ Libra,	♒ Aquarius,
♋ Cancer,	♏ Scorpio,	♓ Pisces.

The Nine Planets.

♄ Saturnus,	☿ Mercurius,	⚵ Juno,
♃ Jupiter,	⛢ { Georgium Sidus,	⚶ Vesta,
♂ Mars,	⚳ Ceres,	☉ Sun,
⊕ Earth,	⚴ Pallas,	○ Moon.
♀ Venus,		

Seven of the Planets sometimes imply the seven days of the week.

Dies Solis—Sunday,   *Dies Mercurii*—Wednesday,
Dies Lunæ—Monday,   *Dies Jovis*—Thursday,
Dies Martis—Tuesday,   *Dies Veneris*—Friday,
                  Dies Saturni—Saturday.

☊ The dragon's Head, or ascending node, and

☋ The Dragon's Tail, or descending node, are the two points in which the eclipses happen.

The Aspects.

♂ Conjunctio; happens when two planets stand under each other in the same sign and degree.

☍ Oppositio; happens when two planets stand diametrically opposite each other.

△ Trigonus; happens when one planet stands from another four signs, or 120 degrees; which make one-third part of the ecliptic.

□ Quadril; happens when two planets stand three signs from each other, which make 90 degrees, or the fourth part of the ecliptic.

✳ Sextil; is the sixth part of the ecliptic, which is two signs, and make 60 degrees.

● New Moon.   ● Full Moon.
☽ First quarter.   ☾ Last quarter.

Many are the signs and symbols which astronomers have invented to impose upon the credulity of the vulgar, who are the chief supporters of almanacs; and especially of such as abound in predictions of any kind: among which we reckon those signs which give notice, on what day it is proper to let blood; to bathe and to cup; to sow and to plant; to take physic; to have one's hair cut; to cut one's nails; to wean children; and many other alike nonsensical observations, to which the lower class of people are particularly bigotted; besides giving credit to the marks that serve to indicate hail, thunder, lightning, or any occult phænomena.

PHYSICAL SIGNS AND ABBREVIATIONS.

℞ stands for *Recipe,* or Take.

ā, aa, of each a like quantity.

℔ a pound.

℥ an ounce.

ʒ a drachm.

℈ a scruple.

j stands for 1 ; ij for 2, and so on.

ß signifies *semi,* or half.

gr. denotes a grain.

One pound makes 12 ounces.

One ounce contains 8 drachms.

One drachm is equal to 3 scruples.

One scruple consists of 20 grains.

One grain has the weight of a barley-corn.

P. stands for *particula,* a little part, and means so much as can be taken between the ends of two fingers.

P. æq. stands for *partes æquales,* or equal parts.

q. s. *quantum sufficit,* or as much as is sufficient.

q. p. *quantum placit,* or as much as you please.

s. a. *secundem artem,* or according to art.

OF GREEK AND HEBREW.

GREEK.

GREEK is more frequently used in printing than the other peculiar characters; it is, therefore, necessary for every respectable printing-office to be furnished with that type, though not to any great amount of weight, as a quantity sufficient to serve for quotations, notes, mottos, &c. may be contained in a pair of cases, by dividing some of the boxes of the upper case for the accents, and omitting useless letters, ligatures, and abbreviations. This was impracticable when ligatures and abbreviations were in use, for then seven hundred and fifty boxes were required for the different sorts in a fount of Greek. The inducement to the first founders of the art to perplex themselves with cutting and casting so many different abbreviations and contractions was probably a desire to imitate Greek writing, and to produce in type the flourishes of the pen; but what could prompt them to confound themselves with an infinite number of ligatures, cannot so well be accounted for. Greek is, however, now cast almost every where without either ligatures or abbreviations, except where founders have express orders for them. Some few, however, not only grace Greek letter, but are also profitable to a compositor who knows how to use them properly.

Having intimated that the useful sorts of a fount of Greek letter may be lodged in a pair of cases that contain no more than two hundred and seven boxes, a scheme will be presented in the following pages for that purpose, which will afford a fair presumption that a great many of the sorts above referred to must be needless, where their number occupies seven hundred and fifty boxes. It must, however, be observed that almost three hundred of these sorts have no other difference than that of being kerned on their hind side; for there has been Greek with capitals kerned on both sides.

We now present to the reader, the Greek alphabet with the name of each letter in English characters, its sound, and numerical value.

THE GREEK ALPHABET.

Characters.	Names in English characters.	Sounds.	Numerical value.
A α . .	Alpha . . .	a	1
B β ϐ .	Beta . . .	b	2
Γ γ ſ . .	Gamma . .	g	3
Δ δ . .	Delta . . .	d	4
E ε . .	Epsilon . .	e short	5
Z ζ ζ .	Zeta . . .	z	7
H η . .	Eta . . .	e long	8
Θ ϑ θ .	Theta . . .	th	9
I ι . .	Iota . . .	i	10
K κ . .	Kappa . . .	k c	20
Λ λ . .	Lambda . .	l	30
M μ . .	Mu	m	40
N ν . .	Nu	n	50
Ξ ξ . .	Xi	x	60
O o . .	Omicron . .	o snort	70
Π π ϖ .	Pi	p	80
P ϱ ρ . .	Rho . . .	r	100
Σ σ ς	Sigma . . .	s	200
T ϑ τ .	Tau . . .	t	300
Υ υ . .	Upsilon . .	u	400
Φ φ . .	Phi	ph	500
X χ . .	Chi	ch	600
Ψ ψ . .	Psi	ps	700
Ω ω . .	Omega . .	o long	800

GREEK UPPER CASE.

A	B	Γ	Δ	E	Z	H
Θ	I	K	Λ	M	N	Ξ
O	Π	P	Σ	T	Υ	Φ
X	Ψ	Ω				

GREEK LOWER CASE.

			in quadrats.	quadrats.	
			n quadrats.		
				—	
				.	
				ꝯ	
				α	
			5 em spaces.	thick and middling Spaces.	
	ε	ν			
	δ	μ	⌐		
γ		λ		ν	
β	ϛ	ξ	ς	ꝫ	
			φ	Φ	

Such compositors and readers as are not Greek scholars, and even those who are, but have not paid attention to accents, will do well to bear in mind the proper situations of the spirits and accents; as many of the faults which so frequently offend the scholar's eye, might thereby be avoided. The following rules may be easily borne in mind:—No accent can be placed over any other than one of the three last syllables of a word. No vowel can have a spirit, or breathing, except at the beginning of a word. The grave accent never occurs but on the last syllable; and this being the case, the asper grave ['] and lenis grave ['] can be wanted only for a few monosyllables, and less than half the quantity usually cast would be enough in a fount. Almost every word has an accent, but very seldom has more than one; and when this happens, it is an acute thrown back upon the last syllable from one of those words called enclitics, which, in that case, has none, unless it be followed by another enclitic. In no other case than this can a last syllable have an acute accent, except before a full point, colon, or note of interrogation, when the grave accent of the last syllable is changed to an acute; a circumstance which has often led printers who were ignorant of the reasons for accenting the same word differently in different situations, to think that there was an error in their copy, and thus to make one in their proof. Most errors, however, proceed from those who do not think at all about the matter.

HEBREW.

In the column No. 1 of the following table, the force of the Hebrew letters, when read without points, is expressed; and the next column, No. 2, gives you their force when the language is complicated with the Masoretic points or vowels, which are certainly of later date than the present Hebrew letters. We also give their names in English characters, and their numerical value.

THE HEBREW ALPHABET.

		No. 1.	No. 2.	Numer. Value.
Aleph אַ	.	Sounded a in *war* (vowel.)	A gentle aspirate.	1
Beth בּ	.		*Bh*	2
Gimel גּ	.	g hard	*Gh*	3
Daleth דּ	.		*Dh*	4
He הּ	.	a in hate (*vow.*)	A rough aspirate.	5
Vau וּ	.	u *vowel*, or before a vowel, *w*		6
Zain זּ	.		*Ds*	7
Cheth חּ	.		*Hh*	8
Teth טּ	.	*Th*		9
Jod יּ	.	Like *ee* in English. (*vowel.*)	*j* consonant, or the softer *y*	10
Caph כ ך		k or c hard		20
Lamed ל				30
Mem מ ם				40
Nun נ ן				50
Samech ם			Soft *s*	60
Ain ע		o long. (*vowel*)	*hg*, or *hgh*, the roughest aspirate.	70
Phe פ ף				80
Tzaddi צ ץ		*j* soft.		90
Koph ק	.	q, or *qu*		100
Resch ר	.			200
Shin שׁ or Sin			*s* hard	300
Thau תּ	.			400

Final Letters.

18

HEBREW UPPER CASE.

HEBREW LOWER CASE.

			quadrats.
		m quadrats.	
		n quadrats.	
			· ·	

hair spaces.

thick and middling Spaces

Spaces and quads for justifying the points.

COMMON HEBREW CASE.

		m quadrate.	quadrats.
		n quadrate.	
	•-		•• ı
	┐		□ ·
	┌		
		hair spaces.	thick and middling Spaces.
	%	•	

Letters that have a likeness to others.

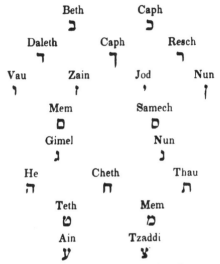

The following five letters are cast broad, and are used at the end of words, viz.

but are not counted among the final letters, being contrived for justifying, because Hebrew is not divided.

The Hebrew has no capitals, and therefore letters of the same shape, but of a larger body, are used at the beginning of chapters, and other parts of Hebrew works.

The Hebrew reads from the right to the left, which is the case with all other Oriental languages, except the Ethiopic and Armenian. In composing Hebrew, therefore, the Jews begin at the end of the composing stick, and justify the vowels and accents over and under the letters after the line of matter is adjusted.

Music,

This music type is a combination of cast characters and rules. The rules are used to form the lines of the stave, and the characters are cast in sections, on a body of the size of the space between the rules, in combination with which they form perfect characters. In this way the same type or section which forms the head of the crotchet serves also for the head of the quaver, semi-quaver and demisemiquaver; the quaver foot-piece is equally applicable to the semi and demisemiquaver; and so of others. In short, the characters are analyzed and reduced to their elements, thirty of these sections producing every imaginable note or combination of notes. There are no kerned characters, and the whole is as easily composed as an ordinary alphabet, the lines being set up first and the rules dropped in afterwards. It is almost superfluous to remark, that the flats, sharps, and other characters belonging to the stave, are adapted in the same manner as the notes, so that the lines of the stave can be extended in one piece across the page. The whole can be laid in one case, a plan of which will accompany every font.

MUSIC, No. 1.

MUSIC, No. 2.

MUSIC, No. 3.

CHAPTER VII.

THE DUTY OF AN OVERSEER.

THOSE persons whose ability or ambition induces them to aspire to the attainment of this important situation, should be endowed with something more than an ordinary capacity, together with an even and forgiving temper; and whose rules of conduct should be founded upon the strict laws of Equity and Justice; not deviating in the least from the above standard in order to favor either the employer or the employed; otherwise he may stand a fair chance of losing the good-will and esteem of one, or perhaps both of the above named parties; he should always bear in mind, in all his actions, that a reciprocity of interests exists between them, which is indispensably necessary to the forwarding an excellent execution of any branch of art, and that it falls precisely within his province to maintain this union of interests to the utmost of his ability.

In houses where several presses are employed, an Overseer is indispensably necessary; it is true a small concern may be conducted by an Employer, if he were not liable to frequent interruptions while in business, together with the necessary absence from home: on which occasions a trustworthy Agent is of course required, not only to answer all applications, but also to attend to every department of the machine; otherwise (compositors and pressmen being at all times dependant on each other) one or both may probably stand idle, from the absence or neglect of duty in either party, or from the employer's engagements abroad. Having presumed thus much, we shall now venture to offer a few hints for the benefit of those who are now, or who may hereafter be selected to fill this highly important situation.

It has been observed, that an Overseer should be the first and last in attendance at the office, in order that he may be satisfied that every person on the premises does his duty; likewise to observe that those on the establishment attend at their regular time: we suggest, that the task of an early attendance in the morning would be more properly filled by the second in authority; because the principal manager would of necessity be frequently required to attend late in the evening to depatch proofs, &c.

The office being now swept, and the type selected from the dust by the errand boy, that found in the body of the rooms should be given to the Overseer, or his deputy, (if any) who ought to see it immediately distributed, and then walk round the house in order that he may discover if the compositors have followed his example, by disposing of the portion found in each respective frame, likewise that no pi be left either on the frames, bulks, or gallies; should there be any, even a single letter, he should insist upon its being immediately distributed. Attention to this particular is of vast importance, because it not only keeps the office clear of pi, but it also prevents useful and valuable sorts from being buried.

He should likewise be possessed of a thorough knowledge of the state of every work in progress, and as a more effectual mode of expediting them, he may adopt the following rules. 1. In companionships, no man should be suffered to hold too large a taking of copy, otherwise he would keep his companions composing at random much longer than were necessary, which would of course retard the imposition of the sheet, and also require a much greater scope of letter to enable them to proceed with the work; from which cause, it is not at all improbable, but that the pressman will have to remain idle in the first instance, and consequently the compositors in the second. 2. The moment a sheet is composed and made up, he should order it to be imposed, provided there be room on the imposing-stone for that purpose. 3. The same expedition should be used in getting the proof pulled when imposed. 4. The Reader should receive it instantly, send it up leaf by leaf to be corrected; which the Overseer of course will direct to be forwarded immediately, should no obstacle occur to prevent it. 5. This duty performed, a second proof should be taken, which the reader should forward to the author, (if required,) or otherwise read it carefully through for press; the same expedition should be used in getting it finally corrected for working off.

A close attention to the above hints will enable an Overseer to conduct and keep in regular motion a concern of great magnitude, not only with satisfaction to himself, but also with credit to his employer, for punctuality and despatch of business.

Sorts not in general use, chases, furniture, leads, &c. should be locked up under the care of the Overseer or his deputy, in order that they may be in readiness when required; he would also find a memorandum book, in which an entry of such sorts should be made, highly beneficial.

He would also find a book, which we shall denominate a *Press Book*, of vast importance, in which he should regularly, every evening, make an entry of the paper that the warehouseman is to give out to wet, for the various works in progress. Upon the pressmen enquiring of him what they are to lay on next, he informs them, and in this book fills up the necessary columns, agreeable with the heads of the annexed table.

When given out to wet.	Names of Works.	No.	Signatures.	Date when laid on.	Names of pressmen.
1844. May 2 4 6 7	Decorative Printing, . . . Physiognomical Portraits, Typographia, ... Musical Library, ...	1000 750 1000 3000	11 82 20 2	1844. May 4 5 8 9	Speer. Flue. Smith. Butt.

It is generally the business of the Overseer to revise the proofs for press, in doing which he will be careful not only to ascertain whether all the corrections marked in the proof are made, but also to cast his eye carefully over the sides, head, and bottom of each page, as it frequently happens that the folios or catch words drop out of the form in lifting it off the imposing stone; also in leaded matter, letters at the beginning and ends of lines frequently fall out of their proper place, and by standing crooked have a slovenly appearance. Before the revise is given to the compositor, the names of the pressmen who are intended to work off the form, should be entered in the *Press*

Book. With foul compositors, the Overseer should invariably require a second revise, in order to ascertain if all the corrections have been made which were marked in the first, as no sort of dependence can be placed on them. He should, (where there is not a person engaged expressly for the purpose, as is the case in houses employing ten or fourteen presses) go regularly round, about every quarter of an hour, to the different presses, and examine their work, point out defects, if any, and glance again over the heads, sides, and bottoms of the pages, to see if any thing has been drawn out by the rollers, which frequently occurs from bad justification of the lines, and careless and improper locking up of the form. An active and conscientious Overseer will not be content with merely managing the concerns of the composing room; he will also see that the business of the warehouse is attended to with regularity and accuracy; and that the warehouseman, errand boys, and apprentices do their duty.

Having, in the present Chapter, presented the Overseer with the plan of a book, called the *Press Book*, we shall introduce another of equal importance, (which we shall call a *Check Book*,) for the purpose of checking the bills of both the Compositors and Pressmen; this book enables him, at a single glance, to discover any overcharges that may have been made.

Plan of a Book for Checking Compositors' and Pressmen's Bills.

Adams' Typographia, 18mo. Double Med. No. 1000.									
	Compositors.					Corrections.	By whom worked at Press.		Observations.
Signature.	Reiter.	Butt.	Rheim.	Denison.	Jones.		Outer Form.	Inner Form.	
B	6	7	9	9	5	81 25	J. Speer.	C. Flue.	
C	12	10	4	4	6	75	C. Flue.	J. Speer.	
D									
E									
F									
G									

After he has entered into the press book an account of the paper intended to be wet, he sets down the same articles with the numbers and date in a book called the *Wetting Book:* from this book the warehouseman receives his instructions for giving out the paper. This book also informs him of the quantity of wet paper, and the length of time it has been wetted; this is of importance when authors sometimes detain proofs so long, that the paper allotted for those sheets will mildew, if it be not hung up to dry in a seasonable time.

In addition to the foregoing tables, we shall now lay before our readers another, equally important in every point of view, which we shall designate with the title of the *Job Book.*

Plan of the Job Book.

Date.	Compos. Names.	Compos. Charge.	Pressm's. Names.	Do. Charge.	Corrections.	No. Printed.	For whom printed.	Size and Description.	Folio of Day-book.	$	Cts.

By means of a *Job Book*, an Employer or Overseer will be enabled, at a single glance, (without referring to the bills of the Compositors and Pressmen,) to discover not only every charge that has been made upon a Job, but also for whom, the number printed, and the size and description, together with the full charge.

An Overseer should be in possession of a thorough knowledge of every branch of his profession. It not unfrequently happens, either from a press of business, or the absence of the reader, that he may be necessitated to read for press; he should make it his study to qualify himself for that important duty: to this point we most particularly invite his earnest attention, and beg to refer him for useful hints upon this subject, to Chapter VI. p. 176, &c. ante. And should he conscientiously sustain the character which we have laid down at the commencement of this article, he will not only acquit himself with credit to his employer, but also prove by his conduct that he is an ornament to society in general.

Th' man who aspires to this high station,
Should for his guide seek moderation;
    And justice keep in view:
But few there are who reach the wish'd for height,
That justly keep strict equity in sight,
    And render each his due.

To the Employer too much court is paid,
When by the men th' entrapping snares are laid,
    To catch the wary elf:
Who, unsuspecting, daily plods along,
Nor heeds the snares placed by the wily throng,
    To entrap his noble self.

The bubble, thus kept up in air so long,
Thro' flattering tales and fulsome tongue,
    By schemes at length is burst;
His office lost, he then most deeply wails,
To hide his shame he now invents new tales,
    And deems his lot most curst.

A warning this, for those who dare aspire,
When in this birth to raise themselves much higher,
    And think 't will last for life;
Should they but once o'erstep the compass bound,
Their folly brings them quickly to the ground,
    To end their days in strife.

RULES AND REGULATIONS TO BE OBSERVED IN A PRINTING-OFFICE.

1. Compositors to receive their cases from the Overseer, or other persons appointed by him, free from all pi, or other heterogeneous matter, with clean quadrat and space boxes, both Roman and Italic, which they are to return to him in the same state.

2. When a compositor receives letter, furniture, &c. from the Overseer, he is to return what he does not use, in the same state he received it, the same day.

3. Compositors to impose their matter when desired by the Employer or Overseer; also to correct proofs, unless in either case it shall appear that all the stones were engaged, in which case he should seize the first opportunity.

4. The proofs when pulled to be given to the reader, or carried into the reading closet, with, if a first proof, the copy, and, if a second, the foul proof.

5. Compositors not to leave a foul stone, either of letter or furniture.

6. A compositor is not to detain an imposing stone longer than the nature of the business may require.

7. When any cases are taken out of the racks, the compositor is to return them into the proper place immediately after he has done with the same.

8. No cases to be placed over others, or under the frames.

9. Gallies, with head-lines, or other useful materials, used during the course of a piece of work, to be cleared the day after the work is all completely at press.

10. When a work is completely finished, the compositor or compositors concerned, shall, before he or they begin another work, unless prevented by the Employer or Overseer, clear away the forms, taking from them the head lines, white lines, direction lines, as also the leads and riglets: which, with the furniture of each sheet, and the matter properly tied up for papering, are to be given to the Overseer.

11. Sweepings of frames to be cleared away before one o'clock every day. Matter broken by accident to be cleared away on the same day.

12. The saw, saw-block, bowl, sponge, letter-brush, shears, bellows, &c., to be returned to their respective places as soon as done with.

13. That pi of any sort, on boards, windows, frames, &c. shall be cleared after five minutes' notice.

14. No person shall take sorts from the frames or cases of another without leave, nor hoard useful sorts, not wanting or likely to want them.

15. Compositors employed by the week, to work not less than ten hours per day.

THE BEST MEANS OF EXPEDITING WORKS OF A
TEMPORARY AND URGENT NATURE.

A judicious distribution of the employment of workmen in every kind of business, is the only means of expediting it. This observation applies very forcibly to the printing business. Pamphlets and other works of a temporary nature, it is sometimes necessary to print in the course of a few hours; to accomplish this, the utmost exertion, accompanied with skilful management, is requisite; we shall, therefore, lay down a plan which we conceive will be found fully to answer this purpose.

As soon as a work of this nature is put in hand, it must be the business of the Overseer to select such men as are able to complete the greatest quantity of work in a given time. We will suppose eight men are ordered to distribute letter for it. Their first concern must be, to appoint one from among them who thoroughly understands his business, and is in other respects qualified to undertake the management of the work, to make it up, and to do every thing which interferes with the regular business of distributing, composing, and correcting.

Having done this, let them proceed to the distribution of their letter; while the *clicker,* or person appointed to manage the job, applies to the Overseer for the copy, receives instructions respecting it, and procures leads and every other necessary sort. He then draws out the following table:

Compositors' Names.	Folios of Copy.	Lines Composed.	Memorandums.

In the first column he sets down the name of each compositor when he takes copy; and, in the second, the folio of the copy, that he may be able to ascertain instantly in whose hands it lies. In the third column he notes down the number of lines each man has composed, opposite to his name, as fast as the gallies are brought to him. In the fourth, he sets down such remarks respecting the copy, &c. as may be necessary, and also any circumstance that may occur in the companionship.

By this means each compositor will receive a share of the amount, according to the number of lines he composes, and the clicker must have an equal share with the person who sets the greatest quantity: or it may be done by limiting the quantity each man is to compose in an hour; whoever is deficient in this quantity, must suffer a proportionate deduction from his share of the work.

When the members of the companionship are ready for their first taking of copy, they are to receive it from the clicker in pieces as short as possible, taking care that the two first have shorter takings than either of the others, to prevent, as much as possible, any delay in the making up. During the time tne first taking is in hand, the clicker sets the half-head, head lines, white lines, and signature lines, together with side notes, and other extraneous matter.

As soon as the first person brings him his matter, he counts off the number of lines, and inserts them in the table; then gives him another taking of copy, and proceeds with the making up. The same plan is observed with the rest of the companionship.

When the first sheet is made up, he lays the pages on the stone, and informs the Overseer of it, who will then immediately procure chases and furniture.

The work will now proceed rapidly, provided the compositors stick close to their business, and there be no hindrance with respect to letter, &c., which depends on the good management of the Overseer. If the clicker finds that he cannot make up the matter as fast as it is composed, he should call one of the compositors to his assistance, who must be the person last in copy. In this case he counts the lines he has composed, sets them down in the table, and takes notice of the time he is off, which is to be made up to him by a deduction from the share of each person.

The proofs should be read immediately after they are pulled, and given to the clicker to be corrected. As soon as this is done, he lays up the forms, and gives the proof to the compositor whose matter stands first, who should immediately correct it, then forward it to the next, and so on, till the sheet be corrected; the clicker then locks it up, and carries the forms to the proof-press.

As soon as one of the companionship is out of copy, and there is no more to be given out, the lines of the whole must be counted off, and set down in the table, which closes the account, and then every one does as much as he can for the general benefit. If there be not work enough to employ the whole, those who are not wanted may go to their regular work, and the time of their absence, till the rest of the companionship return to theirs, be deducted from their respective shares.

It would save time in making calculations, could the companionship agree to divide the amount of the bill between them in equal proportions, and merely fine those who absent themselves from the office; but as some compositors will set considerably more than others, the above mode will, we conceive, be found to answer best, as it excites a spirit of emulation, and induces them to pursue their work with vigor.

RULES TO BE OBSERVED IN COMPANIONSHIP.

THE disputes which frequently arise in printing-office upon trifling as well as intricate points, can only be settled by a reference to the general custom and usage of the trade. These misunderstandings, which annoy and retard business, often take place in companionships consisting of three or four compositors; it is therefore highly desirable that the generally received rules and regulations on this subject, should be explicitly and clearly laid down for the future comfort and government of the compositor.

TAKING COPY.

IF printed copy, and the compositor is desired to follow page for page, each sheet, as it is given out, should be divided into as many parts as the companionship may consist of, in which case the bulk of the copy must not be subject to the inspection of the companionship, but kept by the Overseer, and dealt out by him as it is wanted, or it will inevitably cause contention; for the compositor likely to be first out of copy, if he has free access to that which remains unfinished, will observe whether the next taking be *fat* or *lean*—if the latter, he will hold back and loiter away his time, in order to avoid it, and thus materially delay the work. On the other hand, if this taking appears to be advantageous, and there should happen to be two or three of the companionship out of copy at the same time, a sort of scramble will take place who shall have it, which will end in dispute and confusion: on no account, therefore, should the copy be open to examination. If the copy be manuscript, or not page for page, the Overseer should give it out in such portions as will, in his judgment, insure regularity in the progress of the work; and should, in all cases, mark the name of the compositor in the margin, opposite the paragraph where he is to commence. Compositors are apt to desire a large portion of copy, with the view of advantage in the making up, though nine times in ten it will, as before observed, operate as a loss to them, by their eventually standing still for want of letter. If by mistake too much copy has been taken, the compositor should hand a part of it to the person next in the making up, to set up to himself.

If parts of the copy should be particularly advantageous or otherwise, each of the companionship may throw for the chance of it: the person to whom it may fall, if he have copy in hand, must turn that copy over to him who is about to receive more copy; but for trifling variations from the general state of the copy, it cannot be worth the loss of time necessary to contest it; though it frequently happens that a litigious man will argue half an hour on a point that would not have made five minutes' difference to him in the course of his day's work.

If one of the companionship absents himself from business, and thereby delays the making up, and there is the smallest probability of standing still for want of letter, the person who has the last taking must go on with this man's copy, whether it be good or bad.

MAKING UP.

THE compositor having the first take on the work, as soon as he has completed it, proceeds without delay to making up his matter into pages, according to the directions laid down in our observations on composing. Having completed as many pages as his matter will make, he passes the overplus, if less than half a page, with the correct head and folio, to the compositor whose matter follows his, at the same time taking an account of the number of lines loaned; if, on the contrary, the overplus makes more than half a page, he borrows a sufficient number of lines to complete his page, each compositor keeping an account of the number of lines borrowed and loaned. His last page being completed, he passes the make up to the compositor next in succession, by handing him the proper head lines and folio for the following page; each compositor passing the make up in like manner without delay.

MAKING UP OF LETTER.

THE number of the companionship, if possible, should always be determined on at the commencement of the work, that they may all proceed upon an equal footing. It should be well ascertained that the letter appropriated for the work will be adequate to keep the persons on it fully employed.

If any part of the matter for distribution, whether in chase or in paper, be desirable or otherwise, for the sorts it may contain, it should be divided equally, or the choice of it thrown for.

When a new companion is put on the work after the respective shares of letter are made up, and if there be not a sufficiency to carry on all the companionship without making up more, he must make up an additional quantity before he can be allowed to partake of any part of that which comes from the press.

MAKING UP FURNITURE.

Two of the companionship who may have the greatest proportion of the first sheet, should make up the furniture for that sheet; and though it may be thought that a disadvantage will be felt in making up the first sheet, they having to ascertain the right margin, yet, properly considered, this disadvantage is sufficiently balanced by their not being likely to meet with a scarcity of furniture, which will frequently occur after several sheets are made up. The other companions in rotation, as their matter is made up, will take an equal share of the furniture. Should an odd sheet be wanted, it will be better to throw for the chance of making it up.

IMPOSING AND DISTRIBUTING LETTER.

THE person to whose turn it falls to impose, must lay up the form for distribution; but as continual disputes arise on this subject, and as it can only be ascertained by comparing the number of pages composed, with the number put in chase by each person, we therefore recommend their keeping an exact account of these pages, which had better be done agreeably to the following

Plan of an Imposition Book.

Signatures.	Frost's United States.						By whom imposed.
	Jones.	Reiter.	Stille.	Rheim.			
B	5	2	2	3			Jones.
C	2	3	5	2			Stille.
D							
E							
F							

This book should always be kept in a convenient place, so that each compositor may mark down the number of pages he has made up, opposite to the proper signature, and under his own name; also when he imposes, he inserts his name in the column appropriated for that purpose. By following strictly this mode, every sort of dispute will be prevented; and though a private account may be necessary for individual satisfaction, yet it will not avail in settling a general misunderstanding, as the various private accounts may differ, and the charge of inaccuracy may be alleged with as much reason against one as the other; but in this general scale a mistake can be immediately detected. It also operates as a check on those who may be inclined to write out of their proper signature, or to charge more pages than they have imposed.

As the letter is laid up, it should be divided in equal proportions; and, if it can be so managed, each person had better distribute the matter originally composed by him; for by this means, the sorts which have made his case uneven will again return to him. It may happen, from one of the companionship absenting himself, that his former share of letter remains undistributed at a time a second division is taking place; under these circumstances, he must not be included in this division. In the event of a scarcity of letter, if any man absent himself beyond a reasonable time, his undistributed matter should be divided equally among his companions, and when he returns, he may then have his share of the next division.

CORRECTING.

THE compositor, whose matter is in the first part of the proof, lays up the forms on the imposing stone, and corrects. He then hands the proof to the person who has the following matter. The compositor who corrects the last part of the sheet, locks up the forms.

The compositor having matter in the first and last part, but not the middle of the sheet, only lays up the form and corrects his matter; the locking up is left to the person who corrects last in the sheet.

A compositor having the first page only of the sheet, is required to lay up one form; also to lock up one form if he has only the last page.

If from carelessness in locking up the form, viz. the furniture binding, the quoins badly fitted, &c.—any letters, or even a page should fall out, the person who thus locked up the form must immediately repair the damage. But if from bad justification, or in leaded matter the letters *ride* upon the ends of the leads, the loss attending any accident from this circumstance, must fall upon the person to whom the matter belongs.

It is the business of the person who locks up the form, to ascertain whether all the pages are of an equal length; and though a defect in this respect is highly reprehensible in the person to whom it attaches, (whose duty it is to rectify it,) yet if not previously discovered by the locker-up, and an accident happen, he must make good the defect.

The compositor who imposes a sheet, must correct the chargeable proof of that sheet, which is also generally at the same time corrected for press, and take it to the ready place. He must also rectify any defect in the register, arising from want of accuracy in the furniture.

Forms will sometimes remain a considerable length of time before they are put to press. When this happens, and particularly in the summer, the furniture is likely to shrink, and the pages will, in consequence, if care be not taken, fall out; it is therefore the business of the person who has locked up the form, to attend to it in this respect, or he will be subject to make good any accident which his neglect may occasion.

The liability to accidents of this nature has been greatly lessened by recent improvements, viz. the introduction of metal furniture and quoins; the former we have previously alluded to—the latter is of recent invention, and has not yet been offered to the trade. The Iron Screw Quoin was invented by Mr. E. M. Maeder, of Philadelphia, and consists of a screw working into a square iron shoulder about two inches in length, and about half an inch in thickness, which is placed against a side stick without bevel, the pointed head of the screw bearing against the inner side of the chase;—by applying a small rack to the cogged head of the screw, the form can be locked or screwed up to any degree of tightness without noise, and with but little exertion on the part of the compositor, and having at least half an inch play, will seldom require to be changed. From our knowledge of the advantages of these quoins, we unhesitatingly recommend them to the favorable notice of the profession. They can be had at our Printers' Warehouse.

When forms are wrought off, and ordered to be kept standing, they are then considered under the care of the Overseer. When they are desired to be cleared away, it is done in equal proportions by the companionship. During the time any forms may have remained under the care of the Overseer, should there have been any alteration as to form or substance, such alterations not having been made by the original compositors, they are not subject to clear away those parts of the form that were altered. If the pressmen unlock a form on the press, and from carelessness in the locking up, any part of it fall out, they are subject to the loss that may happen in consequence.

The compositor who locks up a sheet, takes it to the proof-press, and after he has pulled a proof of it, hands it, together with the foul proof, to the reader, and deposits the form in a place appointed for that purpose.

TRANSPOSITION OF PAGES.

EACH person in the companionship must lay down his pages properly on the stone for imposition. The compositor, whose turn it is to impose, looks them over to see if they are rightly placed; should they, after this examination, lay improperly, and be thus imposed, it will be his business to transpose them; but should the folios be wrong, and the mistake arise from this inaccuracy, it must be rectified by the person to whom the matter belongs. Pages being laid down for imposition, without folios or head lines, must be rectified by the person who has been slovenly enough to adopt this plan.

CHAPTER VIII.

THE PRESS.

From thee, O Press! what blessings flow
T' unworthy mortals here below!
   Life's path to smooth:
The Widow's cause, the Infant's tear,
In thee a friend are sure to rear;
   Their loss to sooth.

Through thee, fair Liberty will stand,
The proudest boast throughout this land;
   See Hist'ry's page!
The Press enslav'd, she'll inly moan,
And freedom's sons in chains may groan,
   From age to age.

HOWEVER laudable it may be to cultivate the art to perfection, it is to its common and more general application that we are to look for its great and beneficial effects upon the human intellect, and upon nations and societies of men. The Press is the great engine by which man is enabled to improve the faculties of his nature; it is the preserver of the knowledge and acquirements of former generations, and the great barrier, when not perverted by the hand of power, against the debasement of the human mind, and the equalizing effects of despotism.

In the accomplishment of what we have here undertaken, we shall strictly adhere to those rules which experience and observation have enabled us to select for our guidance, and which, we feel persuaded, are in accordance with the advanced state of this important branch of the art, a branch which is the very end and consummation of all the compositor's previous care and labor—a branch which, if in the least degree neglected, will cause all his taste and skill in composition, and the employer's expenses in beautiful type, to be passed over disregarded.

In former works upon this subject the directions to Pressmen have been found to be quite inadequate, being in a great measure confined to the two-pull Press, and to the minutiæ of balls, beating, &c. The various improvements in the art since those directions were written, have rendered them entirely obsolete, and it therefore devolves upon us to offer such new directions as will suffice to acquaint the beginner with the peculiarities of modern press-work.

Industrious and careful pressmen must stand high in the estimation of every master printer, yet it is to be lamented that so few endeavor to merit so desirable an appellation, and one so easily acquired by a little care and attention.

We shall now lay down a few directions, which, if properly attended to, will enable the pressman to execute his work in a manner that will do credit to himself and justice to his employer.

SETTING UP A PRESS.

UNDER this head might be introduced an almost unlimited variety of operations, yet it is our intention here to confine ourselves to a few remarks upon putting up those hand presses now in general use.

Having placed our frame in an erect position upon its feet, we next place the ribs in their allotted situation, where they are fastened by means of screws, and the stay put under the near end; we then lift the bed into the ribs, and commence nailing the girths in their proper places upon the barrel of the rounce, after which they are secured at the end of the bed; when the press is run out, the double girths should be about half a turn or more round the barrel; the off single girth about two or three turns round it. The position of the rounce when run out should incline a little forward of a perpendicular line, and when run in, a little above a horizontal line on the near side; to accomplish which it may be necessary to loosen the girths at one end of the bed, and to draw them up at the other. We then commence levelling our bed, which should be done with a spirit-level if convenient, if not, an ordinary carpenters' level, raising either end of the press by small blocks or wedges under the feet, or fore stay, as may be required.

Having ascertained our bed to lie truly horizontal, and having placed bearers at each end, upon which to rest the platen, we run it in to its proper place, where it is attached to the suspending rods; being careful to observe that the marked end of the platen is front, and that the marks on the nuts or screws correspond with those on the platen. In screwing down the springs we should avoid compressing them too much, as it would be likely to weaken them, at the same time screwing them sufficiently tight to hold the toggles in their place, and to cause the platen to rise quickly after an impression has been given. We also take notice that the platen falls perfectly horizontal, and that all four corners touch the type at the same time, which may be regulated by screwing or unscrewing the nuts at either corner, and inserting between them and the platen, if necessary, a piece of tin or rule.

The levers, toggles and oil cups being well oiled in their joints, and placed in their respective places, we then proceed to

SETTING UP THE ROLLER STAND.

THE roller stand containing the distributing cylinder, should be regulated to the height of the press, bringing the shelf or bridge even with the corner irons, and of sufficient distance from the bed to allow it to run clear; the stand should then be firmly braced, as the constant turning of the rounce is very apt to loosen it, meanwhile being cautious to observe that the rounce in its revolutions does not come in contact with the frame of the tympan when up. The position of the distributing cylinder should be sufficiently high to allow the two composition rollers, at least one inch apart, to rest on its top without danger of touching the shelf or bridge in front; we have found it advantageous to nail two narrow strips of sole leather on the face of the shelf, about eight or ten inches from each end, which, acting as bearers, cause the rollers to pass very smoothly over them.

The roller handle while in use should lie in a horizontal position, the back end being supported by a bar of wood or iron running parallel with the distributing cylinder. There should be a notch, or hook, about two inches from the end of the handle to catch on the wooden supporter, to prevent the rollers

20

from jumping forward while distributing or changing. It is also necessary to have a back-board for the end of the roller to strike against in coming off the form, to prevent the rollers from falling backwards.

The ink-block is placed about five or six inches to the right of the roller handle, and about on a level with it; it is furnished with the ink slice, and a brayer, or a small roller about four or five inches long, and of the same circumference with the large rollers, being cast in the same mould.

A few years since a great improvement was effected by having the ink-block made of cast iron, for the following reason :— it had been found necessary for the purpose of enabling the men to work the fine and stiff inks in cold weather, to have in the press room what was denominated a moveable ink-stand; this was a small square table, with an iron plate for the top, under which was a shelf to contain a lamp to warm the ink, and render it free to work; this was, of course, moved to the side of each press as wanted, but often proved a cumbrous article in a crowded room, when not wanted. The iron ink-block, with a little shelf underneath it, answers every purpose of the above described apparatus, with this additional advantage over the wooden one, it keeps the ink cooler in hot weather.

COVERING TYMPANS.

The tympans are generally covered with parchment. They should be of an even thickness, and about two inches and a half wider, and three inches longer than the tympans. Tympans have been sometimes covered with linen, which, on account of its evenness, would answer the purpose; but it is so apt to stretch, that the tympans become slack in a short time, and bag, (as it is termed,) which occasions a slur on the work. Muslin and silk have been used, but are likewise subject to the same objection as linen. They are, however, still used for newspapers, and other large works, where parchment cannot be obtained of sufficient dimensions.

Having provided some stiff paste, he lays so much of it on the edges of the skin, as will cover the frame of the tympan, which is also well pasted. He then lays the skin on the inner side of the frame, with the flesh side to face the type, and draws it regularly, as tight as possible, on all sides. That part of the skin that comes on the grooves of the tympan which receives the point-screws, is cut and wrapt round the inside edge of the groove, which admits a free passage for the screws. After having fastened the skin on the sides of the tympan, he draws it towards the joints which receive the frisket, and with a knife cuts across these joints to let them through the skin; he then puts the frisket pins through the same, and makes that end of the tympan fast. He next proceeds to the lower joints, and brings the skin as tight as he can round that part of the tympan. The point-screws and duck-bill are then put on, which prevent the skin from starting. The inner tympan, or drawer, is covered in the same manner. To prevent their warping when the skin begins to draw, pieces of furniture, or wood of any kind, should be placed across the centre till they are perfectly dry.

The skins are put on either wet or dry; if dry, they should be afterwards well wet, which makes them give for the moment; but as they dry, they contract, and are by this means rendered much tighter than they would be if put on wet.

WETTING PAPER.

PAPER should be wet in a trough kept for the purpose, filled with clean water. The size of this trough should be about two inches longer and wider (when folded,) than the largest sized paper that it is probable will have to be wet in it, and about six inches deep. It should have a cover with hinges on the left side, that the cover may fall over on that side, and, resting horizontally, serve the purpose of a shelf to lay the paper upon previous to its being wet.

Having received a sufficient quantity of paper from the Warehouseman, counted out, the pressmen lays one heap on the shelf attached to the paper trough, laying the first token across the heap with the back of the quires towards his right hand, that he may know when to turn the token sheet, and that he may the readier catch at the back of each quire with that hand, for the purpose of dipping it. He then places his paperboard with its breadth before him on his right, usually on the ley trough, laying a wrapper, or a waste sheet of paper on the board, that it may not soil the first sheet of the heap.

He then takes a quire by the centre of the back with his right hand, and the edge of it in his left, and closing his hands a little, that the quire may bend downward between his hands, he dips the back of the quire into the left hand side of the trough, and relinquishing his hold with the left hand, draws the quire briskly through the water with his right; as the quire comes out, he quickly catches the edge of it again in his left hand, and brings it to the heap; and by lifting up his left hand, bears the under side of the quire off the paper previously laid down, till he has placed the quire in an even position. But this drawing the quire through the water he performs either quick or slow; if the paper be weak and spongy, he performs it quickly; if strong and stubborn, slowly. To place the quire in an even position, he lays the back of it exactly upon the open crease of the former, and then lets the side of the quire in his left hand fall flat down upon the heap, and discharging his right hand, brings it to the edge of the quire, and with the assistance of his left thumb, still in its first position, opens or divides either a third or a half of the quire, according to the quality of the paper; then spreading the fingers of his right hand as much as he can through the length of the quire, turns over his opened division of it upon his right hand side of the heap.

Drawing and plate papers, being occasionally used by the letter-press printer, it is proper to observe that a different process must be used in the wetting. These papers are usually sent in from the Stationers quite flat; that is not folded into quires or half quires. The best method of wetting these papers is to use a brush, such as is called a banister brush; and instead of dipping the paper into the trough, lay it on the paper board by the side of the trough, and dipping the brush into the water, give it a gentle shake over the whole surface to give an equal degree of moisture to all parts; and continue to follow up the process upon the same principle as in wetting paper after the ordinary mode, as before described. The drawing-paper being very hard-sized in the making, will require the brush, and much water, three, four, and sometimes five times a quire; while the plate-paper will take as little water as it is possible to give it, so as to cover it all over; and twice a quire will often be too much. This same mode must also be adopted in wetting paper of extraordinary dimensions.

Having wet his first token, he doubles down a corner of the upper sheet of it on his right hand, so that the further corner may be a little towards the left hand of the crease in the middle of the heap, and that the other corner may hang out on the near side of the heap, about an inch and a half; this sheet is called the *token sheet*, as being a mark for the pressman, when he is at work, to know how many tokens of that heap are worked off.

Having wet the whole heap, he lays a wrapper, or waste sheet of paper upon it, that the paper board may not soil the last sheet of the heap; then, three or four times, takes up as much water as he can in the hollow of his hand, and throws it over the waste sheet, that it may moisten and soak downwards into the wet part of the last division of the quire, after which he places the label which the warehouseman must always furnish for each heap, and upon which is written, in legible characters, the title of the work and the date of wetting, in the heap, one half hanging out so as to be easily read.

The paper being thus wetted, he sets it by in a part of the room appropriated for that purpose, and lays another board upon it; and in the middle of the board sets about a half a hundred weight, and lets it stand by to press, commonly till the next morning; for pressmen generally wet their paper after they have left work at night. All wetted paper would be better if it were separated and turned in the course of the following morning, and pressed for ten or twenty hours in a standing press.

20*

But the wetting of paper must, in all cases, depend entirely upon its fabric: and since the printer has seldom, when employed by a bookseller, the choice of the paper, it will require all his skill and patience to adapt his labors to the materials upon which he is to work. The paper for fine work must increase in firmness of texture, as the ink is increased in fineness and tenacity. To attempt doing fine work upon common paper, is but throwing away time and expense. A paper to take the best ink must be made entirely of linen rags, and not bleached by any chemical or artificial means. A fine hand-made paper, fabricated a sufficient time to get properly hardened, and well and equally saturated with size so as not to imbibe more water in one part of the dip than in another, nor resisting the water like a duck's back, is what we have found most suitable for fine printing. The paper having been wetted with the greatest care as to equality of water, should be pressed for twelve hours, and then carefully turned by each three or four sheets, so as no lift be relaid in the same position with respect to the adjoining lift; at the same time every fold and wrinkle must be carefully rubbed out by the action of the hand, so that nothing but a flat and even surface shall remain; the heap should then be pressed for about twenty-four hours in a screw press, and it will be in good order for working.

THE BLANKETS.

The next matter of importance towards obtaining good press work, is the substance which is fixed in the tympans to intervene between the type and the platen, in order, when the power is applied, to cause an impression into the substance of the paper. Whatever is used for this purpose, it is now become technically correct to denominate the blankets. For this purpose there has been generally used a kind of blanket, manufactured for the purpose, of a more even fibre than ordinary blanketing, free from knots, and having a very fine surface, or pile; and to vary the impression as different kinds of work might require, very thin, or Welsh flannel, Cassimeres, or fine broad-cloth are used. These are varied by the judgment of the master or pressman, according to the type, paper, ink, &c. with which he works: thus for very close or heavy forms, small type, he must select the softest woollen blanket, and for yet larger type and more open work, he must continue the change to the thinnest blanket, and sometimes even to two or three sheets of soft paper. Again, a discretion will be required, according to the state or wear of the types—the newer the letter and sharper the ceriphs, the finer may be the work, the stronger the ink, and the harder the impression; while, on the contrary, in order to make type which has been worn, appear *well up to paper*, additional softness must be given. In fact, nothing but observation, experience, and good mechanical common sense can guide the judgment of the pressman in this most material point of *making ready*. By the various changes and combinations of his blankets, adding a soft to a hard, or a hard to a soft one; reversing them in regard to the one or the other falling next the type; adding a sheet of paper between, or under, or over, he must, with necessary judgment and patience, regulate his pull according to the various combinations of circumstances which may attend his work.

We have been thus lengthy upon this subject in order to impress more particularly upon the minds of pressmen, the importance of their paying particular attention to this material requisite in the production of fine printing; being fully aware that it has heretofore been regarded as a matter of but little importance, and having been altogether too much neglected by many pressmen, who have scarcely deemed it necessary to look into their tympans previous to going to work, frequently working ordinary forms with two or three blankets, when one or less would have been amply sufficient.

MAKING READY A FORM.

BEFORE a form is laid on the press, the pressman should carefully wipe the back side of the form and the bed perfectly clean; for if any hard particle, though ever so small, should remain on it, it will cause that part of the form to rise, and not only make a stronger impression, but in all probability injure the letters.

The form should be laid on the press, if an octavo, with the signature page to the left hand, or nearest the platen; if a duodecimo, or its combinations, with the signature at the right hand, or nearest the tympan. The form should be laid under the centre of the platen, and properly quoined up; he then lays down the tympan, wetting it if necessary, and puts in his blankets, which should be well rubbed if they are the least hard. It was customary, formerly, to wet the tympans, for all works, and even jobs of almost every description; but since the introduction of fine printing, and particularly the iron presses, this old custom is well nigh banished, excepting for extraordinary heavy forms, composed with old letter, which of course require more softness to bring them off. After putting in the inner tympan or drawer, he fastens it with the hooks for that purpose, which serve to keep it from springing out. Then lifting up the tympan, he next folds a sheet of the paper he is about to work, in quarto, and lays the short crease over the middle of the grooves of the short cross, if it lie in the middle of the form, for in twelves it does not, and then he folds the paper accordingly in thirds, the long crease of it upon the middle of the long cross, and the short crease over the grooves; having laid his sheet even upon the form, he then lays down the tympan, and pulls gently upon the sheet, which, with the least possible damp, will cause it to adhere to the tympan; should it happen to have been laid uneven, it is much better to relay it, because this sheet (which is denominated the tympan sheet,) is the guide by which the whole impression of the form of white paper is worked. He next selects his points, for large paper short-shanked, and for small, long-shanked points, and screws them to the tympan; if an octavo, the off point will bear to be a trifle longer than the near one, but if twelves, they must be exactly of a length, or placed at exact distances from the edge of the paper, and the more the distance between the point holes, the less the liability of the registers varying by the stretching of the holes. By placing the points unequally in octavos, &c. as before mentioned, he also secures himself the more from a turned heap when he works the reiteration. When a press has a run upon the same work, they seldom ever remove the quoins on the offside of the bed, but let them remain as guages for the following forms; for by thrusting the chase close against those quoins, the register is almost, if not quite made, provided the chases run equal as to size. Having fixed on his points, he then lays down the tympan, within about an inch and a half of the form, in which position he holds it at the upper part with his left hand, while he sinks his body till he can see between the form and the tympan, and with the ball of the middle finger of his right hand, presses gently upon the tympan over the end of each point successively, to ascertain if they fall in the middle of the grooves of the short cross; if not, he moves them: should the sheet have been taken up properly, and the points carefully fixed according to it, there can be little doubt but the points will fall in their places. Under the head of making ready the form, are comprehended several operations, viz.—1. The frisket should be covered with stout paper, in the manner described for putting on parchment, being careful to place the paper on the inside of the frame, so as to lie close to the tympan, and to confine the sheet in its place when laid on for printing; when the paste is sufficiently dried, the frisket should be put on the tympan, and after inking the form, an impression should be pulled upon it, the frisket is then taken off and laid on a board, or on his bank, and the pages cut round with a sharp knife about a Nonpareil from the edge of the margin of each page, it is then replaced on the tympan; after which it would be advisable to put a few cords across, not only to strengthen the bars of paper, but also to keep the sheets closer to the tympan than would otherwise have been the case if the paper bars had been left to perform this office alone; at times it is necessary to work with cords only, where the margin is too small to admit bars of paper.

2. He next examines his form, to see that it is properly locked up and planed down.

3. That no letters or spaces lie in the white lines of the form, nor between the lines in leaded matter; which may happen if the compositors have made any corrections since the form was laid on the press.

4. Should there be any wood cuts in the form, they must be brought to a proper height, which will depend much upon the judgment of the pressman; if the cuts are heavy, they must be at least type high, but should they be light, they will perhaps require to be about a lead or more lower than the type, and the solid parts, if any, brought up by overlays nicely cut from an impression, with a pair of sharp scissors; should any particular part then be too high, it may be humored a little by cutting it out of the tympan sheet; but should the whole appear too heavy, an underlay must be taken out, and if necessary, the cut filed or scraped away at the bottom. This part of the press-man's duty has heretofore been altogether too much neglected, either from inattention, or a want of knowledge of the proper course to be pursued, much to the detriment of the engraver, whose labor, unassisted by the printer, is entirely thrown away.

5. If a white page or pages happen in the form, and he uses a newly covered frisket, he does not cut out that page; but if he works with an old frisket, and that page is already cut out, he pastes on a piece of paper to cover the white page in the form, that it may not black; he then puts on a bearer, to keep the adjoining pages from having too hard an impression; some pressmen use reglets, others have furniture cut to a proper height, and a third class adopt cork, which, from its elasticity, in many cases is very useful; spring bearers, made of hard paper rolled up, are also very serviceable to guard the sides and bottoms of light and open pages, when there is an inclination to slur, which, with some presses, cannot be prevented.

6. He examines whether the frisket bites; that is, whether it keeps off the impression from any part of the pages; if it does, he cuts away so much, and about a Nonpareil more, off the frisket where this happens.

7. He considers whether the catch of the frisket stands either too forward or too backward: if too forward, he may be much delayed by its falling down, and if too backward, after he has given the frisket a touch to bring it down, it will be too long before it will follow, and retard the progress of the work, and not unfrequently cause the sheet to slip out of its proper place; he therefore places the catch so that the frisket may stand a

little beyond a perpendicular backwards, that with a near-guessed strength in the tossing up, it may just stand, and not come back.

8. He fits the gallows so that the tympan may stand as much toward an upright as he can; because it is the sooner let down upon the form and lifted up again. But yet he will not place it so upright as to prevent the white sheets of the paper from lying secure on the tympan; and for reiteration sheets, their laying upon the points secures them.

9. Few pressmen will set the range of the paper bank to stand at right angles with the bed of the press; but they draw the further end of the bank so that the near side may make an angle of about seventy-five degrees, more or less, with the near side of the bed.

10. The pressman brings his heap, and sets it on the horse, on the near end of the paper bank, as near the tympan as he can, yet not to touch it, and places an end of the heap towards him. He then takes the uppermost, or outside sheet, and lays it on the bank; and taking three, or four, or five quires off his heap, he shakes them at each end, to loosen the sheets, that with pressing stick close together; and not finding them loose enough, he shakes them long-ways and side-ways, to and fro, till he finds he has sufficiently loosened or hollowed the heap. Then with the nail of his right hand thumb, he draws or slides forward the upper sheet, and two or three more commonly follow gradually with it, over the hither edge of the heap, to prepare those sheets ready for laying on the tympan.

11. Having attended to the foregoing directions, he next proceeds to pull a *revise* sheet, which must be sent up to the Overseer for a final revision, and that he may discover whether any letters have dropped out of the form in putting it on the press, &c.

12. While the sheet is undergoing a revision, the pressman proceeds to *make register*, (if half sheet-wise) which he does by pulling a waste sheet, and turning it, (without inking, as the sheets may afterwards be used for *slip* sheets,) being particular not to stretch the point holes in the least, or to draw the hand along the sheet in leaving it, as it will be impossible to

make good register while these particulars are neglected. In making register, the points should be knocked up or down in such a direction as would bring the first impression under the last, only knocking the point half the distance apparent on the sheet. Should we be unable to make register with the points, the difficulty must then be either in the furniture, the length of the pages, or what is too frequently the case, in the springing of the cross-bars, from being locked up by careless and indifferent compositors, who commence at one quarter of the form, locking it up tightly, and so going round, instead of gently tapping it at opposite sides till the whole is secure. In locking up a form, the quoins at the feet should be gently struck first, to force up the pages and prevent their hanging; but in unlocking, the side quoins are first slackened, otherwise, should the matter be leaded, the leads are very liable to be bent, if not broke, by the foot of the page being first unlocked.

In making register, it may sometimes be necessary to move the forms, particularly in twelves, in order to avoid the inconvenience of moving the points, or in some cases where they cannot be moved to answer the purpose.

But it sometimes happens that the compositor has not made the white exactly equal between all the sides of the crosses; in this case, altering the quoins will not make good register; the pressman therefore observes which side has too much or too little white, and, unlocking the form, takes out or puts in such a number of leads or reglets as he thinks will make good register, which he tries by pulling a sheet, and if it be necessary, alters it again, till he has pulled a sheet with good register.

PULLING.

To take a sheet off the heap, the puller places his body almost straight before the near side of the tympan; but nimbly twists the upper part of his body a little backwards towards the heap, the better to see that he takes but one sheet off, which he loosens from the rest of the heap by drawing the back of the nail of his right thumb quickly over the bottom part of the heap, (but in the reiteration, care should be observed to draw the thumb on the margin, or between the gutters, that the sheet may not smear or set off,) and, receiving the near end of the sheet with his left hand fingers and thumb, catches it by the further edge with his right hand, about four inches from the upper corner of the sheet, and brings it swiftly to the tympan, and having the sheet thus in both his hands, lays the further side and two extreme corners of the sheet down even upon the further side and extreme further corners of the tympan sheet; the sheet being now properly laid on, he supports it in the centre by the fingers of the left hand, while his right hand, being disengaged, is removed to the back of the ear of the frisket, to bring it down upon the tympan, laying, at the same moment, the tympan on the form. He then, with his left hand, grasps the rounce, and with a moderate strength quickly turns it in; after pulling, he gives a quick and strong pressure upon the rounce, to turn it back, and run the carriage out again: as soon as he has given this pressure, he disengages his left hand from the rounce, and claps the fingers of it towards the bottom of the tympan, to assist the right hand in lifting it up, and also to be ready to catch the bottom of the sheet when the frisket rises, which he conveys quick and gently to the catch; and while it is going up, he slips the thumb of his left hand under the near lower corner of the sheet, which, with the assistance of his two fore-fingers, he raises, and by so doing allows the right hand also to grasp it at the top, in the same manner, which lifts the sheet carefully and expeditiously off the points, and nimbly twisting about his body towards the paper bank, carries the sheet over the heap of white paper to the bank, and lays it down upon a waste sheet or wrapper, put there for that purpose; but while it is coming over the white paper heap, though he has the sheet between both his fore-fingers and thumbs, yet he holds it so loosely, that it may move between them as on two centres, as his body twists about from the side of the tympan towards the side of the paper bank.

Thus, both the pressman's hands at the same time are alternately engaged in different operations; for while his right hand is employed in one action, his left is busy about another; and

these exercises are so suddenly varied, that they seem to slide
into one another's position, beginning when the former is but
half performed.

Having thus pulled a sheet, and laid it down, he turns his
body towards the tympan again, and, as he is turning, gives
the next sheet on the white paper heap a touch with the back
of the nail of his right thumb, as before, to draw it a little over
the hither edge of the heap, and lays it on the tympan, &c. as
he did the first; and so successively every sheet, till the whole
heap of white paper be worked off.

As he comes to a token sheet, he undoubles it, and smooths
out the crease with the back of the nails of his right hand, that
the face of the letter may print upon smooth paper. And being
printed off, he folds it again, as before, for a token sheet when
he works the reiteration.

Having worked off the white paper of twelves, he places his
right hand under the heap, and his left hand supporting the
end near him, turns it over on the horse, with the printed side
downwards: if octavo, he places his left hand under the heap,
supporting the outside near end with his right hand, and turns
it one end over the other; all turning of the paper for reiteration is regulated by this principle, and called by the pressmen
twelve-ways, or *octavo-ways*. In performing this operation, he
takes from the heap so much at once as he can well govern,
without disordering the evenness of the sides of the paper, viz.
a token or more, and lays that upon the horse; then takes
another lift, and so, successively, till he has turned the whole.

Having turned the heap, he proceeds to work it off, as before
described, except that with the left hand he guides the point
holes over the points, moving the sheet with the right hand,
more or less, to assist him in so doing. The token sheets, as
he meets with them, he does not fold down again, as he did the
white paper.

When within a quire or so of the end of the heap, the warehouseman should be called, whose duty it is to count the paper,
and if it falls short, he brings the pressman the number of dry
sheets, which he turns into the heap from which the wet sheets
are taken.

RULES AND REMEDIES FOR PRESSMEN.

ABOUT every five or six sheets a small quantity of ink should be taken; yet this will be subject to considerable variation from the nature of the individual work, and quality of the ink; a form of large type, or solid matter, will require the taking of ink more frequently, and a light form of small type less frequently; during the intervals in which the roller boy is not employed in braying out or taking ink, he should be almost constantly engaged in distributing or changing his rollers. In taking ink, he should invariably take it on the back roller, as it will the sooner be conveyed to the other roller, and consequently save time in distributing. When, through carelessness, too much ink has been taken, it should be removed by laying a piece of clean waste paper on one of the rollers, and distributing them till the ink is reduced to the proper quantity. If letters, quadrats, or furniture, rise up and black the paper, they should be put down with the bodkin, and the quarter locked up tighter. If any letters are battered, the quarter they are in must be unlocked, and perfect ones put in by the compositor. When bearers become too thin by long working, they should be replaced by thicker ones. When the form gets out of register, which will often happen by the starting of the quoins which secure the chase, it must be immediately put in again, as there can scarcely be a greater defect in a book, than a want of uniformity in this particular. If picks, which are produced by bits of paper, composition, or film of ink and grease or filth, get into the form, they are removed with the point of a pin or needle; but if the form is much clogged with them, it should be well rubbed over with clean lie, or taken off, and washed: in either case, before the pressman goes on again, it should be made perfectly dry by pulling several waste sheets upon it, in order to suck up the water deposited in the cavities of the letter. The pressman should habituate himself to glance his eye over every sheet, as he takes it off the tympan; by following this plan, he will be enabled not only to observe any want of uniformity in the color, but also to detect many imperfections which might otherwise escape unnoticed.

In order to make perfect uniformity in the color, the roller boy should be made to keep his ink well brayered out with the small roller, in proper quantities for the work in hand, and also to change his rollers well after taking ink, and at other times; the rollers are changed by moving the roller handle slowly to the right and left, while the crank is being turned briskly with the left hand.

Torn or strained sheets met with in the course of work, are thrown out and placed under the bank. Creases and wrinkles will frequently happen in the sheets through careless wetting of the paper, and which escaped the pressman's notice in turning; these should be carefully removed by smoothing them out with the back of the nails of the right hand.

Slurring and mackling arise from various causes; the following, among many others, are the causes of, and remedies for this evil. If the frame of the tympan rub against the platen, it will inevitably cause a slur or mackle. This can easily be remedied by moving the tympan so as to clear the platen. The joints or hinges of the tympans should be kept well screwed up, or slurring will be the consequence. The thumb piece of the frisket being so long as to cause it to rub against the cheek of the press, always produces a slur; this can be prevented by filing off a part of it. Loose tympans will at all times slur the work, great care must therefore be observed in drawing them perfectly tight. The paper drying at the edges will also cause a slur; this may be remedied by wetting the edges frequently with a sponge.

Independent of the above causes, slurring and mackling will sometimes happen; it will be better in this case to paste corks on the frisket, or to tie as many cords as possible across it, to keep the sheet close to the tympan.

In rolling the form, the pressman should see that the boy rolls it slowly, or the rollers will be apt to jump, which occasions a *friar;* to prevent the rollers from jumping or bounding, various experiments have been tried, as the most successful of which, we would recommend bridges or springs made of thin steel, to reach across the gutters; these springs should taper off at the ends, and have an oblong hole in each end, through which they may be tacked to the gutter sticks. In very open forms, it will perhaps be necessary to put bearers, or pieces of reglet where the blank pages occur at the end of the form, to prevent that end of the roller from falling down and leaving a friar at the opposite end. Of late years this difficulty has, in a great measure, been obviated by imposing the form in such a manner, as in most cases, to bring the blank pages in the centre. (See pages 14, 15, 20, and 21 of the impositions.) This mode should always be adopted for title pages and other light matter, as great advantages must arise from working such pages in the centre of the form.

Before the pressman leaves his work, he covers his heap. He first turns down a sheet like a token sheet, where he leaves off, then puts a quantity of the worked off sheets on it, and a paper board if convenient. Laying the blanket on the heap, after leaving off work, is a bad custom. If the paper be rather dry, it will be better to put wet wrappers on it, after wetting the edges well.

The pressman next observes whether his form be clean; if so, he puts a sheet of waste paper between the tympan and frisket, and lays them down on the form; if it be dirty, it must be rubbed over with clean ley, and several waste sheets pulled on it as before directed, to suck the dirty ley out of the cavities of the letter. On his return to work in the morning, should the type be much worn, he takes care to wet the tympan. If there should be any pages in the form particularly open, those parts of the tympan where they fall must not be wetted.

THE LEY TROUGH.

THE form being worked off, it becomes the pressman's duty to wash it clean and free from every particle of ink, not only for the cleanly working and well standing of the letter in the subsequent composing, but to save his own time in making ready when the same letter gets to press again; for if a pressman is at all remiss in this duty, he will perhaps at last be obliged to do it, and wait the drying of the form, before he can go on with his work in a fit and proper manner. Many an hour is lost from a pressman not bestowing a minute or two in thoroughly cleansing and rinsing his form.

For this purpose, every printing office is provided with a ley trough, suspended on a cross frame, and swinging by iron ears fixed something out of the precise centre, so as the gravity of the trough will cause it to fall in a slanting position forward. This trough is lined with lead, the top front edge being guarded from the pitching of the forms by a plate of iron. The form having been placed in the trough on its side, he takes hold of the rim of the chase by the hook, or instrument for that purpose, and laying it gently down, pours the ley upon it, and sluices it by swinging the trough on its pivots, two or three times to and fro, then taking the *ley-brush*, he applies it to the whole form, type, furniture, and chase; the ley is then let out into a receptacle for that purpose, and the form well rinsed with clean water, by swinging the trough as before; the form is then lifted out, and consigned to the care of the compositor.

The ley is made of pot or pearl-ash. A large earthen jar is usually chosen for the purpose; a sufficient quantity of pearl-ash is added to the water to make it bite the tongue sharply in tasting.

The ley brush is made large, the hairs close, fine, and long, in order not to injure the type, while sufficient force is applied to search every interstice in the letter, where the ink can have insinuated itself.

———

ON FINE PRINTING.

It is to be regretted, that uncontrolable causes preclude us from partaking of those benefits, which are so essentially necessary in the production of Fine Printing; we allude to the very changeable nature of this climate, the temperature of which is so variable, that it acts powerfully upon the oil of which our ink is composed, disposing it at one hour to spread equally over the rollers, and at another rendering it so glutinous and stiff, as to tear the surface of the paper, and thereby baffle the utmost efforts of the pressman; even though he raise the temperature to summer heat, if the frost be intense, it will be of little avail: it has been proved that heat will not entirely counteract the effects of a freezing atmosphere upon some kinds of printing ink. It is not the ink alone that is thus affected, but also the rollers which are so out of order at certain times, that it is utterly impossible for the pressman to produce even passable common work, much less that of a superior kind: of these evils the public are little aware, but they are severely felt both by the employer and the men. But there are other obstacles against the production of Fine Printing, or indeed work of any description; we allude to the introduction of cotton rags, and likewise ground plaster of Paris (called *gypsum*,) into the manufacture of fine and other papers, also the application of the oxygenated muriatic acid for the purpose of obtaining despatch and delicacy of color, and thereby producing a good paper in appearance, from an inferior staple. Nothing can be more perplexing to a printer, nor more detrimental to his labors, than what is termed *bleached* paper: for although it may be thick, and seem strong in the ream, no sooner does the water penetrate through it, than it loses its adhesive quality, and becomes so loose and soft, as scarcely to bear handling, and in working sinks down into the letter, leaving a portion of its substance on the form after the impression, until it so clogs the type, that the work is often rendered scarcely legible. Hence it is that works printed in this country are less valued than those from the English press, whose works are printed on paper of a fine fabric made mostly of linen rags, and sufficiently strong to bear a fine ink; while in this country the pressman is obliged to accommodate the ink to the softness of his paper, which will seldom bear any thing above the lowest priced book ink.

The printers who have paid most attention to fine printing, have endeavored to produce that delicacy and sharpness of appearance on paper which is peculiar to the copper-plate work; but though such an effect may be very nearly approximated, it can never be perfectly attained, the impression being, as I have before remarked, accomplished by such completely different means. In seeking, therefore, after that which peculiarly belongs to another art, we are liable to a neglect of those excellencies which exclusively characterize our own; nor needs the mortification be very great that we cannot produce close imitation of copper-plate printing, when we see the difficult and abortive attempts of the copper-plate printer and engraver to imitate us; and when we consider how much more than the other, our art is capable of performing. With proper materials, properly employed, the impressions from letter-press exhibit peculiar fine relief and outline, which, in many respects, must be allowed to excel in beauty, even the finest productions of copper-plate.

Those who have had opportunities of inspecting the early productions of the press, will be convinced that the art became retrograde in the course of time; for there are yet in existence works of the fifteenth and beginning of the sixteenth centuries, which, whether examined with regard to case or press, will bear a near comparison with any that are now produced. It has been previously remarked that printing, immediately on its invention, made singularly rapid advances to perfection, which may be easily accounted for by the facilities it afforded to the purposes of society, and more especially to the cause of literature; and the unexampled patronage it thus obtained, as being one of the most honorable vestibules to human glory.

The improvements which have taken place in all the arts connected with letter-press printing, have acted, no doubt, powerfully in stimulating the printers of this country to that extraordinary exertion by which such fine specimens of typographic beauty are now so frequently produced. As engraving on copper and on wood progressively improved, it became necessary that the typography which accompanied them should not, by a coarse and common appearance, serve but to disgrace that which it should rival, and abridge the gratification which might be reasonably expected from a union of the arts.

Although the powers of wood engraving are limited, yet, as an art most intimately connected with our own, its importance is worthy of being held in the highest estimation; and were we not to attempt to force it beyond its capabilities, its advantages would be more esteemed. In consequence of several first-rate artists having put their genius to the stretch, in order that their works might vie with copper-plate, a false taste has been produced. It is true that some have sent out very beautiful specimens, affording a vast variety; but how curious soever these productions may appear, yet, on a comparison with impressions from copper, they will be found different things. The two species of printing has each its peculiar feature, which it is a vain attempt for the other to strive to equal. The deep, soft, regular black ground which can be given to a broad surface by completely covering it with fine ink, is a property of letterpress printing which the copper-plate can never be able to accomplish; and there is a receding in perspective, and a general sharpness of outline belonging entirely to the latter, which it is impossible for the former fully to attain. As it is a natural consequence of the different methods of engraving and working off, it is a species of dissimilarity that can never be entirely prevented. In speaking upon this subject, the author of a Printer's Grammar, says: "We are as much disappointed in examining a wood-engraving, in hopes of finding the softness of flesh and delicacy of skin which is produced by an artist on copper, as we are disappointed in not meeting in copper with that broad, deep shade, and strength of contrast, which the engraver on wood may always exhibit." Now with regard to the great defect of wood engravings in general thus spoken of, it is presumed that a considerable advance has been made towards perfection by many artists.

No kind of engraving is better calculated than that of which we are here speaking, to preserve the real outline and proportions of the designer. Indeed, this will be more easily credited when it is stated that he generally makes the drawing with pencil on the block; and the duty of the engraver is to leave those lines standing, by cutting away the interstices with the greatest exactness possible. Thus, as the most unfinished etchings on copper of the ancient masters are more valuable than any imitations of them by a second hand, so are the powers of the engraver on wood preferable for giving, as far as drawings and proportions are concerned, a faithful transcript of the original design. The great point, therefore, seems to be, to consider properly what is the real province of the art, so that expectation may not be raised from it, which, from its nature, cannot be gratified; and the art and the artist be unjustly depreciated in consequence of a disappointment which it is beyond the possibilities of either to prevent.

The difficulties attending the printing of wood engravings, are such as to require the greatest care and attention in the printer, otherwise all the labor previously bestowed by the designer and engraver will prove abortive: the printer of fine wood engravings should have some knowledge of light and shade, without which he must of necessity find himself at a loss in preparing his subjects for the press, however great his skill may be in other respects; for it is from the nice touches alone that the beauty and effect of the engravings are brought out; of these difficulties the public are not aware, otherwise they would more highly prize works of Art on wood, than they have hitherto done.

A difference of opinion exists respecting the color of printing ink; some admire the glaring effect of a dark black, while others prefer the softened richness and warmth of a deep mellow tone, which is always pleasing to behold, without in the least being fatiguing to the sight. The printer must exercise his judgment respecting the color and quality of the ink.

With respect to the Press nothing need be advanced; in several of them, every requisite for Fine Printing is attained.

The paper to be wet in such a manner as to retain its firmness, yet to be sufficiently soft to apply closely to the surface of the letter, and take up all the ink; if too wet, it will be impossible to produce a clear or black impression.

The rollers, on which so much depend, ought to be particularly attended to. (For further directions, see subsequent Chapter.)

The tympans should always be kept in a state of tension, by changing or drying the blanket, and removing the slip sheets, as they become damp.

The blankets must be of fine broad cloth, or kerseymere, and only one to be used.

When printing large letter, the surface of which requires to be well filled with ink, a sheet of tissue paper, or common paper damped, should be laid between every impression, to prevent the sheets from setting off on the back of each other.

Different opinions exist respecting what constitutes Fine Printing; some imagine, if they make their pages sufficiently black, that the end is answered; others, if they are pale and clear; so that each has a style peculiar to himself: therefore persons contend on this head, as though they were criticising a painting or an engraving.

PRINTING ENGRAVINGS ON WOOD.

HAVING previously alluded to this subject in our articles on Fine Printing and Making Ready a Form, it will only be necessary for us here to introduce such practical directions, as are indispensable in obtaining superior impressions from engravings on wood.

Where a single block is to be worked in the centre of a large press, it should be imposed in a small job chase, and this chase again imposed in a larger one, to prevent the springing of the furniture. Bearers, letter-high, placed round the block, serve to equalize the impression, and protect the edges from the severity of the pull; they also render the subject more manageable, by enabling the pressman to add to, or diminish the pressure on particular parts, so as to produce the desired effect. The first pulls made after the block has been laid on the press, require a great deal of care, lest by too hard a pull, the delicate lines of the engraving should be crushed; these remarks are equally applicable to the printing of cards and other light forms.

The impression in an engraving on wood should not be uniformly equal; if it be, some parts will be too hard and black, and other parts have neither pressure nor color enough, with obscurity and roughness, and without any of the mildness of the middle tint, on which the eye seeks to repose after viewing the strong lights and deep shades.

To produce the desired effect, the pressman pulls a few impressions on soiled or damaged India paper, out of which he can cut overlays to the precise shape and size that are wanted, which he does with a penknife and a pair of small scissors, scraping the edges of the overlay in many cases, to cause the additional pressure to blend with the surrounding parts. The overlays being nicely cut, he lays them on the engraving precisely where he wishes them, and having slightly pasted that part of the tympan sheet, puts the tympan slowly down, and presses with his hand over the block sufficiently hard to cause the overlays to adhere to the tympan; this he repeats till his dark shades are sufficiently strong, and should the light parts then be too heavy, he proceeds to cut them out of the tympan sheet, and the sheets in the tympan if necessary; for in the printing of highly finished wood cuts, blankets should never be used, a couple of sheets of fine smooth paper being sufficient.

The pressman will find it an advantage to have a good impression from the engraver before him as a pattern, and then arrange the overlays, &c. until he produces a fac-simile in effect; but it would be still better for him, could he obtain the assistance of the artist at the press side.

It is indispensably necessary in the production of fine printing, of whatever kind, that the workman should be supplied with the finest ink, and a smooth hard paper, and that his rollers or balls, the latter being preferable for wood engravings, should be in the best order.

A fine engraving on wood should always be washed with Spirits of Wine, and when out of use should invariably be kept with its face downward in a cool place. If an engraving warp, it may be straightened by laying the concave side on a few sheets of damp paper for a short time.

ORNAMENTAL PRINTING.

Under this general head, we will attempt to describe the various kinds of Ornamental Printing which have sprung into existence, as it were, within the last twenty years; and from our having been almost exclusively engaged in that branch of the art during the greater portion of that period, it will no doubt be expected of us to explain, for the benefit of the uninitiated, the result of our experience.

CARD PRINTING has, perhaps, since the introduction of Enamelled or Polished Cards, made more rapid strides towards perfection than any other branch of the art; the fine absorbing quality of the Enamel, under proper management, producing the most beautiful results, in many cases scarcely discernable from copper-plate. A card, to be well printed, requires the same treatment as a wood engraving, (see article on that subject) at least so far as the making ready is concerned, and also in being worked without blankets, and with the finest ink. Having made a light impression on our tympan sheet, we place our pins so as to bring the impression as nearly as possible in the centre of the card, one pin at the lower side, and two at the off side, taking care that the head of the pin does not come in contact with the types. The pull should be exceedingly light until properly regulated, having at no time more than is actually necessary to bring up the *face* of the type. Composition Balls should be used for all small forms on the ordinary hand presses, where fine printing is required. (See Balls.) The printing of Cards has, however, been carried to such an extent of late, that they are now printed on small card machines at the rate of one, two, and even three thousand per hour; we have two of these machines in use, one capable of printing one thousand, and the other three thousand per hour. All prepared cards must be printed without wetting, and it is now very common to print all kinds dry.

GOLD PRINTING, like most other novelties, has had its day, but is now more sparingly used; the process, even now, is not generally known by the profession, although within the power of all. The types are composed, and made ready at the press in the usual manner. A pot of gold size is then procured from the Ink maker, or Printers' Warehouse, with which the form is inked in the ordinary manner, and the impression taken upon the paper. The book of Leaf Gold having been previously cut, if for a large job, by merely taking off the back, if for a small one, by cutting it into pieces the size of the printed impression, which is done by pressing a straight edge across it, and cutting it through with the point of a sharp penknife, we proceed to laying on the gold in the following manner: we slightly wet the end of the fore finger of our right hand, and having placed the thumb of that hand on the pile of gold, we raise the edge of the paper with the fore finger sufficiently to dampen it with the moisture of that finger, then pressing the moistened edge of the paper on the gold, it will adhere sufficiently to enable us to lift gold and paper together, and place it on the impression, and so we proceed until it is entirely covered; we then gently pat the gold with the balls of the fingers, or any soft pliable substance, until it is set, when with a very soft hat brush, we brush off the superfluous gold, leaving a clear and beautiful impression of the subject in hand. The sharpness of the print will vary with the judgment of the printer in the quantity of sizing applied to the type; for if the press-work be bad, the print will be bad also.

BRONZE PRINTING is more extensively used than gold printing, being attended usually with less than half the expense in the cost of the material; the method of printing is the same, except that instead of laying on the gold leaf, the impression is rubbed over with the bronze, by dipping a small block covered with a short fine fur into the powder, and brushing off the superfluous bronze with a soft brush, as in gold printing. Bronze can be procured of various colors, and when laid on with judgment, the effect is beautiful. The palest bronze is best.

POLYCHROMATIC PRINTING is a new mode of printing, by which any number of colors can be printed at one impression, with the usual rapidity, and for which we have applied for letters patent of the United States. Rights can be had by applying to us.

XYLOGRAPHIC PRINTING, signifies literally, printing from wooden blocks, but it is commonly applied to a species of Ornamental Bordering cut in type metal, the printing of which is from the surface, usually in colored inks. In 1827 we discovered a mode, which is practised to some extent, by which two colors can be printed at one impression; this is done by having two plates, the inner one blocked in the usual manner, the outer one moveable, and made to fit over it, resting on the same block.

PRINTING IN COLORS.

THE art of printing in colors has heretofore been almost entirely neglected in this country; at least as far as relates to the
embellishing works of ordinary excellence with vignettes, capitals, tail-pieces, and other devices of fancy, in beautiful tints,
in the manner of the early typographers. This may very easily
be accounted for. To print in two colors occupies more than
twice the time necessary to print in one; and it also requires
more skill and ingenuity. These, unfortunately, must be paid
for; and this pecuniary consideration is sufficient to banish
from our pages this lovely art. So did not our forefathers;
they took pride in choosing the most tasteful designs, the most
harmonious colors, to illuminate their productions, and beguile
the reader into study by the illusive charms of gold, and blue,
and crimson. Fortunately, either time was of little value, or
the exclusive possession of the market enabled them to demand
remunerating prices for the time thus well bestowed; but in the
bustle and competition of our more mercantile days, time is
money, and blue and gold, scarlet and green, give way to the
equally useful but infinitely less beautiful uniformity of unre-
deemed black. In this article we propose to give, only the
method of printing in colors, as now in general use, having
under the head of Ornamental Printing, adverted to a new
method which we have recently invented, called Polychromatic
Printing, for further particulars in relation to which, we refer
the reader to that article. The following remarks relate to the
printing of red and black, the same process being applicable to
all other colors.

When red and black are to be printed on the same sheet, the
form is made ready in the usual way, and a line traced all
round the outside of the chase on the press with chalk, or any
thing that will accurately show the exact situation in which the
form must be placed after it has been taken off the press. The
pressman then pulls a sheet in order to get those words or lines
marked, which are to be worked red; while this is doing, he
washes the form thoroughly, as the least dirt remaining on it
will destroy the beauty of the red. The form is then laid with

its face downwards on a letter-board covered with the press-
blankets. Those words marked to be red are then forced down,
(which the soft and spongy nature of the blankets readily admit
of,) and Nonpareil reglets nicely fitted into the vacancies, which
raise the red lines and words all of an equal distance from the
other matter. A sheet of paper is then pasted on the form,
which keeps the Nonpareil underlays in their proper places.
The form is again laid on the press, observing the utmost care
in placing it agreeable to the marks before made on the press.

It must then be made perfectly fast to the corner irons, as it
is highly important that it remain firm and immoveable during
its stay on the press. The frisket (which is covered with strong
paper,) is then put on, the form rolled over with the red ink,
and an impression made on it. The red words are then cut out
with a sharp pointed penknife, with so much nicety as not to
admit the smallest soil on the paper from the other matter.

The red being finished, and the form washed, the compositor
unlocks it, (which is best done on the imposing stone, as the
pressman can easily lay it agreeable to the marks made on the
press,) and draws out the red lines, and fills up the space with
quadrats. When this is done, the pressman cuts out the frisket
for the black. An extra pair of points are used to prevent the
black from falling on the red, which is termed *riding*. When a
great number is to be printed, two forms are generally used,
one for the red, and another for the black, or as many forms as
there are colors to be printed. There is another method of
placing the underlays, which is adopted for broadsides, &c.
with large letter, and with perhaps only two or three lines of
red in them. The red lines are taken out on the press, and the
underlays put in with a bodkin, upon which these lines are
placed, and the frisket cut out as before mentioned.

The custom of printing broadsides, &c. with various colors,
having become so much into general use, has induced most
of our ink makers to turn their attention to the manufacture
of colored inks; consequently the printer can now be supplied
with that article without the delay and labor of making. We
give the following particulars, however, for the benefit of those
who wish to prepare their own colors.

Varnish is the common menstruum adopted for all colors in printing. Red is the color generally used with black. Trieste, or English Vermillion, with a small portion of lake, produces a beautiful red, which should be well ground with a muller on a marble slab, till it be perfectly smooth. If it be in the smallest degree gritty, it clogs the form, and consequently produces a thick and imperfect impression; no pains should therefore be spared to render it perfectly smooth; it may then be made to work as clear and free from picks as black. A cheaper red, but not so brilliant, may be prepared with orange mineral, rose pink, and red lead. The Prussian blue makes also an excellent color, and will require a good deal of time and labor to make it perfectly smooth. It is also ground with the best varnish, but made considerably thicker by allowing a greater portion of color with the same quantity of varnish, than the red; it will then work clear and free from picks. As this color dries rather rapidly, the rollers or balls will require to be frequently washed.

Other colors may be made, viz. lake and indian red, which produce a deep red; verditure and indigo, for blues; orpiment, pink, yellow ochre, for yellows; verdigris and green verditure, for green, &c. All these colors should be ground with soft varnish, being in themselves dryers, or they will so choke up the form, as to require it to be frequently washed; the consistency of the ink must be governed by the quality of the work to be executed; for a posting-bill or coarse job, the ink should be very thin, the proportion of varnish being much greater than when required for fine work; should the work be a wood cut, or small type, the pigment should be made as thick as possible.

In working the above colors, there will be a great deal of difficulty, unless they are ground perfectly smooth; too much care and labor cannot therefore be bestowed upon them.

The best colors for printing, are those of the lightest body and brightest color.

Boiling ley, made of American potash, should be used for washing the forms.

CHAPTER IX.

INKING APPARATUS.

To procure a good press being a printer's first care, his next is the best manner of applying the ink to the type, so as to preserve a perfect uniformity of color; to gain this end, has been the study of many in the profession; and various have been their experiments to accomplish this desirable object.

BALLS.

PELTS were formerly used, and when in perfect order would produce good work; but rhe difficulty of putting them in order, and the filthiness attending them, led to the introduction of the dressed sheep shins, now in use with those who still continue the practice of beating; a practice which must, in general, give place to the more perfect mode of rolling.

Composition Balls are made as described below, substituting instead of the skin, a cotton cloth; the ball being properly knocked up, must then be dipped into the melted composition, and held in the hand till it forms a smooth surface on the face, and is perfectly cool, after which we repeat the dipping until a sufficient thickness of composition is obtained, when it will require the same treatment laid down for rollers.

We introduce the following account of Pelt Balls, in order to show the important alteration which has taken place in this respect, but more particularly to give the printer proper directions for

KNOCKING UP BALLS.

PELTS are used for this purpose, and such are chosen as have a strong grain, and the grease well worked out of them. They are purchased either wet or dry; if dry, they are put to soak in chamber-ley. One skin generally makes two proper sized balls.

When the skin has soaked sufficiently, which will require about fourteen or fifteen hours, it is taken out of the ley, and *curried;* that is, by putting the skin round the currying iron, or any upright post, and taking hold of each end of it, and drawing it with as much force as possible, backwards and forwards, against the post, which discharges a good deal of the water and lime, and renders it more pliable; he then cuts the skin exactly in two, and puts them under his feet, and continues to tread them till he is unable to discover the smallest particle of water, or till it sticks to the foot in treading. The skin is then laid on a wetting board, or a vacant stone, and stretched, by rubbing the ball stock on it, as much as possible. He then places a lining (which is a worn out skin, and which has been previously soaked, but not trodden,) on the skin, and nails them with one nail to the ball stock; he then proceeds to lay the different cardings of the wool one upon the other, crossways, till he has sufficient for the ball; he then takes it up by the bottom corners, and grasps it into a circular form, with which he fills the ball stock, then brings the skin opposite the part already nailed, and makes that also fast with another nail. He then puts two nails immediately opposite each other, between the fastenings already made, and proceeds to put the skin in plaits, about an inch wide; through each plait a nail is driven; the superfluous skin should then be cut off, within half an inch of the nails. Balls are well knocked up when the wool is so placed as to form a full even face, that every part of the skin may bear upon the letter; not rising in hillocks, or falling into dales; not having too much wool in them, for that will render them soon hard and uneasy for the pressman to work with; or too little, for that will make the skin, as the wool settles with working, soon flap, and wrap over into wrinkles, so that he cannot so well distribute the ink on his balls.

SKIN ROLLERS.

It appears that the skin rollers were not used in England. They were first introduced in this country by a Mr. Maxwell, of Philadelphia, about the year 1807, and soon after by him abandoned, not being able to make them work properly : they remained out of use for several years, until they were again introduced by Mr. Fanshaw, of New York, about 1815. They were never considered so good as balls: being too heavy for the hand, they were always used behind the press.

COMPOSITION ROLLERS.

In noticing the composition rollers, we shall present to the reader all the information that we have been able to collect, together with the observations resulting from a practice of nearly twenty years.

This composition appears to have been discovered by the mere chance observation of a process in the Staffordshire potteries, in which they use what are there called dabbers. These were formed of a composition which appeared to possess every requisite for holding and distributing the ink, imparting it equally over the form, and being easily kept clean, soft, and pliable. Mr. B. Foster, a compositor at Weybridge, England, was the first who applied it to letter-press printing, (about the year 1815) by spreading it, in a melted state, upon coarse canvass; and making balls, in all other respects, in the usual manner. The inventors of printing *machinery* soon caught the idea, and by running the composition as a coat upon wooden cylinders, produced the apparatus so long and unsuccessfully sought for, and without which, machine printing would never have succeeded.

Rollers, like most other improvements, have met with considerable opposition ; yet their superiority must certainly be acknowledged by all who have become perfectly acquainted with them.

As this composition has now become one of the most essential requisites of a printing office, and as most printers are desirous of making their own *rollers*, (which plain name seems to have been generally adopted for the revolving cylinder,) we shall endeavor to describe the proportion of its ingredients, and its principal advantages : the first, and most important, is that of doing clean work; in this respect they are decidedly better than balls, as it is seldom necessary to take out picks, or clean the head lines; and a roller is frequently worked all day without the necessity of cleaning it. The next consideration is in point of cheapness, when compared with balls. The pressman will also find that they require but little attention when he has become perfectly acquainted with them. The softness and delicacy of the composition render it less liable than balls, to injure the fine hair strokes of the letter—this consideration alone is sufficient to warrant an experiment. The great saving of ink is also an object worthy of attention, for as it cannot penetrate the surface of the composition, there can be but little wasted.

The composition is made of the following ingredients, viz. For a Medium roller,

> Three lbs. of best Glue.
> Three pints of sugar-house Molasses.
> One table-spoonful of Tar.

This is calculated for approaching cold weather, but it is necessary to reduce the quantity of molasses to one quart for summer heat; and in proportion for any intermediate temperature. The mould best calculated to receive the composition, should be made of brass, copper, or iron, with the interior well polished. The above quantity of composition is intended for a roller of twenty-seven inches in length, and three and a half inches diameter, with a wooden cylinder of two and a half inches diameter, which will give half an inch thickness of composition. The thickness of the composition may be varied according to the size of the wooden cylinder.

DIRECTIONS FOR MAKING COMPOSITION.

THE glue must be put into a bucket, or vessel containing water enough to cover it, and remain in soak five or six hours, or until it shall have soaked nearly through, leaving about one-third dry in the centre, which may be ascertained by breaking a piece of it; it is then taken out of the water, and laid on a board to dry for ten or twelve hours, when it becomes pliable like a piece of sole leather, the water having penetrated through the centre; it is then in a proper state for melting, and should be put into the *melting kettle*.

This must be a double vessel like a glue-kettle, so that the composition in the inner kettle may be melted by the heat of the boiling water in the outer one. For this purpose, an iron pot or a strong boiler may be the best or readiest thing found, into which let a tin vessel be fitted, with a flanch to rest on the rim, so as to leave one or two inches under it. This vessel may be two or three inches above the top of the boiler, and so that the lid of one may fit the other; it must also have a lip for pouring out the composition.

Being thus prepared, put the glue into the inner vessel, the boiler having in it as much water as it will contain when the inner vessel is in its place. Put it on the fire, and keep the water boiling, the heat of which will soon cause the glue to dissolve, and evaporate part of the water. When the glue is all melted, the molasses should be poured slowly into it, stirring it all the while, and shortly after the tar should be added; the latter ingredient, however, is not considered important in the composition, as but few printers make use of it; the water should then be kept boiling for at least two or three hours, occasionally replenishing it, during which time the composition should be frequently stirred, when it will be ready for pouring.

Having given the receipt which we think most favorably of, and which our long experience has fully tested, we will now present the reader with several, the merits of which we are unable to appreciate, never having tried them.

Mr. Hansard, an eminent English printer, and to whom we are indebted for much valuable information in relation to our Art, says—"Take glue, made from the cuttings of parchment or vellum, fine green molasses, pure as from the sugar refiners, and a small quantity of the substance called Paris-white, and you will have every ingredient requisite for good composition. The proportion as follows:—

Glue, 2 lbs.   Molasses, 6 lbs.   Paris-white, ½ lb.

Put the glue in a little water for a few hours to soak, pour off the liquid; put the glue over the fire, and when it is dissolved, add the molasses, and let them be well incorporated together for at least an hour; then with a very fine sieve, mix the Paris-white,* frequently stirring the composition. In another hour, or less, it will be fit to pour into the mould.

Another receipt says 2 lbs. of Glue to 1 lb. of Molasses.

Another . . . 2 . . . . . 3 . . . . .

Another . . . 3 . . . . . 6 . . . . .

Add to the last receipt 12 drops of the following liquid:

"A piece of sal ammonia about the size of a nut, powder the same with about two ounces of Pearl-ash, and dissolve them in a glass of clear water."

---

* This is the carbonate of barytes, *terra pondrosa*, or ponderous earth; the most active of alkaline earths; and acts upon the animal economy as a violent poison. It is found in combination either with the sulphuric acid, forming the native sulphate of barytes, or heavy spar. It is chiefly used in adulteration of paint, giving a body almost equal to white lead. It is very difficult to be obtained pure, being often substituted with Paris-white of the oil shops, which is nothing more than a finer kind of whiting.

In the Printer's Manual, a small work, published in New York, we see recommended two pounds and a half of glue, and two quarts and a pint of molasses. With such proportions, we cannot doubt the necessity of his introducing something like the following:—

" *Washing Rollers.*—A method has long been sought, by which rollers might be cleaned, *without washing the molasses from the glue*. It has at length been found. Take a sufficient quantity of common ley, and add a little fine salt; it is by far better than any other way by which rollers can be washed. The potash destroying the oil in the ink, it no longer adheres to the composition; and the salt counteracts the effect the water would otherwise have on the molasses."

It will be observed that the above receipts differ very materially; and as the composition is subject to the changes of the weather, its consistency must greatly depend on the judgment of the workmen. Of the above receipts, we are disposed to think most favorably of Mr. Hansard's; but cannot admit its superiority over the one previously laid down.

PREPARING THE MOULD.

In preparing the mould, care should be taken to have its interior surface perfectly free from any particles of dirt, or composition; it should then be well oiled with a swab, kept for that purpose, at the same time being particular not to leave too much on the surface, as it will run when the heat of the composition comes to it, and cause an imperfect face on the roller: the end pieces should then be oiled, and, together with the cylinder, placed in the mould, the upper end piece being very open to allow the composition to pass down between the interior of the mould and the cylinder. The cylinder must be well secured from rising, before the composition is poured in, by placing a stick upon the end of it, sufficiently long to reach above the end of the mould, and be tied down with twine. The composition should be poured very slowly, and in such a manner as to cause it only to run down *one side* of the cylinder, allowing the air to escape freely up the other.

If the mould is filled at night, the roller may be drawn on the following morning, but should not be used, for at least twenty-four hours, except in very cold weather; it should be cleaned before it is used, by rolling it about the floor until its surface is covered with dust, then with a sponge wash it off quickly with water, wipe it dry, and let it remain until in a proper state for working.

GENERAL DIRECTIONS FOR WORKING ROLLERS.

HAVING cast three or four rollers for each press, we select two of them for immediate use, which are put into the roller frame for working. To determine when a roller is in order for working, we press the hand gently to it, to discover whether it is adhesive or not, if so, and the fingers can be drawn lightly and smoothly over its surface, it may then be said to be in order; but should it be adhesive, and the fingers will not glide smoothly over its surface, it is then not sufficiently dry, and should be exposed to the air until it possesses the above qualities: a roller well washed at night, and put into an air-tight box till morning, will generally be found in good order for working. For that purpose, every press-room should be furnished with a large upright box or closet of sufficient size to contain all the rollers in a horizontal position, their journals resting on supporters at the end of the box.

To wash the rollers, nothing more is requisite than the application of water, after rolling them in the dust; in cold weather a little warmed, but cold as possible in warm weather, which needs only to be used with the hand or a sponge; some pressmen, however, prefer washing them with ley, after which they should be well rinsed with clean water.

In very warm weather, the rollers should be occasionally changed, to prevent them from getting too soft, or from melting; it is frequently found when a roller is *sick,* or soft, or you do not know what is its ailment, that washing it clean, and hanging it to rest for a time, restores it to as good a state as ever, but it should not be washed till after it has cooled a little, as the cold water has a tendency to wrinkle it very much when over-heated. Great care should also be taken to keep them from the effects of the sun, as they are easily melted, and in warm weather they should be kept in as cool a place as possible during the night. Should any accident happen to the roller, to injure its surface, it may be melted again and re-moulded as before.

Since the introduction of composition, a great annual expense is saved in skins and wool, and a vast deal of the precious time of the men. Upon the introduction of the balls, it was calculated that the saving to each man was a half a day in a week; and we conceive that still more is saved by the rollers. But what is above every other consideration, the quality of the work is materially improved, and the labor is reduced to comparative ease by rolling over a form instead of beating it.

It is curious to contemplate the various changes which have taken place in a press-room, as far as regards manual labor, within a very few years. Previous to the introduction of the iron presses, the *beating* was the lighter labor, and *pulling* the heavier; to the latter of which an apprentice was seldom put, except for very light work, for the first twelve months. Then pulling became the lighter—the stronger beat, and the weaker pulled. But when the rollers were introduced, the stronger again took the bar, and the weaker rolled: and a well-grown lad was capable of taking both parts in the first month of his service. The pulling is now the only hard labor, the rolling requiring only a due degree of adroitness and attention.

About twelve years since, a machine was introduced to supply the place of a boy in rolling the form, &c. which was acted upon by weights and springs wound up by the running in of the bed; this machine performed the various offices of rolling, taking ink, and distributing, but owing to its complicated construction, was very liable to get out of order. Within a few years, however, various improvements have been made upon them, and their construction much simplified; those manufactured by F. J. Austin, of New York, have been favorably received, and are, we think, calculated to supercede the expense and annoyance of a roller boy.

CHAPTER X.

IMPROVED PRESSES.

AMONG the various improvements which have taken place in many branches of our Art, we conceive that none have tended more to the advancement of beauty in execution, and the comfort and convenience of the workman, than the improved presses of the present day.

THE COLUMBIAN PRESS.

THE press thus called was invented by Mr. George Clymer, of Philadelphia, about thirty years since, and made the subject of a patent; shortly after its invention, Mr. Clymer proceeded to Europe, where he introduced them to the notice of the profession in 1818, greatly improved in their manufacture.

They were held in high estimation in Europe, and are still in use there; but in this country they have been superceded by the simplicity, lightness, and cheapness of the Washington Press. They have not, however, been manufactured in this country since the removal of Mr. Clymer to Europe.

THE AMERICAN PRESS.

Tʜɪs press was invented by Mr. Shelden Graves, and is now manufactured by Mr. Ramage, of Philadelphia. It is a combination of the toggles of the Washington Press, and the lever or elbow of the Smith.

THE WASHINGTON PRESS

Wᴀs invented by Mr. Samuel Rust, of New York, to whose ingenuity and skill we are indebted for a valuable combination of levers. They are now manufactured by Messrs. Hoe & Co., Taylor, H. Worrall & Co., and others, of New York, and Mr. F. J. Cosfeldt, of Philadelphia. The frame represented in the engraving seems to have been adopted by most modern press makers, and is an essential improvement on the old cast iron rims; the columns at the sides of the press are cast iron hollow cylinders, with wrought iron bars running perpendicularly through them, which are attached to the head and winter of the press, rendering the frame less liable to be broken, more portable, and certainly much neater in appearance.

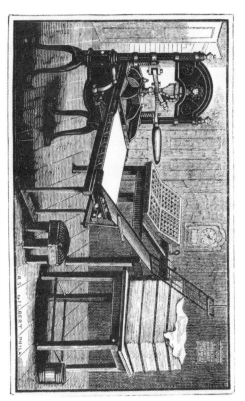

WASHINGTON PRESS

R. S. GILBERT, PHILA.

THE WELLS PRESS.

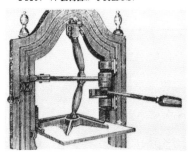

THIS press was invented by John I. Wells, of Hartford, Conn. about the year 1816; when well made, they were excellent presses, but they have given place to those of more recent invention.

MACHINE PRINTING.

THIS term is usually applied to cylindrical printing, but of course literally applies to all kinds of printing where steam power can be used. The first cylinder press was invented in England, about the year 1814, and has caused a great revolution in the art, from the facilities which it affords for printing sheets of paper of a size which could not be worked on a hand press, enabling the proprietors of newspapers to enlarge them to a previously unparalleled extent, and to afford them at prices so greatly reduced, that the circulation of many of them have been more than doubled.

In the following page we present an engraving of the best platen power press now in use; they are manufactured by Seth Adams & Co., of Boston. Mass.

The most prominent manufacturers of Double and Single Cylinder Presses, are A. B. Taylor, and Hoe & Co. The press represented in the frontispiece to this work, is justly entitled to our preference, on account of its simplicity, strength, and speed. Invented and manufactured by A. B. Taylor, of New York, and for sale by T. F. Adams, Philadelphia.

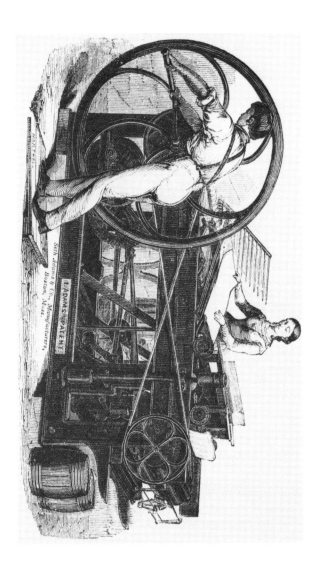

THE RAMAGE PRESS.

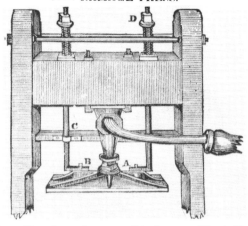

THIS Screw Press bears the name of its inventor, Mr. A. Ramage; it has been improved by substituting an iron bed and platen instead of the old wooden ones, the application of spiral springs, &c. &c.

THE PHILADELPHIA PRESS.

A wrought iron press, invented and manufactured by Mr. A. Ramage. The principal difference between this and other presses, is the use of a frame entirely of wrought iron, judiciously constructed.

THE SMITH PRESS.

THIS press was invented by Mr. Peter Smith, of New York, and is now manufactured by Hoe & Co., and Worrall & Co.

We have deemed it quite unnecessary to present the reader with a representation of this press, as the only difference between this and the Washington, and other presses, is the application of the wedge power between the toggles. They are not considered as powerful as the Washington Press by the same makers.

CHAPTER XI.

WAREHOUSE DEPARTMENT.

THE warehouse department of a printer is a highly important part of his concern; the management of which involves his own credit, and materially affects the interest of his employers: it is therefore indispensably necessary to appoint a man for the management of it, who has been regularly brought up to the business; on whom the utmost reliance may be placed for sobriety and honesty, and who can be taught to feel and act upon the principle of making his employer's interest the object of his constant solicitude. Those who have not such qualifications will be continually liable, through ignorance and carelessness, to fall into many serious mistakes. The employer or overseer should frequently look to the concerns of the warehouse, and see that the people employed there, forward the different works with expedition, neatness, and accuracy.

Having made these observations, we shall now proceed to speak of the different stages of this department, and begin by supposing the warehouse to be quite clear, business coming in, and the warehouseman just entering upon his office. He should first be provided with a book, which is termed " *The Warehouse Book*," agreeable to the plan in the following page, about the size of a foolscap quarto. When the porter or carman brings paper from the stationer or bookseller, the warehouseman should demand the bill of delivery, order the paper to be brought in, and see if it is right according to the bill, before he discharges him; and if right, dismiss him, and enter it immediately into the warehouse book.

This plan will prevent disputes with the bookseller or author, relative to the receipt of paper, or delivery of sheets, as the signature of the person to whom the sheets were delivered can be

THE WAREHOUSE BOOK.

JACKSON'S SHAKSPEARE'S GENIUS JUSTIFIED. NO. (PRINTED) 1000.				
Date.	Receipt of Paper, and of whom.	No. of Copies delivered.	To whom delivered with his signature.	For whom.
1843. Nov. 3.	90 reams of Messrs. F. A. Server & Co.			
Dec. 8.	40 Ditto.			
24.		100	John Troxell.	Jno. Murphy.
30.		300	R. Williams, Binder.	Ditto.
1844. May 4.		400	Edward Hughes.	Ditto.
5.	with waste.	230	John Warwick.	Ditto.
		1030		

immediately produced. It also enables the warehouseman to distinguish, with more ease, the different articles he might have occasion to refer to.

Having entered the receipt of the paper, the warehouseman should then write on each bundle, with red chalk, the title of the book it is intended for, and remove it into a part of the warehouse most out of his way, or into a store-room for that purpose, observing to place it so as to take up as little room as possible.

OF GIVING OUT PAPER TO WET.

A bundle of paper contains two reams, or forty quires, and twenty-four sheets to each quire, if perfect; if not, twenty quires to the ream, of which the two outside quires are called *corded* or *cassie*, as they only serve for cases to the ream. These outside quires are by the paper maker made up of wrinkled, torn, stained, and other damaged sheets, yet the whole quire very rarely consists of such sheets; but frequently some good sheets may be found in looking them over. It is the warehouseman's business to lay by the two outside quires, and cull them when most convenient; likewise so to dispose of them, that they may neither be at the beginning nor end, but about the middle of the volume, or use them for jobs or proof paper; for they are seldom so perfect as the inside quires.

It is the general custom to print of every work what is termed an *even* number, either 250, 500, 750, 1000, &c. These quantities are given out for the wetter in *tokens*, viz. for 250 (sheets) one token, containing 10 quires 18 sheets; for 500, two tokens —one 11 quires, and the other 10 quires and a half; for 750, three tokens, two of them 11 quires each, and the other 10 quires 6 sheets; and for 1000, four tokens, three of them 11 quires each, and the other 10 quires. If a work is printed in half-sheets, it of course requires only half the above quantities.

It would be difficult to form any positive and invariable rule for the quantity to be given out for short numbers, as it must depend, in some degree, upon the quality of the paper. The more expensive papers, on which, generally, short numbers or fine copies are printed, must be given out more sparingly than common paper; and the tympan and register sheets be supplied by a more common sort, cut to the size of the finer.

For numbers up to 150, on ordinary paper, six sheets over, will, generally speaking, be necessary: the warehouseman always bearing in mind to reckon for each 25, so many quires of 24 sheets, and the same number of sheets in the first instance, and then to add the necessary overplus.

In giving out paper for what are termed *jobs*, a little further observation will be necessary. It has been usual to give tables for this purpose, but we have not been convinced of its utility, as few printers would refer to a book for such calculations on every occasion, when they could be so easily made by a simple calculation in division.

For example, a job, (label or any thing else) 750 number, 32 on a sheet, will require 24 sheets, which will give an overplus of 18. If this is not thought sufficient, a remnant or sheet more must be given out, calculating that where a sheet has to be cut into many parts, some further allowance must be made for accidents. The overplus sheets being partly allowed for tympan sheets, register sheets, and other incidents; such as bad sheets, faults committed in rolling, pulling, bad register, &c.; in any of these casualties, the pressman doubles the sheet in the middle, and lays it across the heap. In setting out the paper, the warehouseman lays each token with the folded side, or back part, one way, and the other token with the folded, or back side, the other way, that the wetter may distinguish the different tokens. When this is done, he writes a label, and puts it into the bundle, thus: *Typographia, May* 25, 1844, that the pressman may know how long it has been wet, and the state it is in for working.

$$32)750(23$$
$$\underline{64}$$
$$110$$
$$\underline{96}$$
$$14$$

OF HANGING UP PAPER TO DRY.

WHEN the paper is worked off and counted, the warehouseman takes the heap and carries it to the drying room, where poles are fixed for the purpose of hanging the sheets upon to dry, and lays it down on a stool, or table, of a convenient height, with one end of the heap from him; he then takes the handle of the peel in one hand, and lays the top part down upon the heap, so that the upper edge may reach near the middle of the sheet; after which, with the other hand, he doubles over so much of the printed paper as he thinks sufficient to hang up at one lift, which should be about seventeen sheets, as near as he can guess, or twelve, &c. as he can allow time to dry, or have pole-room to hang them on.

In hanging up the lifts, he places them so that each lift may lap about an inch over the preceding one, till he has disposed of all the paper, or until he comes to the end of the pole. It will sometimes be necessary, where the end of a pole is exposed to any strong current of air, as a window, &c. to *lock* the last lift. This is done by folding a lift two or three times, so as to concentrate its weight in a small compass, and hanging this over the last lift near the window, it will generally prevent the air taking the sheets off the poles.

OF TAKING DOWN SHEETS WHEN DRY.

WHEN the sheets are sufficiently dry, the warehouseman takes his peel, and begins with the last lift hung up, on account of the wrapper being with that lift, and continues to proceed to the other, in the reverse order to that of hanging them up, successively taking them down and brushing them, if dusty, till he has finished the whole; taking care that he lays the single signature of each lift one over the other; if this is not done, it will occasion considerable trouble to turn them when they are to be folded.

There is also another way of taking the sheets down from the poles, which is, by laying the flat side of the peel against the edge of that lift which hangs over the other sheets, and pushing the peel forward, forcing them to slide, one doubling over the other, and so finishing the business with more expedition. But this method cannot be recommended, because the dust, which flies about while the sheets are hanging, must lodge on them, and by pushing them forward, is rubbed in, instead of being brushed off.

OF FILLING IN AND PRESSING SHEETS.

WHEN the sheets are taken down, the warehouseman removes them to the warehouse, where they are filled in between smooth paste-boards made for the purpose. This operation is generally performed by boys or girls, who, after a little practice, become exceedingly expert at it. We shall endeavor to be somewhat minute in our description of this operation, as it seems to have been entirely overlooked by former writers on this subject; we will suppose the paste-boards to have sheets between them, which will be the case after they have been once used. The warehouse being provided with long tables or benches, secured to the wall, and a sufficient number of moveable tables about the size of the largest paper, the warehouseman places one of the small tables endwise against the long one, forming a right angle, and upon which to lay the pressed sheets, as they come out of the boards; the boy then takes his stand at the right side of the table, with the dry unpressed sheets at his right hand, and the paste-boards at his left, somewhat elevated, leaving sufficient space before him to fill in the sheets; he then proceeds as follows:—He first moistens the thumb of his right hand, and reaches across to the paste-boards at his left, drawing one off with his thumb, and placing it before him; he then catches a sheet of the dry paper also with his right hand, and places it as near the centre of the paste board as possible, then twisting his body nimbly round to the left, he slides the pressed sheet from the pile of paste-boards, to the table at his left side, and in resuming his former position, again draws off a paste-board with his thumb, and so on, till the gross or bundle is filled. It is then laid aside, and another bundle filled and laid across the former, taking care always to keep the bundles separated until they are put in press, when they are separated by smooth boards made of cherry or other hard wood. The bundles being all filled in, the warehouseman then proceeds to fill up the standing press, putting in one bundle at a time, and placing a pressing board between them; there should also be a stout plank introduced between the top board and the platen. In case the press should not hold quite as much as we wish, more may sometimes be added by unscrewing the press, after it has been once screwed down, which so compresses the bundles, that one or two more may often be admitted. The press is then finally screwed down as tight as possible, and should remain so for at least twelve hours, when it should be entirely emptied before the sheets are taken out of the boards. In all these operations, care should be taken to keep the sides of the piles or heaps perfectly even.

OF COUNTING OUT AND PUTTING BY SHEETS.

WHEN the sheets are taken out, the warehouseman knocks them up, and after counting them into quires, proceeds to tie them up in wrappers, marking the name of the work and signature on each bundle; he then puts them by in that part of the room where they will be most out of his way, till wanted. But two or three sheets of each signature should be put by, in case the author, bookseller, or employer, should want a copy of the work, or a specimen of as many sheets as are finished. If this has not been done, and clean sheets should be wanted, he would then be obliged to lift every signature to get a sheet out of each, which will occasion a great loss of time; this may easily be prevented by reserving a few sheets as they are worked off.

SIZES OF PAPER AS MADE BY MACHINERY.

Double Imperial, ...	32 by 44.
Do. Super Royal, . . .	27 by 42.
Do. Medium, 23 by 36—24 by 37½—25 by 38.	
Royal and Half, ...	25 by 29.
Imperial and Half, ...	26 by 32.
Imperial, ...	22 by 32.
Super Royal, ...	21 by 27.
Royal, . . .	19 by 24—20 by 25.
Medium, ...	18½ by 23½
Demy, . . . , . .	17 by 22.
Folio Post, ...	16 by 21.
Fools Cap, ...	14 by 17.
Crown, ...	15 by 20.

TECHNICAL TERMS USED IN PRINTING.

Bank. A stage about four feet high, to lay sheets on at press.

Beard of a letter. The outer angle of the square shoulder of the shank which reaches almost to the face of the letter.

Bearer. A piece of reglet to bear off the impression from a blank page.—A long piece of furniture, type high, used in working jobs.—A solid faced type interspersed in the blank parts of a page, in composing for stereotyping, to resist the force of the knife in shaving the plates.

Bite. Is when the inked impression of the page, or any part of it, is prevented by the frisket's not being sufficiently cut out.

Blankets. Woollen cloth to lay between the tympans.

Body. The shank of the letter.

Bottled-arsed. When letter is wider at the bottom than the top.

Brayer. A round wooden rubber, flat at the bottom, used to bray or rub out the ink. Now substituted by a small roller about five inches long.

Break. A short line.

Broadside. A form of one full page, printed on one side of a whole sheet of paper.

Broken Matter. When the orderly succession in which the letters stood, in a line, page, or form is broken or mingled together, which mingled letters are called pi.

Bur. When the founder has neglected to take off the roughness of the letter in dressing.

Cassie Paper. Broken paper.

Clean Proof. When a proof has but few faults in it.

Close matter. Matter with few breaks.

Correct. A compositor is said to correct when he mends the faults marked in a proof.

Corrections. The letters marked in a proof.

Devil. The Errand-boy of a Printing house.

Double. Among compositors, a repetition of words; also, among pressmen, a sheet that is twice pulled and mackled.

Dressing a Chase or Form. The fitting the pages and chase with furniture and quoins.

Drive out. When a compositor sets wide.

Fat face, or fat Letter, is a broad stemmed letter.

Fat work. Is when there are many break-lines in a work.

First Form. The form that contains the first page of a sheet.

Fly. The person that takes off the sheets from the press in cases of expedition.

Form. The pages when fitted into a chase.

Foul Proof. When a proof has many faults marked in it.

Fount. The whole number of types cast to one body and face.

Friar. Where any part of the form has not received the ink.

Full Press. When two men work at the press with hand rollers or balls.

Get in. To set close.

Good color. Sheets printed neither too black nor too light.

Good work. Is so called in a two-fold sense; the master printer calls it good work when the compositors and pressmen have done their duty; and the workmen call it good work, if it be light, easy work, and they have a good price for it.

Half Press. When but one person works at the press.

Hell. The receptacle for broken or battered letters, the old metal box—the shoe.

Horse. The stage on which pressmen set the heaps of paper on their banks.

Keep in. Is a caution either given to, or resolved on, by the compositor, where there may be doubt of driving out his matter beyond his counting off, wherefore he sets close, to keep in.

Keep out. A caution either given to, or resolved on, by the compositor, when there may be doubt of getting in his matter too fast, wherefore he sets wide, to drive or keep out.

Kern of a Letter. That part which hangs over the body.

Letter Hangs. When the page is out of square.

Low Case. When the compositor has composed almost all the letters out of his case.

Macule. When part of the impression appears double.

Matter. The series of the discourse of the compositor's copy.

Measure. The width of a page.

Monk. When the ink is not distributed, or lies in blotches.

Naked Form. When the furniture is taken from the pages.

Off. When the pressman has worked off the designed number.

Out. When a compositor has set all his copy.

Out of Register. When the pages do not back each other.

Pick. When any dirt gets into the hollows of the letter, which chokes up the face of it, and occasions a spot.

Pi. When a page is broken, and the letters squabbled.

Quarters. Octavos and twelves are said to be imposed in quarters, not from their equal divisions, but because they are imposed and locked up in four parts.

Ratting. Working at less than the established prices.

Register sheet. Sheet or sheets printed to make register with.

Reiteration. The form printed on the second side.

Reglet. Is a thin sort of furniture, of an equal thickness all its length. It is made to the thickness of type.

Rise. A form is said to rise, when in rearing it off the correcting stone, no letter or furniture, &c. drop out.

Runs on sorts. When matter uses only a few sorts of letter.

Set off. When sheets that are newly worked off, black those that come in contact with them.

Shank. The square metal upon which a letter stands.

Signature. Any letter of the alphabet or figure used at the bottom of the first page of a sheet, as a direction for the binders to place the sheets in a volume.

Slur. When the impression of the sheets appear smeared.

Smouting. When either compositors or pressmen are employed for a short time, and not engaged for a constancy.

Sorts. The letters that lie in every box of the case, are separately called sorts in printers' and founders' language.

Squabble. A page or form is squabbled when the letter or letters are twisted about out of their square position.

Stem. The straight flat strokes of a straight letter.

Superior Letters. Letters of a small face, justified by the founder in the mould near the top of the line.

Turn for a letter. When a sort runs short, a letter of the same thickness is substituted, placing it bottom upwards.

White line. A line of quadrats.

White page. A page that no matter comes in.

White paper. Although the first form be printed off, yet pressmen call that heap white paper, till the reiteration be printed.

INDEX.

PART I.

HISTORY OF THE ART.

PART II.

CHAPTER I.

PRACTICE OF THE ART.

CHAPTER II.

LETTER FOUNDERS' SORTS.

CHAP. III.

RULES, SIZES OF LETTER, &c.

CHAP. IV.

OBSERVATIONS ON COMPOSING, &c.

CHAPTER V.

IMPOSING, &C.

CHAPTER VI.

CORRECTORS AND CORRECTING.

CHAPTER VII.

OVERSEER'S DEPARTMENT.

CHAPTER VIII.

THE PRESS.

CHAPTER IX.

INKING APPARATUS.

CHAPTER X.

IMPROVED PRESSES.

CHAPTER XI.

WAREHOUSE DEPARTMENT.

THOMAS F. ADAMS'
PRINTERS' FURNISHING WAREHOUSE,

No. 8 Franklin Place,

UNDER SANDERSON'S FRANKLIN HOUSE,

PHILADELPHIA,

Where he has for Sale,

BRUCE'S PRINTING TYPES,

Wells & Webb's Wood Types, Furniture, &c.

LIGHTBODY'S PRINTING INKS,

TAYLOR'S PRINTING MACHINERY,

ADAMS' PLATEN POWER PRESSES,

With every article used in the Art,

of the *best* quality.

ALSO,

SECOND HAND MATERIALS SUITABLE FOR NEWSPAPERS.

~~~~~~~~~~~

STEREOTYPING

in all its branches executed in the best manner,

and at the lowest prices.

The List of Titles